ESSENTIAL
book of
POETRY

ESSENTIAL
~ *book of* ~
POETRY

Five Centuries
~ *of Verse* ~

CHANCELLOR
PRESS

First published in Great Britain in 1994 by Chancellor Press
an imprint of Reed Consumer Books Limited
Michelin House, 81 Fulham Road, London SW3 6RB
and Auckland, Melbourne, Singapore and Toronto

Compilation: Alex Bennion, Edel Brosnan
Design: Gwyn Lewis

ISBN 1 85152 500 9

A CIP catalogue record for this book is available from
the British Library

Printed in Great Britain by the Bath Press

Contents

CONTENTS

CONTENTS

CONTENTS

CONTENTS

Preface

We have attempted in this volume to select poems that are familiar favourites, as well as some that are less well known but are enjoyable and stimulating to read.

In addition, although people often take pleasure in dipping into an anthology, these poems can be read in sequence, and we have tried to capture the changing mood of the times, both in movements in poetry such as the sea-change from the Augustans to the Romantics at the end of the eighteenth century, and in external historical events. Outside events have always influenced poets and their choice of subject, and poetry was above all the medium chosen by individuals to express their profound emotions during the two world wars. We have traced, for example, the course of World War I from the patriotic poems of Kipling and others, through the early idealism of the soldiers to disillusionment, despair and Kipling's bitter 'Epitaphs of the War' after the loss of his only son.

With regard to the earlier poems in this collection, we have used modern translations in most cases. The poems by Sir Philip Sidney are taken from his sonnet sequence *Astrophel and Stella*, and 'The Cave of Despair' and 'The Bower of Bliss' are from Edmund Spenser's *The Faerie Queene*. Shakespeare presented a problem in that so much of his greatest poetry is to be found in his plays, but, with the exception of 'All the World's a Stage' from *As You Like It* and Ariel's songs from *The Tempest*, we decided to include only his best-known and best-loved songs, poems and sonnets.

In the case of Milton, we have included an extract from *Paradise Lost*, as it is impossible to ignore its influence on later poets. The vast breadth of Milton's work was difficult to represent fully in the space available here, so we have omitted extracts from his other lengthy classics such as *Lycidas* and *Paradise*

Regained. Instead, we have chosen some shorter pieces which share the themes and issues featured in these longer works. The poetry of Swift and Pope, though comic rather than epic, is likewise represented mainly by extracts from their longer works.

We have tried to include examples from as many English-speaking countries as possible – Ireland, North America, the Caribbean – and to bring the collection up to date with works by Margaret Atwood, Benjamin Zephaniah, Paul Durcan and Wendy Cope, amongst others.

Here, we hope, the reader will find poems to memorise, to read aloud and – above all – to enjoy.

JOHN SKELTON

To Mistress Margaret Hussey

Merry Margaret,
As midsummer flower,
Gentle as falcon
Or hawk of the tower:
With solace and gladness,
Much mirth and no madness,
All good and no badness;
So joyously,
So maidenly,
So womanly
Her demeaning
In every thing,
Far, far passing
That I can indite,
Or suffice to write
Of Merry Margaret
As midsummer flower,
Gentle as falcon
Or hawk of the tower.
As patient and still
And as full of good will
As fair Isaphill,
Coriander,
Sweet pomander,
Good Cassander,
Steadfast of thought,
Well made, well wrought,
Far may be sought
Ere that ye can find
So courteous, so kind
As Merry Margaret,
This midsummer flower,
Gentle as falcon
Or hawk of the tower.

To Mistress Margery Wentworth

With marjoram gentle,
 The flower of goodlihead,
Embroidered the mantle
 Is of your maidenhead.
Plainly I cannot glose;
 Ye be, as I devine,
The pretty primrose,
 The goodly columbine.
With marjoram gentle,
 The flower of goodlihead,
Embroidered the mantle
 Is of your maidenhead.
Benign, courteous, and meek,
 With wordės well devis'd;
In you, who list to seek,
 Be virtues well compris'd.
With marjoram gentle,
 The flower of goodlihead,
Embroidered the mantle
 Is of your maidenhead.

SIR THOMAS WYATT

Remembrance

They flee from me, that sometime did me seek
 With naked foot, stalking in my chamber.
I have seen them gentle, tame, and meek,
 That now are wild, and do not remember
 That sometime they put themselves in danger
  To take bread at my hand; and now they range
  Busily seeking with a continual change.

Thanked be fortune it hath been otherwise
 Twenty times better; but once, in special,
In thin array, after a pleasant guise,
 When her loose gown from her shoulders did fall,
 And she me caught in her arms long and small,
  Therewith all sweetly did me kiss
  And softly said, 'Dear heart, how like you this?'

It was no dream; I lay broad waking:
 But all is turned, thorough my gentleness,
Into a strange fashion of forsaking;

And I have leave to go of her goodness,
And she also to use newfangleness.
But since that I so kindly am served,
I would fain know what she hath deserved.

EDMUND SPENSER

'One day I wrote her name upon the strand'

One day I wrote her name upon the strand,
But came the waves and washèd it away:
Again I wrote it with a second hand,
But came the tide, and made my pains his prey.
'Vain man,' said she, 'thou do'st in vain assay,
A mortal thing so to immortalize,
For I myself shall like to this decay,
And eek my name be wipèd out likewise.'
'Not so,' quoth I, 'let baser things devise
To die in dust, but you shall live by fame:
My verse your virtues rare shall eternize,
And in the heavens write your glorious name,
Where, whenas death shall all the world subdue,
Our love shall live, and later life renew.'

The Cave of Despair

Ere long they come, where that same wicked wight
His dwelling has, low in an hollow cave,
Farre underneath a craggie clift ypight,
Darke, dolefull, drearie, like a greedie grave,
That still for carrion carcases doth crave:
On top whereof aye dwelt the ghastly Owle,
Shrieking his balefull note, which ever drave
Farre from that haunt all other chearefull fowle;
And all about it wandring ghostes did waile and howle.

And all about old stockes and stubs of trees,
Whereon nor fruit, nor leafe was ever seene,
Did hang upon the ragged rocky knees;
On which had many wretches hanged beene,
Whose carcases were scattered on the greene,
And throwne about the cliffs. Arrived there,
That bare-head knight for dread and dolefull teene,
Would faine have fled, ne durst approchen neare,
But th'other forst him stay, and comforted in feare.

That darkesome cave they enter, where they find
That cursed man, low sitting on the ground,
Musing full sadly in his sullein mind;
His griesie lockes, long growen, and unbound,
Disordred hong about his shoulders round,
And hid his face; through which his hollow eyne
Lookt deadly dull, and stared as astound;
His raw-bone cheekes through penurie and pine
Were shronke into his jawes, as he did never dine.

His garment nought but many ragged clouts,
With thornes together pind and patched was,
The which his naked sides he wrapt abouts;
And him beside there lay upon the gras
A drearie corse, whose life away did pas,
All wallowd in his owne yet luke-warme blood,
That from his wound yet welled fresh, alas;
In which a rustie knife fast fixed stood,
And made an open passage for the gushing flood.

Which piteous spectacle, approving trew
The wofull tale that Trevisan had told,
When as the gentle Redcrosse knight did vew,
With firie zeale he burnt in courage bold,
Him to avenge, before his bloud were cold,
And to the villein said, 'Thou damned wight,
The author of this fact we here behold,
What justice can but judge against thee right,
With thine owne bloud to price his bloud, here shed in sight?

'What franticke fit' (quoth he) 'hath thus distraught
Thee, foolish man, so rash a doome to give?
What justice ever other judgement taught
But he should die who merites not to live?
None else to death this man despayring drive
But his owne guiltie mind deserving death.
Is then unjust to each his due to give?
Or let him die that loatheth living breath?
Or let him die at ease that liveth here uneath?

'Who travels by the wearie wandring way
To come unto his wished home in haste,
And meetes a flood, that doth his passage stay,
Is not great grace to helpe him over past,
Or free his feet, that in the myre sticke fast?
Most envious man, that grieves at neighbours good,
And fond, that joyest in the woe thou hast,
Why wilt not let him passe, that long hath stood
Upon the banke, yet wilt thy selfe not passe the flood?

'He there does now enjoy eternall rest
And happie ease, which thou doest want and crave,
And further from it daily wanderest:
What if some litle paine the passage have,
That makes fraile flesh to feare the bitter wave?
Is not short paine well borne, that brings long ease,
And layes the soule to sleepe in quiet grave?
Sleepe after toyle, port after stormie seas,
Ease after warre, death after life does greatly please.'

The knight much wondred at his suddeine wit,
And said, 'The terme of life is limited,
Ne may a man prolong, nor shorten it;
The souldier may not move from watchfull sted,
Nor leave his stand, untill his Captaine bed.'
'Who life did limit by almightie doome,'
(Quoth he) 'knowes best the termes established;
And he that points the Centonell his roome
Doth license him depart at sound of morning droome.

'Is not his deed, what ever thing is donne,
In heaven and earth? did not he all create
To die againe? all ends that was begonne.
Their times in his eternall booke of fate
Are written sure, and have their certaine date.
Who then can strive with strong necessitie,
That holds the world in his still chaunging state,
Or shunne the death ordaynd by destinie?
When houre of death is come, let none aske whence, nor why.

'The lenger life, I wote the greater sin,
The greater sin, the greater punishment:
All those great battels, which thou boasts to win,
Through strife and bloud-shed and avengement,
Now praysd, hereafter deare thou shalt repent:
For life must life, and bloud must bloud repay.
Is not enough thy evill life forespent?
For he that once hath missed the right way,
The further he doth goe, the further he doth stray.

'Then do not further goe, no further stray,
But here lie downe, and to thy rest betake,
Th'ill to prevent, that life ensewen may.
For what hath life, that may it loved make,
And gives not rather cause it to forsake?
Feare, sicknesse, age, losse, labour, sorrow, strife,
Paine, hunger, cold, that makes the hart to quake;
And ever fickle fortune rageth rife,
All which, and thousands mo do make a loathsome life.'

The Bower of Bliss

Eftsoones they heard a most melodious sound,
  Of all that mote delight a daintie eare,
Such as attonce might not on living ground,
  Save in this Paradise, be heard elswhere:
  Right hard it was, for wight which did it heare,
To read what manner musicke that mote bee:
  For all that pleasing is to living eare,
Was there consorted in one harmonee,
Birdes, voyces, instruments, windes, waters, all agree.

The joyous birdes shrouded in chearefull shade,
  Their notes unto the voyce attempred sweet;
Th'Angelicall soft trembling voyces made
  To th'instruments divine respondence meet:
  The silver sounding instruments did meet
With the base murmure of the waters fall:
  The waters fall with difference discreet,
Now soft, now loud, unto the wind did call:
The gentle warbling wind low answered to all.

There, whence that Musick seemed heard to bee,
  Was the faire Witch her selfe now solacing,
With a new Lover, whom through sorceree
  And witchcraft she from farre did thither bring:
  There she had him now layd a slombering,
In secret shade, after long wanton joyes:
  Whilst round about them pleasauntly did sing
Many faire Ladies, and lascivious boyes,
That ever mixt their song with licentious toyes.

And all that while, right over him she hong,
  With her false eyes fast fixed in his sight,
As seeking medicine, whence she was stong,
  Or greedily depasturing delight:
  And oft inclining downe with kisses light,
For feare of waking him, his lips bedewd,
  And through his humid eyes did sucke his spright,
Quite molten into lust and pleasure lewd;
Wherewith she sighed soft, as if his case she rewd.

The whiles some one did chaunt this lovely lay;
  'Ah see, who so faire thing doest faine to see,
In springing flowre the image of thy day;
  Ah see the Virgin Rose, how sweetly shee
  Doth first peepe forth with bashfull modestee,
That fairer seemes, the lesse ye see her may;
  Lo, see soone after, how more bold and free
Her bared bosome she doth broad display;
Loe, see soone after, how she fades, and falles away.

'So passeth, in the passing of a day,
Of mortall life the leafe, the bud, the flowre,
Ne more doth flourish after first decay,
That earst was sought to decke both bed and bowre,
Of many a Ladie, and many a Paramowre:
Gather therefore the Rose, whilest yet is prime,
For soone comes age, that will her pride deflowre:
Gather the Rose of love, whilest yet is time,
Whilest loving thou mayst loved be with equall crime.'

SIR PHILIP SIDNEY

To Sleep

Come, Sleep, O Sleep, the certain knot of peace,
The baiting-place of wit, the balm of woe,
The poor man's wealth, the prisoner's release,
The indifferent judge between the high and low;
With shield of proof shield me from out the press
Of those fierce darts Despair at me doth throw:
O make in me those civil wars to cease;
I will good tribute pay, if thou do so.
Take thou of me smooth pillows, sweetest bed,
A chamber deaf to noise and blind to light,
A rosy garland and a weary head;
And if these things, as being thine by right,
Move not thy heavy grace, thou shalt in me,
Livelier than elsewhere, Stella's image see.

To the Moon

With how sad steps, O moon, thou climb'st the skies!
How silently, and with how wan a face!
What! may it be that even in heavenly place
That busy archer his sharp arrows tries?
Sure, if that long-with-love-acquainted eyes
Can judge of love, thou feel'st a lover's case
I read it in thy looks; thy languished grace
To me, that feel the like, thy state descries.
Then, even of fellowship, O Moon, tell me,
Is constant love deemed there but want of wit?
Are beauties there as proud as here they be?
Do they above love to be loved, and yet
Those lovers scorn whom that love doth possess?
Do they call 'virtue' there – ungratefulness?

Look in thy Heart

Loving in truth, and fain in verse my love to show,
That She, dear She, might take some pleasure of my pain,
Pleasure might cause her read, reading might make her know,
Knowledge might pity win, and pity grace obtain,
I sought fit words to paint the blackest face of woe;
Studying inventions fine, her wits to entertain,
Oft turning others' leaves, to see if thence would flow
Some fresh and fruitful showers upon my sun-burn'd brain.
But words came halting out, wanting Invention's stay;
Invention, Nature's child, fled stepdame Study's blows;
And others' feet still seem'd but strangers in my way.
Thus, great with child to speak, and helpless in my throes,
Biting my truand pen, beating myself for spite,
'Fool,' said my Muse to me, 'look in thy heart and write.'

'My true love hath my heart, and I have his'

My true love hath my heart, and I have his,
  By just exchange, one for the other given.
I hold his dear, and mine he cannot miss,
  There never was a better bargain driven.
His heart in me keeps me and him in one,
  My heart in him his thoughts and senses guides;
He loves my heart, for once it was his own,
  I cherish his, because in me it bides.
His heart his wound receivèd from my sight,
  My heart was wounded with his wounded heart;
For as from me on him his hurt did light,
  So still methought in me his hurt did smart.
    Both equal hurt, in this change sought our bliss:
    My true love hath my heart and I have his.

'Dear, why make you more of a dog than me?'

Dear, why make you more of a dog than me?
  If he do love, I burn, I burn in love:
  If he wait well, I never thence would move:
If he be fair, yet but a dog can be.
Little he is, so little worth is he;
  He barks, my songs thine own voice oft doth prove:
  Bidd'n, perhaps he fetcheth thee a glove,

But I unbid, fetch even my soul to thee.
  Yet while I languish, him that bosom clips,
That lap doth lap, nay lets, in spite of spite,
This sour-breath'd mate taste of those sugar'd lips.
Alas, if you grant only such delight
  To witless things, then Love I hope (since wit
  Becomes a clog) will soon ease me of it.

SIR EDWARD DYER

'My mind to me a kingdom is'

My mind to me a kingdom is;
  Such present joys therein I find,
That it excels all other bliss
  That world affords or grows by kind.
Though much I want which most would have
Yet still my mind forbids to crave.

No princely pomp, no wealthy store,
  No force to win the victory,
No wily wit to salve a sore,
  No shape to feed a loving eye;
To none of these I yield as thrall,
For why, my mind doth serve for all.

I see how plenty suffers oft,
  And hasty climbers soon do fall;
I see that those which are aloft
  Mishap doth threaten most of all.
They get with toil, they keep with fear;
Such cares my mind could never bear.

Content I live, this is my stay,
  I seek no more than may suffice;
I press to bear no haughty sway;
  Look, what I lack my mind supplies.
Lo! thus I triumph like a king,
Content with that my mind doth bring.

Some have too much, yet still do crave;
  I little have, and seek no more.
They are but poor, though much they have,
  And I am rich with little store.
They poor, I rich; they beg, I give;
They lack, I leave; they pine, I live.

I laugh not at another's loss,
  I grudge not at another's gain;
No wordly waves my mind can toss;
  My state at one doth still remain.
I fear no foe, I fawn no friend;
I loathe not life, nor dread my end.

Some weigh their pleasure by their lust,
  Their wisdom by their rage of will;
Their treasure is their only trust,
  A cloaked craft their store of skill.
But all the pleasure that I find
Is to maintain a quiet mind.

My wealth is health and perfect ease;
  My conscience clear my choice defence;
I neither seek by bribes to please
  Nor by deceit to breed offence.
Thus do I live, thus will I die;
Would all did so as well as I!

A Silent Love

The lowest trees have tops, the ant her gall,
The fly her spleen, the little spark his heat;
The slender hairs cast shadows, though but small,
And bees have stings, although they be not great;
  Seas have their source, and so have shallow springs;
  And love is love, in beggars and in kings.

Where waters smoothest run, there deepest are the fords,
The dial stirs, yet not perceives it move;
The firmest faith is found in fewest words,
The turtles do not sing, and yet they love;
  True hearts have ears and eyes, no tongues to speak;
  They hear and see, and sigh, and then they break.

CHRISTOPHER MARLOWE

The Passionate Shepherd to His Love

Come live with me, and be my love,
And we will all the pleasures prove
That valleys, groves, hills and fields,
Woods, or steepy mountain yields.

And we will sit upon the rocks,
Seeing the shepherds feed their flocks
By shallow rivers, to whose falls
Melodious birds sing madrigals.

And I will make thee beds of roses,
And a thousand fragrant posies;
A cap of flowers, and a kirtle,
Embroider'd all with leaves of myrtle.

A gown made of the finest wool,
Which from our pretty lambs we pull;
Fair lined slippers for the cold,
With buckles of the purest gold.

A belt of straw and ivy buds,
With coral clasps and amber studs,
An if these pleasures may thee move,
Come live with me, and be my love.

The shepherd swains shall dance and sing
For thy delight each May-morning:
If these delights thy mind may move,
Then live with me, and be my love.

SIR WALTER RALEIGH

The Nymph's Reply to the Shepherd

If all the world and love were young,
And truth in every Shepherd's tongue,
These pretty pleasures might me move,
To live with thee, and be thy love.

Time drives the flocks from field to fold,
When Rivers rage, and Rocks grow cold,
And Philomel becometh dumb,
The rest complains of cares to come.

The flowers do fade, and wanton fields,
To wayward winter reckoning yields,
A honey tongue, a heart of gall,
Is fancy's spring, but sorrow's fall.

Thy gowns, thy shoes, thy beds of Roses,
Thy cap, thy kirtle, and thy posies,
Soon break, soon wither, soon forgotten:
In folly ripe, in reason rotten.

Thy belt of straw and Ivy buds,
Thy Coral clasps and Amber studs,
All these in me no means can move,
To come to thee, and be thy love.

But could youth last, and love still breed,
Had joys no date, nor age no need,
Then these delights my mind might move,
To live with thee, and be thy love.

The Lie

Go, soul, the body's guest,
  Upon a thankless arrant;
Fear not to touch the best;
  The truth shall be thy warrant.
    Go, since I needs must die,
    And give the world the lie.

Say to the court, it glows
  And shines like rotten wood;
Say to the church, it shows
  What's good, and doth no good:
    If church and court reply,
    Then give them both the lie.

Tell potentates, they live
  Acting by other's action,
Not loved unless they give,
  Not strong but by affection:
    If potentates reply,
    Give potentates the lie.

Tell men of high condition
  That manage the estate,
Their purpose is ambition,
  Their practice only hate:
    And if they once reply,
    Then give them all the lie.

Tell them that brave it most,
  They beg for more by spending,
Who, in their greatest cost,
  Seek nothing but commending:
    And if they make reply,
    Then give them all the lie.

Tell zeal it wants devotion;
  Tell love it is but lust;
Tell time it metes but motion;
  Tell flesh it is but dust:
    And wish them not reply,
    For thou must give the lie.

Tell age it daily wasteth;
  Tell honour how it alters;
Tell beauty how she blasteth;
  Tell favour how it falters:
    And as they shall reply,
    Give every one the lie.

Tell wit how much it wrangles
  In tickle points of niceness;
Tell wisdom she entangles
  Herself in over-wiseness:
    And when they do reply,
    Straight give them both the lie.

Tell physic of her boldness;
  Tell skill it is prevention;
Tell charity of coldness;
  Tell law it is contention:
    And as they do reply,
    So give them still the lie.

Tell fortune of her blindness;
  Tell nature of decay;
Tell friendship of unkindness;
  Tell justice of delay:
    And if they will reply,
    Then give them all the lie.

Tell arts they have no soundness,
  But vary by esteeming;
Tell schools they want profoundness,
  And stand to much on seeming:
    If arts and schools reply,
    Give arts and schools the lie.

Tell faith it's fled the city;
  Tell how the country erreth;
Tell, manhood shakes off pity;
  Tell, virtue least preferreth:
    And if they do reply,
    Spare not to give the lie.

So when thou hast, as I
  Commanded thee, done blabbing,
Although to give the lie
  Deserves no less than stabbing,
    Stab at thee he that will,
    No stab thy soul can kill.

CHIDIOCK TICHBOURNE

Written the Night Before his Execution

My prime of youth is but a frost of cares;
  My feast of joy is but a dish of pain;
My crop of corn is but a field of tares;
  And all my good is but vain hope of gain;
My life is fled, and yet I saw no sun;
And now I live, and now my life is done.

The spring is past, and yet it hath not sprung;
  The fruit is dead, and yet the leaves be green;
My youth is gone, and yet I am but young;
  I saw the world and yet I was not seen;
My thread is cut, and yet it is not spun;
And now I live, and now my life is done.

I sought my death and found it in my womb,
  I look'd for life and saw it was a shade,
I trod the earth and knew it was my tomb,
  And now I die, and now I was but made;
My glass is full, and now my glass is run,
And now I live, and now my life is done.

THOMAS LODGE

Rosalind's Madrigal

Love in my bosom like a bee
    Doth suck his sweet;
Now with his wings he plays with me,
    Now with his feet.
Within mine eyes he makes his nest,
His bed amidst my tender breast;
My kisses are his daily feast,
And yet he robs me of my rest.
  Ah, wanton, will ye?

And if I sleep, then percheth he
    With pretty flight,
And makes his pillow of my knee
    The livelong night.
Strike I my lute, he tunes the string;
He music plays if so I sing;
He lends me every love thing;
Yet cruel he my heart doth sting.
  Whist, wanton, still ye!

Else I with roses every day
    Will whip you hence,
And bind you, when you long to play,
    For your offence.
I'll shut mine eyes to keep you in,
I'll make you fast it for your sin,
I'll count your power not worth a pin.
Alas! what hereby shall I win
  If he gainsay me?

What if I beat the wanton boy
    With many a rod?
He will repay me with annoy,
    Because a god.
Then sit thou safely on my knee,
And let thy bower my bosom be;
Lurk in mine eyes, I like of thee.
O Cupid, so thou pity me,
  Spare not, but play thee!

ROBERT GREENE

o

Sephestia's Lullaby

Weep not, my wanton, smile upon my knee;
When thou art old there's grief enough for thee.
    Mother's wag, pretty boy,
    Father's sorrow, father's joy.
    When thy father first did see
    Such a boy by him and me,
    He was glad, I was woe:
    Fortune changed made him so,
    When he left his pretty boy,
    Last his sorrow, first his joy.

Weep not, my wanton, smile upon my knee;
When thou art old there's grief enough for thee.
Streaming tears that never stint,
Like pearl drops from a flint,
Fell by course from his eyes,
That one another's place supplies:
Thus he grieved in every part,
Tears of blood fell from his heart,
When he left his pretty boy,
Father's sorrow, father's joy.

Weep not, my wanton, smile upon my knee;
When thou art old there's grief enough for thee.
The wanton smiled, father wept;
Mother cried, baby lept;
More he crowed, more we cried;
Nature could not sorrow hide.
He must go, he must kiss
Child and mother, baby bliss;
For he left his pretty boy,
Father's sorrow, father's joy.

Weep not, my wanton, smile upon my knee;
When thou art old there's grief enough for thee.

THOMAS BONHAM

In Praise of Ale

When that the chill Charocco blows
And winter tells a heavy tale,
When pies and daws and rooks and crows
Do sit and curse in frost and snows,
Then give me ale.

Ale in a Saxon rumkin then,
Such as will make grimalkin prate,
Bids valour burgeon in tall men,
Quickens the poet's wit and pen,
Despises fate.

Ale, that the absent battle fights,
And scorns the march of Swedish drum;
Disputes of princes, laws and rights;
What's done and past tells mortal wights,
And what's to come.

Ale, that the ploughman's heart up keeps
  And equals it to tyrants' thrones;
That wipes the eye that fain would weep,
And lulls in sweet and dainty sleep
    The o'erwearied bones.

Grandchild of Ceres, barley's daughter,
  Wine's emulous neighbour if but stale,
Ennobling all the nymphs of water
And filling each man's mouth with laughter–
    Oh, give me ale!

JOHN DAVIES

Homely Meats

The author loving these homely meats specially, viz.: cream, pancakes, buttered pippin-pies (laugh, good people) and tobacco; writ to that worthy and virtuous gentlewoman, whom he calleth Mistress, as followeth

If there were, oh! an Hellespont of cream
Between us, milk-white mistress, I would swim
To you, to show to both my love's extreme,
Leander-like,–yea! dive from brim to brim.
But met I with a buttered pippin-pie
Floating upon't, that would I make my boat
To waft me to you without jeopardy,
Though sea-sick I might be while it did float.
Yet if a storm should rise, by night or day,
Of sugar-snows and hail of caraways,
Then, if I found a pancake in my way,
It like a plank should bring me to your kays;
  Which having found, if they tobacco kept,
  The smoke should dry me well before I slept.

MICHAEL DRAYTON

Agincourt

Fair stood the wind for France
  When we our sails advance,
Nor now to prove our chance
  Longer will tarry;
But putting to the main,

At Caux, the mouth of Seine,
With all his martial train
  Landed King Harry.

And taking many a fort,
Furnish'd in warlike sort,
Marcheth tow'rds Agincourt
  In happy hour;
Skirmishing day by day
With those that stopp'd his way,
Where the French gen'ral lay
  With all his power.

Which, in his height of pride,
King Henry to deride,
His ransom to provide
  Unto him sending;
Which he neglects the while
As from a nation vile,
Yet with an angry smile
  Their fall portending.

And turning to his men,
Quoth our brave Henry then,
'Though they to one be ten
  Be not amazèd:
Yet have we well begun;
Battles so bravely won
Have ever to the sun
  By fame been raisèd.

'And for myself' (quoth he)
'This my full rest shall be:
England ne'er mourn for me
  Nor more esteem me:
Victor I will remain
Or on this earth lie slain,
Never shall she sustain
  Loss to redeem me.

'Poitiers and Cressy tell,
When most their pride did swell,
Under our swords they fell:
  No less our skill is
Than when our grandsire great,
Claiming the regal seat,
By many a warlike feat
  Lopp'd the French lilies.'

The Duke of York so dread
The eager vaward led;
With the main Henry sped
  Among his henchmen.
Excester had the rear,
A braver man not there;
O Lord, how hot they were
  On the false Frenchmen!

They now to fight are gone,
Armour on armour shone,
Drum now to drum did groan
  To hear was wonder;
That with the cries they make
The very earth did shake:
Trumpet to trumpet spake,
  Thunder to thunder.

Well it thine age became,
O noble Erpingham,
Which didst the signal aim
  To our hid forces!
When from a meadow by,
Like a storm suddenly
The English archery
  Stuck the French horses.

With Spanish yew so strong,
Arrows a cloth-yard long
That like to serpents stung,
  Piercing the weather;
None from his fellow starts,
But playing manly parts,
And like true English hearts
  Stuck close together.

When down their bows they threw,
And forth their bilbos drew,
And on the French they flew,
  Not one was tardy;
Arms were from shoulders sent,
Scalps to the teeth were rent,
Down the French peasants went–
  Our men were hardy!

This while our noble king,
His broadsword brandishing,
Down the French host did ding
  As to o'erwhelm it;

And many a deep wound lent,
His arms with blood besprent,
And many a cruel dent
  Bruisèd his helmet.

Gloster, that duke so good,
Next of the royal blood,
For famous England stood
  With his brave brother;
Clarence, in steel so bright,
Though but a maiden knight,
Yet in that furious fight
  Scarce such another.

Warwick in blood did wade,
Oxford the foe invade,
And cruel slaughter made
  Still as they ran up;
Suffolk his axe did ply,
Beaumont and Willoughby
Bare them right doughtily,
  Ferrers and Fanhope.

Upon Saint Crispin's Day
Fought was this noble fray,
Which fame did not delay
  To England to carry.
O when shall English men
With such acts fill a pen?
Or England breed again
  Such a King Harry?

A Summer's Evening

Clear had the day been from the dawn,
  All chequer'd was the sky,
Thin clouds, like scarfs of cobweb lawn,
  Veil'd Heaven's most glorious eye.

The wind had no more strength than this,
  That leisurely it blew,
To make one leaf the next to kiss
  That closely by it grew.

The rills that on the pebbles play'd
  Might now be heard at will;
This world they only music made,
  Else everything was still.

The flowers like brave embroidered girls,
  Look'd as they most desired
To see whose head with orient pearls
  Most curiously was tired;

And to itself the subtle air
  Such sovreignty assumes,
That it receiv'd too large a share
  From Nature's rich perfumes.

The Parting

Since there's no help, come let us kiss and part –
Nay, I have done, you get no more of me;
And I am glad, yea, glad with all my heart,
That thus so cleanly I myself can free.
Shake hands for ever, cancel all our vows,
And when we meet at any time again,
Be it not seen in either of our brows
That we one jot of former love retain.
Now at the last gasp of Love's latest breath,
When, his pulse failing, Passion speechless lies,
When Faith is kneeling by his bed of death,
And Innocence is closing up his eyes,
  – Now if thou wouldst, when all have given him
    over,
  From death to life thou might'st him yet recover.

Verses Made the Night Before he Died

So well I love thee as without thee I
Love nothing; if I might choose, I'd rather die
Than be one day debarred thy company.

Since beasts and plants do grow and live and move,
Beasts are those men that such a life approve:
He only lives that deadly is in love.

The corn, that in the ground is sown, first dies,
And of one seed do many ears arise;
Love, this world's corn, by dying multiplies.

The seeds of love first by thy eyes were thrown
Into a ground untilled, a heart unknown
To bear such fruit, till by thy hands 'twas sown.

Look as your looking-glass by chance may fall,
Divide, and break in many pieces small,
And yet shows forth the selfsame face in all,

Proportions, features, graces, just the same,
And in the smallest piece as well the name
Of fairest one deserves as in the richest frame;

So all my thoughts are pieces but of you,
Which put together makes a glass so true
As I therein no other's face but yours can view.

THOMAS CAMPION

Jack and Joan

Jack and Joan they think no ill,
But loving live, and merry still;
Do their week-days' work, and pray
Devoutly on the holy day;
Skip and trip it on the green,
And help to choose the Summer Queen;
Lash out at a country feast
Their silver penny with the best.

Well can they judge of nappy ale,
And tell at large a winter tale;
Climb up to the apple loft,
And turn the crabs till they be soft.
Tib is all the father's joy,
And little Tom the mother's boy.
All their pleasure is content,
And care to pay their yearly rent.

Joan can call by name her cows,
And deck her windows with green boughs;
She can wreaths and tutties make,
And trim with plums a bridal cake.
Jack knows what brings gain or loss,
And his long flail can stoutly toss;
Make the hedge which others break,
And ever thinks what he doth speak.

Now you courtly dames and knights,
That study only strange delights,
Though you scorn the home-spun gray
And revel in your rich array;

Though your tongues dissemble deep
And can your heads from danger keep:
Yet for all your pomp and train,
Securer lives the silly swain.

Love-Charms

Thrice toss these oaken ashes in the air;
Thrice sit thou mute in this enchanted chair;
Then thrice three times tie up this true love's knot,
And murmur soft: 'She will, or she will not.'

Go burn these poisonous weeds in yon blue fire,
These screech-owl's feathers and this prickling briar,
This cypress gathered at a dead man's grave,
That all they fears and cares an end may have.

Then come, you fairies, dance with me a round;
Melt her hard heart with your melodious sound.
In vain are all the charms I can devise;
She hath an art to break them with her eyes.

THOMAS NASHE

In Time of Pestilence

Adieu, farewell earth's bliss,
This world uncertain is;
Fond are life's lustful joys,
Death proves them all but toys,
None from his darts can fly.
I am sick, I must die.
        Lord, have mercy on us!

Rich men, trust not in wealth,
Gold cannot buy you health;
Physic himself must fade,
All things to end are made.
The plague full swift goes by.
I am sick, I must die.
        Lord, have mercy on us!

Beauty is but a flower
Which wrinkles will devour;
Brightness falls from the air,
Queens have died young and fair,

Dust hath closed Helen's eye.
I am sick, I must die.
    Lord, have mercy on us!

Strength stoops unto the grave,
Worms feed on Hector brave,
Swords may not fight with fate,
Earth still holds ope her gate.
Come! come! the bells do cry.
I am sick, I must die.
    Lord, have mercy on us!

Wit with his wantonness
Tasteth death's bitterness;
Hell's executioner
Hath no ears for to hear
What vain art can reply.
I am sick, I must die.
    Lord, have mercy on us!

Haste, therefore, each degree,
To welcome destiny.
Heaven is our heritage,
Earth but a player's stage;
Mount we unto the sky.
I am sick, I must die.
    Lord, have mercy on us!

THOMAS HEYWOOD

An Epitaph

I was, I am not; smiled, that since did weep;
Laboured, that rest; I waked, that now must sleep;
I played, I play not; sung, that now am still;
Saw, that am blind; I would, that have no will;
I fed that which feeds worms; I stood, I fell;
I bade God save you, that now bid farewell;
I felt, I feel not; followed, was pursued;
I warred, have peace; I conquered, am subdued;
I moved, want motion; I was stiff, that bow
Below the earth; then something, nothing now;
I catched, am caught; I travelled, here I lie;
Lived in the world, that to the world now die.

FRANCIS BACON

Life

The world's a bubble and the Life of Man
    Less than a span
In his conception wretched, from the womb
    So to the tomb;
Curst from his cradle, and brought up to years
    With cares and fears.
Who then to frail mortality shall trust,
But limns on water, or but writes in dust.

Yet whilst with sorrow here we live opprest,
    What life is best?
Courts are but only superficial schools
    To dandle fools:
The rural parts are turn'd into a den
    Of savage men:
And where's a city from foul vice so free,
But may be termed the worst of all the three?

Domestic cares afflict the husband's bed,
    Or pains his head:
Those that live single, take it for a curse
    Or do things worse:
Some would have children: those that have them moan
    Or wish them gone:
What is it, then, to have, or have no wife,
But single thraldom or a double strife?

But our affections still at home to please
    Is a disease:
To cross the seas to any foreign soil,
    Peril and toil:
Wars with their noise affright us: when they cease,
    We are worse in peace;–
What then remains, but that we still should cry
For being born, or being born, to die?

WILLIAM SHAKESPEARE

Spring

When daisies pied and violets blue
And lady-smocks all silver-white
And cuckoo-buds of yellow hue
Do paint the meadows with delight,
The cuckoo then, on every tree,
Mocks married men; for thus sings he,
Cuckoo!
Cuckoo, cuckoo! O, word of fear,
Unpleasing to a married ear!

When shepherds pipe on oaten straws,
And merry larks are ploughmen's clocks,
When turtles tread, and rooks, and daws,
And maidens bleach their summer smocks,
The cuckoo then, on every tree,
Mocks married men; for thus sings he,
Cuckoo!
Cuckoo, cuckoo! O, word of fear,
Unpleasing to a married ear!

Winter

When icicles hang by the wall,
And Dick the shepherd blows his nail,
And Tom bears logs into the hall,
And milk comes frozen home in pail;
When blood is nipped, and ways be foul,
Then nightly sings the staring owl.
Tu-whit, to-who! a merry note,
While greasy Joan doth keel[1] the pot.

When all aloud the wind doth blow,
And coughing drowns the parson's saw,
And birds sit brooding in the snow,
And Marian's nose looks red and raw,
When roasted crabs hiss in the bowl,
Then nightly sings the staring owl,
Tu-whit, tu-who! a merry note,
While greasy Joan doth keel the pot.

[1]cool

'It was a lover and his lass'

It was a lover and his lass,
  With a hey, and a ho, and a hey nonino,
That o'er the green corn-field did pass,
  In spring time, the only pretty ring time,
When birds do sing, hey ding a ding, ding;
Sweet lovers love the spring.

Between the acres of the rye,
  With a hey, and a ho, and a hey nonino,
Those pretty country folks would lie,
  In spring time, the only pretty ring time,
When birds do sing, hey ding a ding, ding;
Sweet lovers love the spring.

This carol they began that hour,
  With a hey, and a ho, and a hey nonino,
How that a life was but a flower
  In spring time, the only pretty ring time,
When birds do sing, hey ding a ding, ding;
Sweet lovers love the spring.

And therefore take the present time,
  With a hey, and a ho, and a hey nonino;
For love is crowned with the prime
  In spring time, the only pretty ring time,
When birds do sing, hey ding a ding, ding;
Sweet lovers love the spring.

Mistress Mine

O Mistress mine, where are you roaming?
O stay and hear! your true-love's coming
    That can sing both high and low;
Trip no further, pretty sweeting,
Journeys end in lovers' meeting–
    Every wise man's son doth know.

What is love? 'tis not hereafter;
Present mirth hath present laughter;
    What's to come is still unsure:
In delay there lies no plenty,–
Then come kiss me, Sweet-and-twenty,
    Youth's a stuff will not endure.

The Phoenix and the Turtle

Let the bird of loudest lay,
  On the sole Arabian tree,
  Herald sad and trumpet be,
To whose sound chaste wings obey.

But thou shrieking harbinger,
  Foul precurrer of the fiend,
  Augur of the fever's end,
To this troop come thou not near.

From this session interdict
  Every fowl of tyrant wing,
  Save the eagle, feathered king;
Keep the obsequy so strict.

Let the priest in surplice white
  That defunctive music can,
  Be the death-divining swan,
Lest the requiem lack his right.

And thou treble-dated crow,
  That thy sable gender mak'st
  With the breath thou giv'st and tak'st,
'Mongst our mourners shalt thou go.

Here the anthem doth commence:
  Love and constancy is dead;
  Phoenix and the turtle fled
In a mutual flame from hence.

So they loved, as love in twain
  Had the essence but in one;
  Two distincts, division none;
Number there in love was slain.

Hearts remote, yet not asunder;
  Distance, and no space was seen
  'Twixt the turtle and his queen;
But in them it were a wonder.

So between them love did shine,
  That the turtle saw his right
  Flaming in the phoenix' sight;
Either was the other's mine.

Property was thus appalled,
  That the self was not the same;
  Single nature's double name
Neither two nor one was called.

Reason, in itself confounded,
  Saw division grow together,
  To themselves yet either neither,
Simple were so well compounded:

That it cried, 'How true a twain
  Seemeth this concordant one!
  Love hath reason, reason none,
If what parts can so remain.'

Whereupon it made this threne
  To the phoenix and the dove,
  Co-supremes and stars of love,
As chorus to their tragic scene.

THRENOS

Beauty, truth, and rarity,
Grace in all simplicity,
Here enclosed in cinders lie.

Death is now the phoenix' nest;
And the turtle's loyal breast
To eternity doth rest,

Leaving no posterity:
'Twas not their infirmity,
It was married chastity.

Truth may seem, but cannot be;
Beauty brag, but 'tis not she;
Truth and beauty buried be.

To this urn let those repair
That are either true or fair;
For these dead birds sigh a prayer.

Ariel's Songs

I

Full fathom five thy father lies;
  Of his bones are coral made;
Those are pearls that were his eyes:
  Nothing of him that doth fade,
But doth suffer a sea-change
Into something rich and strange:
Sea nymphs hourly ring his knell.
                Ding-dong!
  Hark! now I hear them,
                Ding-dong, bell!

II

Where the bee sucks, there suck I,
In a cowslip's bell I lie,
There I couch when owls do cry,
On the bat's back I do fly
After summer merrily.
  Merrily, merrily, shall I live now
  Under the blossom that hangs on the bough.

All the World's a Stage

All the world's a stage,
And all the men and women merely players:
They have their exits and their entrances;
And one man in his time plays many parts,
His acts being seven ages. At first the infant,
Mewling and puking in the nurse's arms.
And then the whining schoolboy, with his satchel,
And shining morning face, creeping like snail
Unwillingly to school. And then the lover,
Sighing like furnace, with a woeful ballad
Made to his mistress' eyebrow. Then a soldier,
Full of strange oaths, and bearded like the pard,
Jealous in honour, sudden and quick in quarrel,
Seeking the bubble reputation
Even in the cannon's mouth. And then the justice,
In fair round belly with good capon lined,
With eyes severe and beard of formal cut,
Full of wise saws and modern instances;
And so he plays his part. The sixth age shifts
Into the lean and slippered pantaloon,
With spectacles on nose, and pouch on side;
His youthful hose, well saved, a world to wide
For his shrunk shank; and his big manly voice,
Turning again toward childish treble, pipes
And whistles in his sound. Last scene of all,
That ends this strange eventful history,
Is second childishness and mere oblivion,
Sans teeth, sans eyes, sans taste, sans everything.

'Shall I compare thee to a summer's day?'

Shall I compare thee to a summer's day?
  Thou art more lovely and more temperate:
Rough winds do shake the darling buds of May,
  And summer's lease hath all too short a date:
Sometime too hot the eye of heaven shines,
  And often is his gold complexion dimmed;
And every fair from fair sometime declines,
  By chance, or nature's changing course untrimmed;
But thy eternal summer shall not fade,
  Nor lose possession of that fair thou owest,
Nor shall Death brag thou wanderest in his shade,
  When in eternal lines to time thou growest;
    So long as men can breathe, or eyes can see,
    So long lives this, and this gives life to thee.

'When in disgrace with fortune and men's eyes'

When in disgrace with fortune and men's eyes
  I all alone beweep my outcast state,
And trouble deaf heaven with my bootless cries,
  And look upon myself, and curse my fate,
Wishing me like to one more rich in hope,
  Featured like him, like him with friends possessed,
Desiring this man's art, and that man's scope,
  With what I most enjoy contented least;
Yet in these thoughts myself almost despising,
  Haply I think on thee, and then my state,
Like to the lark at break of day arising
  From sullen earth, sings hymns at heaven's gate;
    For thy sweet love remembered such wealth brings
    That then I scorn to change my state with kings.

'When to the sessions of sweet silent thought'

When to the sessions of sweet silent thought
  I summon up remembrance of things past,
I sigh the lack of many a thing I sought,
  And with old woes new wail my dear time's waste:
Then can I drown an eye, unused to flow,
  For precious friends hid in death's dateless night,
And weep afresh love's long since cancelled woe,
  And moan the expense of many a vanished sight:
Then can I grieve at grievances foregone,
  And heavily from woe to woe tell o'er

The sad account of fore-bemoanèd moan,
Which I new pay as if not paid before.
But if the while I think on thee, dear friend,
All losses are restored and sorrows end.

'Farewell! thou art too dear for my possessing'

Farewell! thou art too dear for my possessing,
And like enough thou know'st thy estimate:
The charter of thy worth gives thee releasing;
My bonds in thee are all determinate.
For how do I hold thee but by thy granting?
And for that riches where is my deserving?
The cause of this fair gift in me is wanting,
And so my patent back again is swerving.
Thyself thou gav'st, thy own worth then not knowing,
Or me, to whom thou gav'st it, else mistaking;
So thy great gift, upon misprision growing,
Comes home again, on better judgement making.
Thus have I had thee, as a dream doth flatter,
In sleep a king, but, waking, no such matter.

'They that have power to hurt and will do none'

They that have power to hurt and will do none,
That do not do the thing they most do show,
Who, moving others, are themselves as stone,
Unmovèd, cold, and to temptation slow–
They rightly do inherit heaven's graces,
And husband nature's riches from expense;
They are the lords and owners of their faces,
Others, but stewards of their excellence,
The summer's flower is to the summer sweet,
Though to itself it only live and die;
But if that flower with base infection meet,
The basest weed outbraves his dignity:
For sweetest things turn sourest by their deeds;
Lilies that fester smell far worse than weeds.

'Let me not to the marriage of true minds'

Let me not to the marriage of true minds
Admit impediments. Love is not love
Which alters when it alteration finds,
Or bends with the remover to remove.

O, no! it is an ever-fixèd mark,
  That looks on tempests and is never shaken;
It is the star to every wandering bark,
  Whose worth's unknown, although his height be taken.
Love's not Time's fool, though rosy lips and cheeks
  Within his bending sickle's compass come;
Love alters not with his brief hours and weeks,
  But bears it out even to the edge of doom.
    If this be error, and upon me proved,
    I never writ, nor no man ever loved.

'The expense of spirit in a waste of shame'

The expense of spirit in a waste of shame
  Is lust in action; and till action, lust
Is perjured, murderous, bloody, full of blame,
  Savage, extreme, rude, cruel, not to trust;
Enjoyed no sooner but despisèd straight;
  Past reason hunted; and no sooner had,
Past reason hated, as a swallowed bait,
  On purpose laid to make the taker mad:
Mad in pursuit, and in possession so;
  Had, having, and in quest to have, extreme;
A bliss in proof, and proved, a very woe;
  Before, a joy proposed; behind, a dream.
    All this the world well knows; yet none knows well
    To shun the heaven that leads men to this hell.

JOHN DONNE

The Flea

Mark but this flea, and mark in this,
How little that which thou deny'st me is;
It suck'd me first, and now sucks thee,
And in this flea, our two bloods mingled be;
Thou know'st that this cannot be said
A sin, nor shame, nor loss of maidenhead,
  Yet this enjoys before it woo,
  And pamper'd swells with one blood made of two,
  And this, alas, is more than we would do.

Oh stay, three lives in one flea spare,
Where we almost, yea more than married are.
This flea is you and I, and this
Our marriage bed, and marriage temple is;

Though parents grudge, and you, we're met,
And cloistered in these living walls of jet.
  Though use make you apt to kill me,
  Let not to that, self murder added be,
  And sacrilege, three sins in killing three.

Cruel and sudden, hast thou since
Purpled thy nail, in blood of innocence?
Wherein could this flea guilty be,
Except in that drop which it suck'd from thee?
Yet thou triumph'st, and say'st that thou
Find'st not thyself, nor me the weaker now;
  'Tis true, then learn how false, fears be;
  Just so much honour, when thou yield'st to me,
  Will waste, as this flea's death took life from thee.

'Go and catch a falling star'

Go and catch a falling star,
  Get with child a mandrake root,
Tell me where all past years are,
  Or who cleft the Devil's foot;
Teach me to hear mermaids singing,
Or to keep off envy's stinging,
    And find
    What wind
Serves to advance an honest mind.

If thou beest born to strange sights,
  Things invisible to see,
Ride ten thousand days and nights
  Till Age snow white hairs on thee;
Thou, when thou return'st, wilt tell me
All strange wonders that befell thee,
    And swear
    No where
Lives a woman true and fair.

If thou find'st one, let me know;
  Such a pilgrimage were sweet.
Yet do not; I would not go,
  Though at next door we might meet.
Though she were true when you met her,
And last till you write your letter,
    Yet she
    Will be
False, ere I come, to two or three.

The Sun Rising

Busy old fool, unruly Sun,
Why dost thou thus,
Through windows and through curtains call on us?
Must to thy motions lovers' seasons run?
Saucy pedantic wretch, go chide
Late school-boys, and sour 'prentices,
Go tell court-huntsmen that the King will ride,
Call country ants to harvest offices;
Love, all alike, no season knows, nor clime,
Nor hours, days, months, which are the rags of time.

Thy beams, so reverend and strong
Why shouldst thou think?
I could eclipse and cloud them with a wink,
But that I would not lose her sight so long:
If her eyes have not blinded thine,
Look, and tomorrow late tell me,
Whether both the Indias of spice and mine
Be where thou left'st them, or lie here with me.
Ask for those kings whom thou saw'st yesterday,
And thou shalt hear, 'All here in one bed lay.'

She's all States, and all Princes I;
Nothing else is.
Princes do but play us; compared to this,
All honour's mimic; all wealth alchemy.
Thou, Sun, art half as happy as we,
In that the world's contracted thus;
Thine age asks ease, and since thy duties be
To warm the world, that's done in warming us.
Shine here to us, and thou art everywhere;
This bed thy centre is, these walls thy sphere.

The Good-Morrow

I wonder by my troth, what thou and I
Did, till we lov'd? were we not wean'd till then?
But suck'd on country pleasures, childishly?
Or snorted we in the seven sleepers' den?
'Twas so; but this, all pleasures fancies be.
If ever any beauty I did see,
Which I desir'd, and got, 'twas but a dream of thee.

And now good-morrow to our waking souls,
Which watch not one another out of fear;
For love all love of other sights controls,

And makes one little room an everywhere.
Let sea-discoverers to new worlds have gone,
Let maps to other, worlds on worlds have shown,
Let us possess one world, each hath one, and is one.

My face in thine eye, thine in mine appears,
And true plain hearts do in the faces rest;
Where can we find two better hemispheres
Without sharp North, without declining West?
What ever dies, was not mixt equally;
If our two loves be one, or thou and I
Love so alike that none do slacken, none can die.

A Valediction: Forbidding Mourning

As virtuous men pass mildly away,
  And whisper to their souls to go,
Whilst some of their sad friends do say
  'The breath goes now,' and some say, 'No':

So let us melt, and make no noise,
  No tear-floods, nor sigh-tempests move,
'Twere profanation of our joys
  To tell the laity our love.

Moving of the earth brings harms and fears,
  Men reckon what it did and meant;
But trepidation of the spheres,
  Though greater far, is innocent.

Dull sublunary lovers' love
  (Whose soul is sense) cannot admit
Absence, because it doth remove
  Those things which elemented it.

But we by a love so much refined
  That ourselves know not what it is,
Inter-assurèd of the mind,
  Care less eyes, lips and hands to miss.

Our two souls therefore, which are one,
  Though I must go, endure not yet
A breach, but an expansion
  Like gold to airy thinness beat.

If they be two, they are two so
  As stiff twin compasses are two;
Thy soul, the fixed foot, makes no show
  To move, but doth, if the other do.

And though it in the centre sit,
  Yet when the other far doth roam,
It leans, and hearkens after it,
  And grows erect, as it comes home.

Such wilt thou be to me, who must
  Like the other foot, obliquely run;
Thy firmness makes my circle just,
  And makes me end where I begun.

Antiquary

If in his study he hath so much care
To hang all old strange things, let his wife beware.

'Death, be not proud'

Death, be not proud, though some have callèd thee
  Mighty and dreadful, for thou art not so;
  For those whom thou think'st thou dost overthrow
Die not, poor Death, nor yet canst thou kill me.
From rest and sleep, which but thy pictures be,
  Much pleasure – then, from thee much more must flow;
  And soonest our best men with thee do go,
Rest of their bones and soul's delivery.
Thou'rt slave to fate, chance, kings and desperate men,
  And dost with poison, war, and sickness dwell;
  And poppy or charms can make us sleep as well,
And better than thy stroke. Why swell'st thou then?
    One short sleep past, we wake eternally,
    And death shall be no more. Death, thou shalt die.

The Anniversary

    All Kings, and all their favourites,
    All glory of honours, beauties, wits,
  The sun itself, which makes times, as they pass,
  Is elder by a year now than it was
  When thou and I first one another saw:
  All other things to their destruction draw,
    Only our love hath no decay;
  This no tomorrow hath, nor yesterday,
  Running it never runs from us away,
But truly keeps his first, last, everlasting day.

Two graves must hide thine and my corse;
If one might, death were no divorce.
Alas, as well as other Princes, we
(Who Prince enough in one another be)
Must leave at last in death these eyes and ears,
Oft fed with true oaths, and with sweet salt tears;
But souls where nothing dwells but love
(All other thoughts being inmates) then shall prove
This, or a love increasèd there above,
When bodies to their graves, souls from their graves remove.

And then we shall be throughly blest;
But we no more than all the rest.
Here upon earth we're Kings, and none but we
Can be such Kings, nor of such subjects be;
Who is so safe as we? where none can do
Treason to us, except one of us two.
True and false fears let us refrain,
Let us love nobly, and live, and add again
Years and years unto years, till we attain
To write threescore: this is the second of our reign.

A Hymn to God the Father

Wilt Thou forgive that sin where I begun,
Which is my sin, though it were done before?
Wilt Thou forgive that sin, through which I run,
And do run still: though still I do deplore?
When Thou hast done, Thou hast not done,
For, I have more.

Wilt Thou forgive that sin by which I have won
Others to sin? and, made my sin their door?
Wilt Thou forgive that sin which I did shun
A year, or two: but wallowed in, a score?
When Thou has done, Thou hast not done,
For I have more.

I have a sin of fear, that when I have spun
My last thread, I shall perish on the shore;
Swear by Thyself, that at my death Thy son
Shall shine as He shines now, and heretofore;
And, having done that, Thou has done,
I fear no more.

BEN JONSON

Ode to Himself

Where dost thou careless lie,
Buried in ease and sloth?
Knowledge that sleeps doth die;
And this security,
It is the common moth,
That eats on wits, and arts, and oft destroys them both.

Are all the Aonian springs
Dried up? lies Thespia waste?
Doth Clarius' harp want strings,
That not a nymph now sings?
Or droop they as disgraced,
To see their seats and bowers by chattering pies defaced?

If hence thy silence be,
As 'tis too just a cause,
Let this thought quicken thee:
Minds that are great and free
Should not on fortune pause,
'Tis crown enough to virtue still, her own applause.

What though the greedy fry
Be taken with false baits
Of worded balladry
And think it poesy?
They die with their conceits,
And only piteous scorn upon their folly waits.

Then take in hand thy lyre,
Strike in thy proper strain;
With Japhet's line, aspire
Sol's chariot for new fire,
To give the world again:
Who aided him will thee, the issue of Jove's brain.

And since our dainty age
Cannot endure reproof,
Make not thyself a page
To that strumpet the Stage,
But sing high and aloof,
Safe from the wolf's black jaw, and the dull ass's hoof.

Hymn to Diana

Queen and huntress, chaste and fair,
  Now the sun is laid to sleep,
Seated in thy silver chair,
  State in wonted manner keep:
    Hesperus entreats thy light,
    Goddess excellently bright.

Earth, let not thy envious shade
  Dare itself to interpose;
Cynthia's shining orb was made
  Heaven to clear when day did close:
    Bless us then with wishèd sight,
    Goddess excellently bright.

Lay thy bow of pearl apart,
  And thy crystal-shining quiver;
Give unto the flying hart
  Space to breathe, how short soever:
    Thou that mak'st a day of night–
    Goddess excellently bright.

Simplex Munditiis

Still to be neat, still to be drest,
As you were going to a feast;
Still to be powdered, still perfumed,
Lady, it is to be presumed,
Though art's hid causes are not found,
All is not sweet, all is not sound.

Give me a look, give me a face
That makes simplicity a grace;
Robes loosely flowing, hair as free:
Such sweet neglect more taketh me
Than all the adulteries of art;
They strike mine eyes, but not my heart.

Inviting a Friend to Supper

Tonight, grave Sir, both my poor house and I
  Do equally desire your company:
Not that we think us worthy such a guest,
  But that your worth will dignify our feast
With those that come; whose grace may make that seem
  Something, which else could hope for no esteem.

It is the fair acceptance, Sir, creates
  The entertainment perfect: not the cates.
Yet shall you have, to rectify your palate,
  An olive, capers, or some better salad,
Ushering the mutton; with a short-legged hen,
  If we can get her, full of eggs, and then
Lemons, and wine for sauce; to these a cony
  Is not to be despaired of for our money;
And though fowl now be scarce, yet there are clerks,
  The sky not falling, think we may have larks.
I'll tell you of more, and lie, so you will come:
  Of partridge, pheasant, wood-cock, of which some
May yet be there; and godwit, if we can;
  Knot, rail and ruff too. How so ere, my man
Shall read a piece of Virgil, Tacitus,
  Livy, or of some better book to us,
Of which we'll speak our minds, amidst our meat;
  And I'll profess no verses to repeat:
To this, if ought appear which I not know of,
  That will the pastry, not my paper show of.
Digestive cheese and fruit there sure will be;
  But that which most doth take my Muse and me
Is a pure cup of rich Canary wine,
  Which is the Mermaid's now, but shall be mine;
Of which had Horace or Anacreon tasted,
  Their lives, as do their lines, till now had lasted.
Tobacco, nectar, or the Thespian spring
  Are all but Luther's beer, to this I sing.
Of this we will sup free, but moderately,
  And we will have no Pooly or Parrot[1] by;
Nor shall our cups make any guilty men,
  But at our parting we will be as when
We innocently met. Not simple word
  That shall be uttered at our mirthful board
Shall make us sad next morning, or affright
  The liberty that we'll enjoy tonight.

[1]two well-known informers

On my First Daughter

Here lies to each her parents' ruth
Mary, the daughter of their youth:
Yet, all Heaven's gifts being Heaven's due,
It makes the father less to rue.
At six months' end she parted hence
With safety of her innocence;
Whose soul Heaven's Queen (whose name she bears)

In comfort of her mother's tears,
Hath placed amongst her virgin-train;
Where, while that severed doth remain,
This grave partakes the fleshly birth,
Which cover lightly, gentle earth.

JOHN WEBSTER

'Call for the robin-redbreast and the wren'

Call for the robin-redbreast and the wren,
Since o'er shady groves they hover,
And with leaves and flowers do cover
The friendless bodies of unburied men.
Call unto his funeral dole
The ant, the field-mouse, and the mole,
To rear him hillocks that shall keep him warm,
And (when gay tombs are robb'd) sustain no harm;
But keep the wolf far thence, that's foe to men,
For with his nails he'll dig them up again.

JOHN FORD

'Can you paint a thought?'

Can you paint a thought? or number
Every fancy in a slumber?
Can you count soft minutes roving
From a dials point by moving?
Can you graspe a sigh? or lastly,
Rob a Virgins honour chastly?
  No, o no; yet you may
    Sooner do both that and this,
    This and that, and never miss,
  Then by any praise display
    Beauties beauty, such a glory
    As beyond all Fate, all Story,
      All arms, all arts,
      All loves, all hearts,
    Greater then those, or they,
    Do, shall, and must obey.

ANON

Tom o' Bedlam

From the hag and hungry goblin
That into rags would rend ye,
The spirit that stands by the naked man
In the Book of Moons defend ye,
That of your five sound senses
You never be forsaken,
Nor wander from yourselves with Tom
Abroad to beg your bacon,
While I do sing, Any food, any feeding,
Feeding, drink, or clothing;
Come dame or maid, be not afraid,
Poor Tom will injure nothing.

Of thirty bare years have I
Twice twenty been enraged,
And of forty been three times fifteen
In durance soundly caged
On the lordly lofts of Bedlam
With stubble soft and dainty,
Brave bracelets strong, sweet whips ding dong
With wholesome hunger plenty,
And now I sing, etc.

With a thought I took for Maudlin
And a cruse of cockle pottage,
With a thing thus tall, sky bless you all,
I befell into this dotage.
I slept not since the Conquest,
Till then I never waked,
Till the roguish boy of love where I lay
Me found and strip't me naked.
And now I sing, etc.

When I short have shorn my sow's face
And swigg'd my horny barrel,
In an oaken inn I pound my skin
As a suit of gilt apparel;
The moon's my constant mistress
And the lovely owl my marrow;
The flaming drake and the night crow make
Me music to my sorrow.
While I do sing, etc.

The palsy plagues my pulses
When I prig your pigs or pullen,
Your culvers take, or matchless make

Your Chanticleer or Sullen.
When I want provant with Humphrey
I sup, and when benighted,
I repose in Paul's with waking souls
Yet never am affrighted.
But I do sing, etc.

I know more than Apollo,
For oft when he lies sleeping
I see the stars at bloody wars
In the wounded welkin weeping;
The moon embrace her shepherd,
And the Queen of Love her warrior,
While the first doth horn the star of morn,
And the next the heavenly Farrier.
While I do sing, etc.

The gypsies, Snap and Pedro,
Are none of Tom's comradoes,
The punk I scorn and the cutpurse sworn,
And the roaring boy's bravadoes.
The meek, the white, the gentle
Me handle, touch, and spare not;
But those that cross Tom Rynosseross
Do what the panther dare not.
Although I sing, etc.

With an host of furious fancies
Whereof I am commander,
With a burning spear and a horse of air,
To the wilderness I wander.
By a knight of ghosts and shadows
I summon'd am to a tourney
Ten leagues beyond the wide world's end:
Methinks it is no journey.
Yet will I sing, etc.

ANON

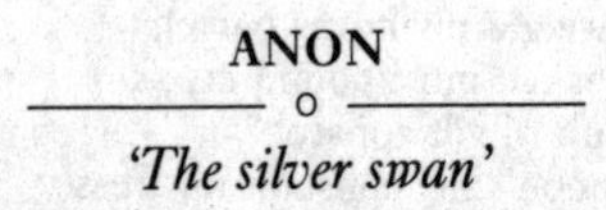

'The silver swan'

The silver swan, who living had no note,
When death approached, unlocked her silent throat,
Leaning her breast against the reedy shore,
Thus sung her first and last, and sung no more:
'Farewell all joys! O death, come close mine eyes;
More geese than swans now live, more fools than wise.'

BISHOP RICHARD CORBET

To his Son, Vincent Corbet

on his Birth Day, November 10, 1630, being then three years old

What I shall leave thee none can tell,
But all shall say I wish thee well;
I wish thee, Vin, before all wealth,
Both bodily and ghostly health:
Nor too much wealth, nor wit, come to thee;
So much of either may undo thee.
I wish thee learning, not for show,
Enough for to instruct, and know;
Not such as gentlemen require,
To prate at table or at fire.
I wish thee all thy mother's graces,
Thy father's fortunes and his places.
I wish thee friends, and one at court,
Not to build on, but support;
To keep thee, not in doing many
Oppressions, but from suffering any.
I wish thee peace in all thy ways,
Nor lazy nor contentious days;
And when thy soul and body part,
As innocent as now thou art.

The Fairies' Farewell

Farewell, rewards and Fairies,
   Good housewives now may say,
For now foul sluts in dairies
   Do fare as well as they;
And though they sweep their hearths no less
   Than maids were wont to do,
Yet who of late for cleanliness
   Finds sixpence in her shoe?

Lament, lament, old Abbies,
   The fairies' lost command;
They did but change priests' babies,
   But some have changed your land;
And all your children sprung from thence
   Are now grown Puritans,
Who live as changelings ever since
   For love of your domains.

At morning and at evening both
   You merry were and glad,
So little care of sleep or sloth
   These pretty ladies had.
When Tom came home from labour,
   Or Ciss to milking rose,
Then merrily, merrily went their tabor,
   And nimbly went their toes.

Witness those rings and roundelays
   Of theirs, which yet remain,
Were footed in Queen Mary's days
   On many a grassy plain;
But since of late Elizabeth,
   And later James, came in
They never danced on any heath
   As when the time hath been.

By which we note the Fairies
   Were of the old profession;
Their songs were Ave Marys,
   Their dances were procession.
But now, alas, they all are dead,
   Or gone beyond the seas,
Or farther for Religion fled,
   Or else they take their ease.

A tell-tale in their company
   They never could endure,
And whoso kept not secretly
   Their mirth, was punished sure.
It was a just and Christian deed
   To pinch such black and blue:
O, how the Common wealth doth need
   Such Justices as you.

Now they have left our quarters
   A Register they have
Who looketh to their Charters,
   A man both wise and grave;
An hundred of their merry pranks
   By one that I could name
Are kept in store, con twenty thanks
   To William for the same.

I marvel who his cloak would turn
   When Puck had led him round,
Or where those walking fires would burn,
   Where Cureton would be found;

How Broker would appear to be
  For whom this Age doth mourn;
But that their spirits live in thee,
  In thee, old William Chourne.

To William Chourne of Staffordshire
  Give laud and praises due,
Who every meal can mend your cheer
  With tales both old and true.
To William all give audience,
  And pray ye for his noddle,
For all the Fairies' evidence
  Were lost if that were addle.

GEORGE WITHER

I Loved a Lass

I loved a lass, a fair one,
  As fair as e'er was seen;
She was indeed a rare one,
  Another Sheba queen.
But, fool as then I was,
  I thought she loved me too,
But now, alas, she's left me,
  Falero, lero, loo.

Her hair like gold did glister,
  Each eye was like a star;
She did surpass her sister,
  Which passed all others far.
She would me 'honey' call,
  She'd, O! she'd kiss me too;
But now, alas, she's left me,
  Falero, lero, loo.

In summer time to Medley
  My love and I would go;
The boatmen there stood ready,
  My love and I to row.
For cream there would we call,
  For cakes, and for prunes too;
But now, alas, she's left me,
  Falero, lero, loo.

Many a merry meeting
  My love and I have had;

She was my only sweeting,
  She made my heart full glad,
The tears stood in her eyes,
  Like to the morning dew;
But now, alas, she's left me,
  Falero, lero, loo.

And as abroad we walkèd,
  As lovers' fashion is,
Oft as we sweetly talkèd
  The sun should steal a kiss,
The wind upon her lips
  Likewise most sweetly blew;
But now, alas, she's left me,
  Falero, lero, loo.

Her cheeks were like the cherry,
  Her skin as white as snow;
When she was blithe and merry,
  She angel-like did show.
Her waist exceeding small,
  The fives did fit her shoe;
But now, alas, she's left me,
  Falero, lero, loo.

In summer time or winter
  She had her heart's desire;
I still did scorn to stint her
  From sugar, sack, or fire;
The world went round about,
  No cares we ever knew;
But now, alas, she's left me,
  Falero, lero, loo.

ROBERT HERRICK

Delight in Disorder

A sweet disorder in the dress
Kindles in clothes a wantonness:
A lawn about the shoulders thrown
Into a fine distraction:
An erring lace which here and there
Enthralls the crimson stomacher:
A cuff neglectful, and thereby
Ribbons to flow confusedly:
A winning wave, deserving note,
In the tempestuous petticoat:

A careless shoe-string, in whose tie
I see a wild civility:
Do more bewitch me than when art
Is too precise in every part.

Julia in Silks

Whenas in silks my Julia goes,
Then, then, methinks, how sweetly flows
The liquefaction of her clothes.

Next, when I cast mine eyes and see
That brave vibration each way free;
O how that glittering taketh me!

To the Virgins to Make Much of Time

Gather ye rose-buds while ye may,
  Old Time is still a-flying;
And this same flower that smiles today,
  Tomorrow will be dying.

The glorious lamp of heaven, the Sun,
  The higher he's a-getting,
The sooner will his race be run,
  And nearer he's to setting.

That age is best, which is the first,
  When youth and blood are warmer
But being spent, the worse, and worst
  Times still succeed the former.

Then be not coy, but use your time,
  And while you may, go marry:
For having lost but once your prime,
  You may for ever tarry.

GEORGE HERBERT

Virtue

Sweet day, so cool, so calm, so bright,
The bridal of the earth and sky:
The dew shall weep thy fall tonight,
  For thou must die.

Sweet rose, whose hue angry and brave
Bids the rash gazer wipe his eye:
Thy root is ever in its grave,
And thou must die.

Sweet spring, full of sweet days and roses,
A box where sweets compacted lie:
My music shows ye have your closes,
And all must die.

Only a sweet and virtuous soul,
Like seasoned timber never gives;
But though the whole world turn to coal,
Then chiefly lives.

The Collar

I struck the board, and cried, 'No more!
I will abroad.
What? shall I ever sigh and pine?
My lines and life are free; free as the road,
Loose as the wind, as large as store.
Shall I be still in suit?
Have I no harvest but a thorn
To let me blood, and not restore
What I have lost with cordial fruit?
Sure there was wine
Before my sighs did dry it: there was corn
Before my tears did drown it.
Is the year only lost to me?
Have I no bays to crown it?
No flowers, no garlands gay? all blasted?
All wasted?
Not so, my heart: but there is fruit,
And thou hast hands.
Recover all thy sigh-blown age
On double pleasures: leave thy cold dispute
Of what is fit, and not. Forsake thy cage,
Thy rope of sands,
Which petty thoughts have made, and made to thee
Good cable, to enforce and draw,
And be thy law,
While thou didst wink and wouldst not see.
Away; take heed:
I will abroad.

Call in thy death's head there: tie up thy fears
He that forbears
To suit and serve his need,
Deserves his load.'
But as I raved and grew more fierce and wild
At every word,
Methoughts I heard one calling, 'Child!'
And I replied, 'My Lord'.

Church Music

Sweetest of sweets, I thank you: when displeasure
Did through my body wound my mind,
You took me thence, and in your house of pleasure
A dainty lodging me assigned.

Now I in you without a body move,
Rising and falling with your wings;
We both together sweetly live and love,
Yet say sometimes, 'God help poor kings.'

Comfort, I'll die; for if you post from me,
Sure I shall do so, and much more;
But if I travel in your company,
You know the way to Heaven's door.

Love

Love bade me welcome; yet my soul drew back,
Guilty of dust and sin.
But quick-eyed Love, observing me grow slack
From my first entrance in,
Drew nearer to me, sweetly questioning,
If I lacked anything.

'A guest', I answered, 'worthy to be here.'
Love said, 'You shall be he.'
'I, the unkind, ungrateful? Ah, my dear,
I cannot look on thee.'
Love took my hand, and smiling did reply,
'Who made the eyes but I?'

'Truth, Lord, but I have marred them; let my shame
Go where it doth deserve.'
'And know you not', says Love, 'who bore the blame?'
'My dear, then I will serve.'
'You must sit down', says Love, 'and taste my meat.'
So I did sit and eat.

Discipline

Throw away thy rod,
Throw away thy wrath:
        O my God,
Take the gentle path.

For my heart's desire
Unto thine is bent:
        I aspire
To a full consent.

Not a word or look
I affect to own,
        But by book,
and thy book alone.

Though I fail, I weep;
Though I halt in pace,
        Yet I creep
To the throne of grace.

Then let wrath remove;
Love will do the deed;
        For with love
Stony hearts will bleed.

Love is swift of foot,
Love's a man of war,
        And can shoot,
And can hit from far.

Who can 'scape his bow?
That which wrought on thee,
        Brought thee low,
Needs must work on me.

Throw away thy rod:
Though man frailties hath,
        Thou art God:
Throw away thy wrath.

THOMAS CAREW

The Spring

Now that the winter's gone, the earth hath lost
Her snow-white robes, and now no more the frost
Candies the grasse, or castes an ycie creame
Upon the silver Lake, or Chrystall streame:
But the warme Sunne thawes the benummed Earth,
And makes it tender, gives a sacred birth
To the dead Swallow; wakes in hollow tree
The drowzie Cuckow, and the Humble-Bee.
Now doe a quire of chirping Minstrels bring
In tryumph to the world, the youthfull Spring.
The Vallies, hills, and woods, in rich araye,
Welcome the comming of the long'd for May.
Now all things smile, onely my *Love* doth lowre:
Nor hath the scalding Noon-day-Sunne the power,
To melt that marble yce, which still doth hold
Her heart congeald, and makes her pittie cold.
The Oxe which lately did for shelter flie
Into the stall, doth now securely lie
In open fields; and love no more is made
By the fire side; but in the cooler shade
Amyntas now doth with his *Cloris* sleepe
Under a Sycamoure, and all things keepe
Time with the season, only shee doth carry
June in her eyes, in her heart *January*.

A Song

Aske me no more where *Jove* bestowes,
When *June* is past, the fading rose:
For in your beauties orient deepe,
These Flowers as in their causes sleepe.

Aske me no more whither doe stray
The golden Atomes of the day:
For in pure love heaven did prepare
Those powders to inrich your haire.

Aske me no more whither doth hast
The Nightingale when May is past:
For in your sweet dividing throat
She winters, and keepes warme her note.

Aske me no more where those starres light,
That downewards fall in dead of night:

For in your eyes they sit, and there,
Fixed become as in their sphere.

Aske me no more if East or West,
The Phenix builds her spicy nest:
For unto you at last shee flies,
And in your fragrant bosome dyes.

WILLIAM STRODE

On Westwall Downes

When Westwall Downes I gan to tread,
Where cleanely wynds the greene did sweepe,
Methought a landskipp there was spread,
Here a bush and there a sheepe:
  The pleated wrinkles of the face
  Of wave-swolne earth did lend such grace,
  As shadowings in Imag'ry
  Which both deceive and please the eye.

The sheepe sometymes did tread the maze
By often wynding in and in,
And sometymes round about they trace
Which mylkmaydes call a Fairie ring:
  Such semicircles have they runne,
  Such lynes across so trymly spunne
  That sheppeards learne whenere they please
  A new Geometry with ease.

The slender food upon the downe
Is allwayes even, allwayes bare,
Which neither spring nor winter's frowne
Can ought improve or ought impayre:
  Such is the barren Eunuches chynne,
  Which thus doth evermore begynne
  With tender downe to be orecast
  Which never comes to haire at last.

Here and there twoe hilly crests
Amiddst them hugg a pleasant greene,
And these are like twoe swelling breasts
That close a tender fall betweene.
  Here would I sleepe, or read, or pray
  From early morn till flight of day:
  But harke! a sheepe-bell calls mee upp,
  Like Oxford colledge bells, to supp.

EDMUND WALLER

Old Age

The seas are quiet when the winds give o'er;
So calm are we when passions are no more.
For then we know how vain it was to boast
Of fleeting things, so certain to be lost.
Clouds of affection from our younger eyes
Conceal that emptiness which age descries.

The soul's dark cottage, battered and decayed,
Lets in new light through chinks that Time has made:
Stronger by weakness, wiser men become
As they draw near to their eternal home.
Leaving the old, both worlds at once they view
That stand upon the threshold of the new.

To a Fair Lady Playing with a Snake

Strange, that such horror and such grace
Should dwell together in one place;
A fury's arm, an angel's face!

'Tis innocence and youth which makes
In Chloris' fancy such mistakes,
To start at love and play with snakes.

By this and by her coldness barr'd,
Her servants have a task too hard:
The tyrant has a double guard.

Thrice happy snake, that in her sleeve
May boldly creep: we dare not give
Our thoughts so unconfin'd a leave.

Contented in that nest of snow
He lies, as he his bliss did know,
And to the wood no more would go.

Take heed, fair Eve, you do not make
Another tempter of this snake;
A marble one so warm'd would speak.

RICHARD CRASHAW

An Epitaph upon Husband and Wife, which Died and Were Buried Together

To these whom death again did wed,
This grave's their second marriage bed;
For though the hand of fate could force
'Twixt soul and body a divorce,
It could not sunder man and wife
Because they both liv'd but one life.
Peace, good reader, do not weep;
Peace, the lovers are asleep.
They, sweet turtles, folded lie
In the last knot that love could tie.
And though they lie as they were dead,
Their pillows stone, their sheets of lead,
(Pillow hard, and sheets not warm)
Love made the bed; they'll take no harm.
Let them sleep, let them sleep on
Till this stormy night be gone,
Til th' eternal morrow dawn:
Till the curtains will be drawn,
And they awake into a light
Whose day shall never die in night.

SIR JOHN SUCKLING

The Constant Lover

Out upon it, I have loved
   Three whole days together!
And am like to love three more,
   If it hold fair weather.

Time shall moult away his wings
   Ere he shall discover
In the whole wide world again
   Such a constant lover.

But a pox upon't, no praise
   There is due at all to me:
Love with me had made no stay,
   Had it any been but she.

Had it any been but she,
   And that very very face,
There had been at least ere this
   A dozen dozen in her place.

'Why so pale and wan'

Why so pale and wan, fond lover?
    Prithee, why so pale?
Will, when looking well can't move her,
    Looking ill prevail?
    Prithee, why so pale?

Why so dull and mute, young sinner?
    Prithee, why so mute?
Will, when speaking well can't win her,
    Saying nothing do 't?
    Prithee, why so mute?

Quit, quit for shame! This will not move;
    This cannot take her.
If of herself she will not love,
    Nothing can make her:
    The devil take her!

SAMUEL BUTLER

Hudibras, The Presbyterian Knight

For his religion it was fit
To match his learning and his wit:
'Twas Presbyterian true blue,
For he was of that stubborn crew
Of errant saints, whom all men grant
To be the true Church Militant:
Such as do build their faith upon
The holy text of pike and gun;
Decide all controversies by
Infallible artillery;
And prove their doctrine orthodox
By apostolic blows and knocks;
Call fire and sword and desolation,
A godly-thorough-Reformation,
Which always must be carry'd on,
And still be doing, never done:
As if religion were intended
For nothing else but to be mended.
A sect, whose chief devotion lies
In odd perverse antipathies;
In falling out with that or this,
And finding somewhat still amiss:
More peevish, cross, and splenetic,

That dog distract, or monkey sick.
That with more care keep Holy-day
The wrong, than others the right way:
Compound for sins, they are inclin'd to;
By damning those they have no mind to;
Still so perverse and opposite,
As if they worshipp'd God for spite,
The self-same thing they will abhor
One way, and long another for.
Free-will they one way disavow,
Another, nothing else allow.
All piety consists therein
In them, in other men all sin.

Sidrophel, the Rosicrucian Conjurer

This said, he turned about his steed,
And eftsoons on th' adventure rid;
Where leave we him and Ralph a while,
And to the conjurer turn our style,
To let our reader understand
What's useful of him beforehand.
He had been long t'wards mathematics,
Optics, philosophy, and statics,
Magic, horoscopy, astrology,
And was old dog at physiology;
But as a dog that turns the spit
Bestirs himself, and plies his feet
To climb the wheel, but all in vain,
His own weight brings him down again:
And still he's in the self-same place
Where at his setting out he was;
So in the circle of the arts
Did he advance his nat'ral parts,
Till falling back still, for retreat,
He fell to juggle, cant, and cheat:
For as those fowls that live in water
Are never wet, he did but smatter;
Whate'er he laboured to appear,
His understanding still was clear;
Yet none a deeper knowledge boasted,
Since old Hodge Bacon, and Bob Grosted.
Th' intelligible world he knew,
And all men dream on 't to be true:
That in this world there's not a wart
That has not there a counterpart;

Nor can there, on the face of ground
An individual beard be found
That has not, in that foreign nation,
A fellow of the self-same fashion;
So cut, so coloured, and so curl'd,
As those are in th' inferior world.

RICHARD LOVELACE

To Lucasta, Going to the Wars

Tell me not, sweet, I am unkind,
That from the nunnery
Of thy chaste breast and quiet mind,
To war and arms I fly.

True, a new mistress now I chase,
The first foe in the field;
And with a stronger faith embrace
A sword, a horse, a shield.

Yet this inconstancy is such
As you too shall adore;
I could not love thee, dear, so much,
Lov'd I not Honour more.

La Bella Bona-Roba

I cannot tell who loves the skeleton
Of a poor marmoset, naught but bone, bone:
Give me a nakedness with her clothes on.

Such whose white-satin upper coat of skin,
Cut upon velvet rich incarnadin,
Has yet a body (and of flesh) within.

Sure it is meant good husbandry in men,
Who so incorporate with airy lean,
T' repair their sides, and get their rib again.

Hard hap unto that huntsman that decrees
Fat joys for all his sweat, whenas he sees,
After his 'say, naught but his keeper's fees.

Then Love, I beg, when next thou takest thy bow,
Thy angry shafts, and dost heart-chasing go,
Pass rascal deer, strike me the largest doe.

To Althea from Prison

When Love with unconfinèd wings
  Hovers within my gates;
And my divine Althea brings
  To whisper at the grates:
When I lie tangled in her hair,
  And fettered to her eye;
The birds that wanton in the air,
  Know no such liberty.

When flowing cups run swiftly round
  With no allaying Thames,
Our careless heads with roses bound,
  Our hearts with loyal flames;
When thirsty grief in wine we steep,
  When healths and draughts go free,
Fishes that tipple in the deep,
  Know no such liberty.

When, like committed linnets, I
  With shriller throat shall sing
The sweetness, mercy, majesty,
  And glories of my King;
When I shall voice aloud, how good
  He is, how great should be;
Enlargèd winds that curl the flood,
  Know no such liberty.

Stone walls do not a prison make,
  Nor iron bars a cage;
Minds innocent and quiet take
  That for an hermitage;
If I have freedom in my love,
  And in my soul am free;
Angels alone that soar above,
  Enjoy such liberty.

The Grasshopper

To My Noble Friend Mr Charles Cotton

O thou that swing'st upon the waving hair
  Of some well-filled oaten beard,
Drunk every night with a delicious tear
  Dropp'd thee from heav'n where now th' art rear'd;

The joys of earth and air are thine entire,
  That with thy feet and wings dost hop and fly;
And when thy poppy works, thou dost retire
  To thy carv'd acorn-bed to lie.

Up with the day, the sun thou welcomest then,
  Sport'st in the gilt plats of his beams,
And all these merry days mak'st merry men,
  Thyself, and melancholy streams.

But ah the sickle! golden ears are cropp'd,
  Ceres and Bacchus bid good night;
Sharp frosty fingers all your flow'rs have topp'd,
  And what scythes spar'd, winds shave off quite.

Poor verdant fool, and now green ice! thy joys,
  Large and as lasting as thy perch of grass,
Bid us lay in 'gainst winter rain, and poise
  Their floods with an o'erflowing glass.

Thou best of men and friends! we will create
  A genuine summer in each other's breast;
And spite of this cold time and frozen fate,
  Thaw us a warm seat to our rest.

Our sacred hearths shall burn eternally
  As vestal flames; the North-wind, he
Shall strike his frost-stretch'd wings, dissolve, and fly
  This Ætna in epitome.

Dropping December shall come weeping in,
  Bewail th' usurping of his reign;
But when in showers of old Greek we begin,
  Shall cry he hath his crown again.

Night as clear Hesper shall our tapers whip
  From the light casements where we play,
And the dark hag from her black mantle strip,
  And stick there everlasting day.

Thus richer than untempted kings are we,
  That asking nothing, nothing need:
Though lord of all what seas embrace, yet he
  That wants himself is poor indeed.

ANNE BRADSTREET

To my Dear and Loving Husband

If ever two were one, then surely we.
If ever man were lov'd by wife, then thee.
If ever wife was happy in a man,
Compare with me, ye women, if you can.
I prize thy love more than whole Mines of gold,
Or all the riches that the East doth hold.
My love is such that Rivers cannot quench,
Nor ought but love from thee give recompence.
They love is such I can no way repay;
The heavens reward thee manifold I pray.
Then while we live, in love lets so persever,
That when we live no more, we may live ever.

ANDREW MARVELL

The Mower against Gardens

Luxurious Man, to bring his Vice in use,
  Did after him the World seduce:
And from the fields the Flow'rs and Plants allure,
  Where Nature was most plain and pure.
He first enclos'd within the Gardens square
  A dead and standing pool of Air:
And a more luscious Earth for them did knead,
  Which stupifi'd them while it fed.
The Pink grew then as double as his Mind;
  The nutriment did change the kind.
With strange perfumes he did the Roses taint.
  And Flow'rs themselves were taught to paint.
The Tulip, white, did for complexion seek;
  And learn'd to interline its cheek:
Its Onion root they then so high did hold,
  That one was for a Meadow sold.
Another World was search'd, through Oceans new,
  To find the Marvel of Peru.
And yet these Rarities might be allow'd,
  To Man, that sov'raign thing and proud;
Had he not dealt between the Bark and Tree,
  Forbidden mixtures there to see.
No Plant now knew the Stock from which it came;
  He grafts upon the Wild the Tame:
That the uncertain and adult'rate fruit

Might put the Palate in dispute.
His green Seraglio has its Eunuchs too;
Lest any Tyrant him out-do.
And in the Cherry he does Nature vex,
To procreate without a Sex.
'Tis all enforc'd; the Fountain and the Grot;
While the sweet Fields do lie forgot:
Where willing Nature does to all dispence
A wild and fragrant Innocence:
And Fauns and Fairies do the Meadows till,
More by their presence than their skill.
Their Statues polish'd by some ancient hand,
May to adorn the Gardens stand:
But howso'ere the Figures do excel,
The Gods themselves with us do dwell.

The Garden

How vainly men themselves amaze
To win the palm, the oak, or bays,
And their uncessant labours see
Crowned from some single herb or tree,
Whose short and narrow-vergèd shade
Does prudently their toils upbraid;
While all flowers and all trees do close
To weave the garlands of repose!

Fair Quiet, have I found thee here,
And Innocence, thy sister dear?
Mistaken long, I sought you then
In busy companies of men:
Your sacred plants, if here below,
Only among the plants will grow:
Society is all but rude
To this delicious solitude.

No white nor red was ever seen
So amorous as this lovely green.
Fond lovers, cruel as their flame,
Cut in these trees their mistress' name:
Little, alas! they know or heed
How far these beauties hers exceed!
Fair trees! wheresoe'er your barks I wound,
No name shall but your own be found.

When we have run our passions' heat,
Love hither makes his best retreat:
The gods, that mortal beauty chase,
Still in a tree did end their race;

Apollo hunted Daphne so,
Only that she might laurel grow;
And Pan did after Syrinx speed
Not as a nymph, but for a reed.

What wondrous life is this I lead!
Ripe apples drop about my head;
The luscious clusters of the vine
Upon my mouth do crush their wine;
The nectarine and curious peach
Into my hands themselves do reach;
Stumbling on melons, as I pass,
Ensnared with flowers, I fall on grass.

Meanwhile the mind from pleasure less
Withdraws into its happiness;
The mind, that Ocean where each kind
Does straight its own resemblance find;
Yet it creates, transcending these,
Far other worlds, and other seas;
Annihilating all that's made
To a green thought in a green shade.

Here at the fountain's sliding foot,
Or at some fruit-tree's mossy root,
Casting the body's vest aside,
My soul into the boughs does glide;
There, like a bird, it sits and sings,
Then whets and combs its silver wings,
And, till prepared for longer flight,
Waves in its plumes the various light.

Such was that happy Garden-state
While man there walked without a mate:
After a place so pure and sweet,
What other help could yet be meet!
But 'twas beyond a mortal's share
To wander solitary there:
Two paradises 'twere in one,
To live in Paradise alone.

How well the skilful gardener drew
Of flowers and herbs this dial new!
Where, from above, the milder sun
Does through a fragrant zodiac run:
And, as it works, the industrious bee
Computes its time as well as we.
How could such sweet and wholesome hours
Be reckoned, but with herbs and flowers.

To His Coy Mistress

Had we but world enough, and time,
This coyness, Lady, were no crime.
We would sit down, and think which way
To walk, and pass our long love's day.
Thou by the Indian Ganges' side
Should'st rubies find: I by the tide
Of Humber would complain. I would
Love you ten years before the Flood:
And you should if you please refuse
Till the conversion of the Jews.
My vegetable love should grow
Vaster than empires, and more slow.
An hundred years should go to praise
Thine eyes, and on thy forehead gaze.
Two hundred to adore each breast:
But thirty thousand to the rest.
An age at least to every part,
And the last age should show your heart.
For, Lady, you deserve this state;
Nor would I love at lower rate.
But at my back I always hear
Time's winged chariot hurrying near:
And yonder all before us lie
Deserts of vast eternity.
Thy beauty shall no more be found;
Nor, in thy marble vault, shall sound
My echoing song: then worms shall try
That long preserved virginity:
And your quaint honour turn to dust;
And into ashes all my lust.
The grave's a fine and private place,
But none I think do there embrace.
Now therefore, while the youthful hue
Sits on thy skin like morning dew,
And while thy willing soul transpires
At every pore with instant fires,
Now let us sport us while we may;
And now, like amorous birds of prey,
Rather at once our time devour,
Than languish in his slow-chapped power.
Let us roll all our strength, and all
Our sweetness, up into one ball:
And tear our pleasures with rough strife,
Thorough the iron gates of life.
Thus, though we cannot make our sun
Stand still, yet we will make him run.

An Horatian Ode upon Cromwell's Return from Ireland

The forward youth that would appear
Must now forsake his muses dear,
  Nor in the shadows sing
  His numbers languishing.
'Tis time to leave the books in dust,
And oil th' unused armour's rust,
  Removing from the wall
  The corslet of the hall.
So restless Cromwell could not cease
In the inglorious arts of peace,
  But through advent'rous war
  Urged his active star.
And, like the three fork'd lightning, first
Breaking the clouds where it was nurst,
  Did through his own side
  His fiery way divide.
For 'tis all one to courage high
The emulous or enemy;
  And with such to inclose
  Is more then to oppose.
Then burning through the air he went,
And palaces and temples rent:
  And Caesar's head at last
  Did through his laurels blast.
'Tis madness to resist or blame
The force of angry heaven's flame:
  And, if we would speak true,
  Much to the man is due.
Who, from his private gardens, where
He liv'd reserved and austere,
  As if his highest plot
  To plant the bergamot,
Could by industrious valour climb
To ruin the great work of time,
  And cast the kingdom old
  Into another mould.
Though justice against fate complain,
And plead the ancient rights in vain:
  But those do hold or break
  As men are strong or weak.
Nature that hateth emptiness,
Allows of penetration less:
  And therefore must make room
  Where greater spirits come.
What field of all the civil wars,
Where his were not the deepest scars?
  And Hampton shows what part

He had of wiser art.
Where, twining subtile fears with hope,
He wove a net of such a scope,
That Charles himself might chase
To Caresbrook's narrow case.
That thence the royal actor borne
The tragic scaffold might adorn:
While round the armed bands
Did clap their bloody hands.
He nothing common did or mean
Upon that memorable scene:
But with his keener eye
The axe's edge did try:
Nor call'd the gods with vulgar spite
To vindicate his helpless right,
But bow'd his comely head,
Down as upon a bed.
This was that memorable hour
Which first assur'd the forced pow'r.
So when they did design
The Capitol's first line,
A bleeding head where they begun,
Did fright the architects to run;
And yet in that the State
Foresaw its happy fate.
And now the Irish are asham'd
To see themselves in one year tam'd:
So much one man can do,
That does both act and know.
They can affirm his praises best,
And have, though overcome, confest
How good he is, how just,
And fit for highest trust:
Nor yet grown stiffer with command,
But still in the republic's hand:
How fit he is to sway
That can so well obey.
He to the commons feet presents
A kingdom, for his first years rents:
And, what he may, forbears
His fame to make it theirs:
And has his sword and spoils ungirt,
To lay them at the public's skirt.
So when the falcon high
Falls heavy from the sky,
She, having kill'd, nor more does search,
But on the next green bough to perch;
Where, when he first does lure,
The Falconer has her sure.

What may not then our isle presume
While victory his crest does plume!
  What may not others fear
  If thus he crown each year!
A Caesar he ere long to Gaul,
To Italy an Hannibal,
  And to all states not free
  Shall clymacterick be.
The Pict no shelter now shall find
Within his party-colour'd mind;
  But from this valour sad
  Shrink underneath the plad:
Happy if in the tufted brake
The English hunter him mistake.
  Nor lay his hounds in near
  The Caledonian deer.
But thou the wars' and fortune's Son
March indefatigably on:
  And for the last effect
  Still keep thy sword erect;
Besides the force it has to fright
The spirits of the shady night,
  The same arts that did gain
  A pow'r must it maintain.

HENRY VAUGHAN

The Waterfall

With what deep murmurs through time's silent stealth
Doth thy transparent, cool, and watery wealth
    Here flowing fall,
    And chide and call,
As if his liquid loose retinue stayed
Lingering, and were of this steep place afraid,
    The common pass
    Where, clear as glass,
    All must descend
    Not to an end;
But quickened by this deep and rocky grave,
Rise to a longer course more bright and brave.

  Dear stream! dear bank, where often I
  Have sat, and pleased my pensive eye,
  Why, since each drop of thy quick store
  Runs thither, whence it flowed before,
  Should poor souls fear a shade or night,

Who came, sure, from a sea of light?
Or since those drops are all sent back
So sure to thee, that none doth lack,
Why should frail flesh doubt any more
That what God takes, he'll not restore?
O useful Element and clear!
My sacred wash and cleanser here,
My first consigner unto those
Fountains of life, where the Lamb goes,
What sublime turths, and wholesome themes
Lodge in thy mystical, deep streams!
Such as dull man can never find,
Unless that Spirit lead his mind,
Which first upon thy face did move,
And hatched all with his quickening love.
As this loud brook's incessant fall
In streaming rings restagnates all,
Which reach by course the bank, and then
Are no more seen, just so pass men.
O my invisible estate,
My glorious liberty, still late!
Thou art the channel my soul seeks,
Not this with cataracts and creeks.

Peace

My soul, there is a country
  Far beyond the stars,
Where stands a wingèd sentry
  All skilful in the wars:
There above noise and danger
  Sweet Peace sits crowned with smiles,
And One born in a manger
  Commands the beauteous files.
He is thy gracious friend
  And – O my soul, awake! –
Did in pure love descend
  To die here for thy sake.
If thou canst get but thither,
  There grows the flower of Peace,
The Rose that cannot wither,
  Thy fortress, and thy ease.
Leave then thy foolish ranges
  For none can thee secure,
But one who never changes,
  Thy God, thy life, thy cure.

'They are all gone into the world of light'

They are all gone into the world of light!
   And I alone sit lingering here;
Their very memory is fair and bright,
   And my sad thoughts doth clear.

It glows and glitters in my cloudy breast
   Like stars upon some gloomy grove,
Or those faint beams in which this hill is dressed,
   After the sun's remove.

I see them walking in an air of glory,
   Whose light doth trample on my days:
My days, which are at best but dull and hoary,
   Mere glimmering and decays.

O holy Hope! and high Humility,
   High as the heavens above!
These are your walks, and you have showed them me,
   To kindle my cold love.

Dear beauteous Death! the jewel of the Just,
   Shining nowhere but in the dark;
What mysteries do lie beyond thy dust,
   Could man outlook that mark!

He that hath found some fledged bird's nest may know,
   At first sight, if the bird be flown;
But what fair well or grove he sings in now,
   That is to him unknown.

And yet, as angels in some brighter dreams
   Call to the soul, when man doth sleep;
So some strange thoughts transcend our wonted themes,
   And into glory peep.

If a star were confined into a tomb,
   Her captive flames must needs burn there;
But when the hand that locked her up gives room,
   She'll shine through all the sphere.

O Father of eternal life, and all
   Created glories under thee!
Resume thy spirit from this world of thrall
   Into true liberty.

Either disperse these mists, which blot and fill
   My perspective still as they pass,
Or else remove me hence unto that hill,
   Where I shall need no glass.

The World

I saw Eternity the other night
Like a great Ring of pure and endless light,
        All calm as it was bright;
And round beneath it, Time, in hours, days, years,
        Driven by the spheres,
Like a vast shadow moved, in which the world
        And all her train were hurled.
The doting Lover in his quaintest strain
        Did their complain;
Near him, his lute, his fancy, and his flights,
        Wit's sour delights;
With gloves and knots, the silly snares of pleasure;
        Yet his dear treasure
All scattered lay, while he his eyes did pour
        Upon a flower.

The darksome Statesman hung with weights and woe,
Like a thick midnight fog, moved there so slow
        He did nor stay nor go;
Condemning thoughts, like sad eclipses, scowl
        Upon his soul,
And clouds of crying witnesses without
        Pursued him with one shout.
Yet digged the mole, and, lest his ways be found,
        Worked under ground,
Where he did clutch his prey; but One did see
        That policy.
Churches and altars fed him, perjuries
        Were gnats and flies;
It rained about him blood and tears, but he
        Drank them as free.

The fearful Miser on a heap of rust
Sat pining all his life there, did scarce trust
        His own hands with the dust;
Yet would not place one piece above, but lives
        In fear of thieves.
Thousands there were as frantic as himself,
        And hugged each one his pelf.
The downright Epicure placed heaven in sense
        And scorned pretence;
While others, slipped into a wide excess,
        Said little less;
The weaker sort, slight, trivial wares enslave,
        Who think them brave;
And poor despisèd Truth sat counting by
        Their victory.

Yet some, who all this while did weep and sing,
And sing and weep, soared up into the Ring;
But most would use no wing.
'O fools', said I, 'thus to prefer dark night
Before true light,
To live in grots, and caves, and hate the day
Because it shows the way,
The way which from this dead and dark abode
Leads up to God,
A way where you might tread the sun, and be
More bright that he.'
But as I did their madness so discuss,
One whispered thus,
This Ring the Bridegroom did for none provide
But for his Bride.

MARGARET CAVENDISH, DUCHESS OF NEWCASTLE

Soul and Body

Great Nature she doth clothe the soul within
A fleshly garment which the Fates do spin.
And when these garments are grown old and bare,
With sickness torn, Death takes them off with care,
And folds them up in peace and quiet rest,
And lays them safe within an earthly chest;
Then scours them, and makes them sweet and clean,
Fit for the soul to wear those clothes again.

JOHN BUNYAN

'He that is down needs fear no fall'

He that is down needs fear no fall,
He that is low, no pride;
He that is humble, ever shall
Have God to be his Guide,

I am content with what I have,
Little be it, or much:
And Lord, contentment still I crave,
Because thou savest such.

Fulness to such a burden is
That go on Pilgrimage;
Here little, and hereafter Bliss,
Is best from age to age.

'What danger is the Pilgrim in'

What danger is the Pilgrim in,
How many are his Foes,
How many ways there are to sin,
No living mortal knows.

Some of the Ditch shy are, yet can
Lie tumbling in the Mire;
Some, though they shun the Frying-pan,
Do leap into the Fire.

JOHN MILTON

Epilogue from Samson Agonistes

All is best, though we oft doubt,
What th'unsearchable dispose
Of highest wisdom brings about,
And ever best found in the close.
Oft he seems to hide his face,
But unexpectedly returns
And to his faithful Champion hath in place
Bore witness gloriously; whence *Gaza* mourns
And all that band them to resist
His uncontroulable intent;
His servants hee with new acquist
Of true experience from this great event
With peace and consolation hath dismist,
And calm of mind all passion spent.

Sabrina

The Spirit. Sabrina fair,
Listen where thou art sitting
Under the glassy, cool, translucent wave,
In twisted braids of lilies knitting
The loose train of thy amber-dropping hair;
Listen for dear honour's sake,
Goddess of the silver lake,
Listen and save.

Listen and appear to us
In name of great Oceanus,
By the earth-shaking Neptune's mace,
And Tethys' grave majestic pace,

By hoary Nereus' wrinkled look,
And the Carpathian wizard's hook,
By scaly Triton's winding shell,
And old soothsaying Glaucus' spell,
By Leucothea's lovely hands,
And her son that rules the strands,
By Thetis' tinsel-slippered feet,
And the songs of Sirens sweet,
By dead Parthenope's dear tomb,
And fair Ligea's golden comb,
Wherewith she sits on diamond rocks
Sleeking her soft alluring locks;
By all the nymphs that nightly dance
Upon thy streams with wily glance,
Rise, rise, and heave thy rosy head
From thy coral-paven bed,
And bridle in thy headlong wave,
Till thou our summons answered have.
Listen and save!

Sabrina. By the rushy-fringèd bank,
Where grows the willow and the osier dank,
My sliding chariot stays,
Thick set with agate, and the azurn sheen
Of turkis blue, and emerald green,
That in the channel strays.
Whilst from off the waters fleet
Thus I set my printless feet
O'er the cowslip's velvet head,
That bends not as I tread.
Gentle swain, at thy request
I am here!

On His Blindness

When I consider how my light is spent,
E're half my days, in this dark world and wide,
And that one Talent which is death to hide,
Lodg'd with me useless, though my Soul more bent
To serve therewith my Maker, and present
My true account, least he returning chide,
Doth God exact day-labour, light deny'd,
I fondly ask; But patience to prevent
That murmur, soon replies, God doth not need
Either man's work or his own gifts, who best
Bear his milde yoak, they serve him best, his State
Is Kingly. Thousands at his bidding speed
And post o're Land and Ocean without rest:
They also serve who only stand and waite.

On the Late Massacre in Piedmont

Avenge, O Lord, thy slaughtered saints, whose bones
  Lie scattered on the Alpine mountains cold,
  Even them who kept thy truth so pure of old
  When all our fathers worshipped stocks and stones,
Forget not; in thy book record their groans
  Who were thy sheep, and in their ancient fold
  Slain by the bloody Piedmontese that rolled
  Mother with infant down the rocks. Their moans
The vales redoubled to the hills, and they
  To heaven. Their martyred blood and ashes sow
  O'er all the Italian fields, where still doth sway
The triple tyrant, that from these may grow
  A hundredfold, who, having learnt thy way,
  Early may fly the Babylonian woe.

from *Paradise Lost*

Of Mans First Disobedience, and the Fruit
Of that Forbidden Tree, whose mortal tast
Brought Death into the World, and all our woe,
With loss of *Eden*, till one greater Man
Restore us, and regain the blissful Seat,
Sing Heav'nly Muse, that on the secret top
Of *Oreb*, or of *Sinai*, didst inspire
That Shepherd, who first taught the chosen Seed,
In the Beginning how the Heav'ns and Earth
Rose out of *Chaos*: Or if *Sion* Hill
Delight three more, and *Siloa's* Brook that flow'd
Fast by the Oracle of God; I thence
Invoke thy aid to my adventrous Song,
That with no middle flight intends to soar
Above th' *Aonian* Mount, while it pursues
Things unattempted yet in Prose or Rhime.
And chiefly Thou O Spirit, that dost prefer
Before all Temples th' upright heart and pure,
Instruct me, for Thou know'st; Thou from the first
Wast present, and with mighty wings outspread
Dove-like satst brooding on the vast Abyss
And mad'st it pregnant: What in me is dark
Illumine, what is low raise and support;
That to the highth of this great Argument
I may assert Eternal Providence,
And justifie the wayes of God to men.
  Say first, for Heav'n hides nothing from they view
Nor the deep Tract of Hell, say first what cause

Mov'd our Grand Parents in that happy State,
Favour'd of Heav'n so highly, to fall off
From their Creator, and transgress his Will
For one restraint, Lords of the World besides?
Who first seduc'd them to that fowl revolt?
Th' infernal Serpent; he it was, whose guile
Stird up with Envy and Revenge, deceiv'd
The Mother of Mankinde, what time his Pride
Had cast him out from Heav'n, with all his Host
Of Rebel Angels, by whose aid aspiring
To set himself in Glory above his Peers,
He trusted to have equal'd the most High,
If he oppos'd; and with ambitious aim
Against the Throne and Monarchy of God
Rais'd impious War in Heav'n and Battel proud
With vain attempt. Him the Almighty Power
Hurld headlong flaming from th' Ethereal Skie
With hideous ruine and combustion down
To bottomless perdition, there to dwell
In Adamantine Chains and penal Fire,
Who durst defie th' Omnipotent to Arms.
Nine times the Space that measures Day and Night
To mortal men, he with his horrid crew
Lay vanquisht, rowling in the fiery Gulfe
Confounded though immortal: But his doom
Reserv'd him to more wrath; for now the thought
Both of lost happiness and lasting pain
Torments him; round he throws his baleful eyes
That witness'd huge affliction and dismay
Mixt with obdurate pride and stedfast hate:
At once as far as Angels kenn he views
The dismal Situation waste and wilde,
A Dungeon horrible, on all sides round
As one great Furnace flam'd, yet from those flames
No light, but rather darkness visible
Serv'd only to discover sights of woe,
Regions of sorrow, doleful shades, where peace
And rest can never dwell, hope never comes
That comes to all; but torture without end
Still urges, and a fiery Deluge, fed
With ever-burning Sulphur unconsum'd:
Such place Eternal Justice had prepar'd
For those rebellious, here their Prison ordain'd
In utter darkness, and their portion set
As far remov'd from God and light of Heav'n
As from the Center thrice to th' utmost Pole.
O how unlike the place from whence they fell!
There the companions of his fall, o'rewhelm'd
With Floods and Whirlwinds of tempestuous fire,

He soon discerns, and weltring by his side
One next himself in power, and next in crime,
Long after known in *Palestine*, and nam'd
Bëëlzebub. To whom th' Arch-Enemy,
And thence in Heav'n call'd Satan, with bold words
Breaking the horrid silence thus began.
  If thou beest he; But O how fall'n! how chang'd
From him, who in the happy Realms of Light
Cloth'd with transcendent brightness didst outshine
Myriads though bright: If he whom mutual league,
United thoughts and counsels, equal hope,
And hazard in the Glorious Enterprize,
Joynd with me once, now misery hath joynd
In equal ruin: into what Pit thou seest
From what highth fal'n, so much the stronger provd
He with his Thunder: and till then who knew
The force of those dire Arms? yet not for those
Nor what the Potent Victor in his rage
Can else inflict do I repent or change,
Though chang'd in outward lustre; that fixt mind
And high disdain, from sence of injur'd merit,
That with the mightiest rais'd me to contend,
And to the fierce contention brought along
Innumerable force of Spirits arm'd
That durst dislike his reign, and me preferring,
His utmost power with adverse power oppos'd
In dubious Battel on the Plains of Heav'n,
And shook his throne. What though the field be lost?
All is not lost; the unconquerable Will,
And study of revenge, immortal hate,
And courage never to submit or yield:
And what is else not to be overcome?
That Glory never shall his wrath or might
Extort from me. To bow and sue for grace
With suppliant knee, and deifie his power
Who from the terrour of this Arm so late
Doubted his Empire, that were low indeed,
That were an ignominy and shame beneath
This downfall; since by Fate the strength of Gods
And this Empyreal substance cannot fail,
Since through experience of this great event
In Arms not worse, in foresight much advanc't,
We may with more successful hope resolve
To wage by force or guile eternal Warr
Irreconcileable, to our grand Foe,
Who now triumphs, and in th' excess of joy
Sole reigning holds the Tyranny of Heav'n.
  So spake th' Apostate Angel, though in pain,
Vaunting aloud, but rackt with deep despare:

And him thus answer'd soon his bold Compeer.
O Prince, O Chief of many Throned Powers,
That led th' imbattelld Seraphim to Warr
Under thy conduct, and in dreadful deeds
Fearless, endanger'd Heav'ns perpetual King;
And put to proof his high Supremacy,
Whether upheld by strength, or Chance, or Fate,
Too well I see and rue the dire event,
That with sad overthrow and foul defeat
Hath lost us Heav'n, and all this mighty Host
In horrible destruction laid thus low,
As far as Gods and Heav'nly Essences
Can Perish: for the mind and spirit remains
Invincible, and vigour soon returns,
Though all our Glory extinct, and happy state
Here swallow'd up in endless misery.
But what if he our Conquerour, (whom I now
Of force believe Almighty, since no less
Then such could hav orepow'rd such force as ours)
Have left us this our spirit and strength intire
Strongly to suffer and support our pains,
That we may so suffice his vengeful ire,
Or do him mightier service as his thralls
By right of Warr, what e're his business be
Here in the heart of Hell to work in Fire,
Or do his Errands in the gloomy Deep;
What can it then avail though yet we feel
Strength undiminisht, or eternal being
To undergo eternal punishment?
Whereto with speedy words th' Arch-fiend reply'd.
Fall'n Cherube, to be weak is miserable
Doing or Suffering: but of this be sure,
To do ought good never will be our task,
But ever to do ill our sole delight,
As being the contrary to his high will
Whom we resist. If then his Providence
Out of our evil seek to bring forth good,
Our labour must be to pervert that end,
And out of good still to find means of evil;
Which oft times may succeed, so as perhaps
Shall grieve him, if I fail not, and disturb
His inmost counsels from their destind aim.
But see the angry Victor hath recall'd
His Ministers of vengeance and pursuit
Back to the Gates of Heav'n: The Suphurous Hail
Shot after us in storm, oreblown hath laid
The fiery Surge, that from the Precipice
Of Heav'n receiv'd us falling, and the Thunder,
Wing'd with red Lightning and impetuous rage,

Perhaps hath spent his shafts, and ceases now
To bellow through the vast and boundless Deep.
Let us not slip th' occasion, whether scorn,
Or satiate fury yield it from our Foe.
Seest thou yon dreary Plain, forlorn and wilde,
The seat of desolation, voyd of light,
Save what the glimmering of these livid flames
Casts pale and dreadful? Thither let us tend
From off the tossing of these fiery waves,
There rest, if any rest can harbour there,
And reassembling our afflicted Powers,
Consult how we may henceforth most offend
Our Enemy, our own loss how repair,
How overcome this dire Calamity,
What reinforcement we may gain from Hope,
If not what resolution from despare.
  Thus Satan talking to his neerest Mate
With Head up-lift above the wave, and Eyes
That sparkling blaz'd, his other Parts besides
Prone on the Flood, extended long and large
Lay floating many a rood, in bulk as huge
As whom the Fables name of monstrous size,
Titanian, or *Earth-born*, that warr'd on *Jove*,
Briarios or *Typhon*, whom the Den
By ancient *Tarsus* held, or that Sea-beast
Leviathan, which God of all his works
Created hugest that swim th' Ocean stream:
Him haply slumbring on the *Norway* foam
The Pilot of some small night-founder'd Skiff,
Deeming some Island, oft, as Sea-men tell,
With fixed Anchor in his skaly rind
Moors by his side under the Lee, while Night
Invests the Sea, and wished Morn delayes:
So stretcht out huge in length the Arch-fiend lay
Chain'd on the burning Lake, nor even thence
Had ris'n or heav'd his head, but that the will
And high permission of all-ruling Heaven
Left him at large to his own dark designs,
That with reiterated crimes he might
Heap on himself damnation, while he sought
Evil to others, and enrag'd might see
How all his malice serv'd but to bring forth
Infinite goodness, grace and mercy shewn
On Man by him seduc't, but on himself
Treble confusion, wrath and vengeance pour'd.
Forthwith upright he rears from off the Pool
His mighty Stature; on each hand the flames
Drivn backward slope their pointing spires, and rowld
In billows, leave i' th' midst a horrid Vale.

Then with expanded wings he stears his flight
Aloft, incumbent on the dusky Air
That felt unusual weight, till on dry Land
He lights, if it were Land that ever burn'd
With solid, as the Lake with liquid fire;
And such appear'd in hue, as when the force
Of subterranean wind transports a Hill
Torn from *Pelorus*, or the shatter'd side
Of thundring *Ætna*, whose combustible
And fewel'd entrals thence conceiving Fire,
Sublim'd with Mineral fury, aid the Winds,
And leave a singed bottom all involv'd
With stench and smoak: Such resting found the sole
Of unblest feet. Him followed his next Mate,
Both glorying to have scap't the *Stygian* flood
As Gods, and by their own recover'd strength,
Not by the sufferance of supernal Power.
  Is this the Region, this the Soil, the Clime,
Said then the lost Arch Angel, this the seat
That we must change for Heav'n, this mournful gloom
For that celestial light? Be it so, since hee
Who now is Sovran can dispose and bid
What shall be right: fardest from him is best
Whom reason hath equald, force hath made supream
Above his equals. Farewel happy Fields
Where Joy for ever dwells: Hail horrours, hail
Infernal world, and thou profoundest Hell
Receive thy new Possessor: One who brings
A mind not to be chang'd by Place or Time.
The mind is its own place, and in it self
Can make a Heav'n of Hell, a Hell of Heav'n.
What matter where, if I be still the same,
And what I should be, all but less then hee
Whom Thunder hath made greater? Here at least
We shall be free; th' Almighty hath not built
Here for his envy, will not drive us hence:
Here we may reign secure, and in my choyce
To reign is worth ambition though in Hell:
Better to reign in Hell, then serve in Heav'n.

APHRA BEHN

And Forgive Us Our Trespasses

How prone we are to Sin, how sweet were made
The pleasures, our resistless hearts invade!
Of all my Crimes, the breach of all thy Laws,
Love, soft bewitching Love! has been the cause;
Of all the Paths that Vanity has trod,
That sure will soonest be forgiven of God;
If things on Earth may be to Heaven resembled,
It must be love, pure, constant, undissembled:
But if to Sin by chance the Charmer press,
Forgive, O Lord, forgive our Trespasses.

JOHN DRYDEN

MacFlecknoe

All human things are subject to decay,
And, when Fate summons, Monarchs must obey:
This Fleckno found, who, like Augustus, young
Was call'd to empire, and had govern'd long:
In prose and verse, was own'd, without dispute
Through all the realms of Non-sense, absolute.
This agèd prince now flourishing in peace,
And blest with issue of a large increase,
Worn out with business, did at length debate
To settle the succession of the state:
And pond'ring which of all his sons was fit
To reign, and wage immortal war with wit;
Cry'd, 'tis resolv'd; for Nature pleads that he
Should onely rule, who most resembles me:
Shadwell alone my perfect image bears,
Mature in dullness from his tender years.
Shadwell alone, of all my sons, is he
Who stands confirm'd in full stupidity.
The rest to some faint meaning make pretence,
But Shadwell never deviates into sense.
Some beams of wit on other souls may fall,
Strike through and make a lucid interval;
But Shadwell's genuine night admits no ray,
His rising fogs prevail upon the day:
Besides his goodly fabrick fills the eye,
And seems design'd for thoughtless majesty:
Thoughtless as Monarch Oakes, that shade the plain,
And, spread in solemn state, supinely reign.

Song: Sylvia the Fair

Sylvia the fair, in the bloom of fifteen
Felt an innocent warmth, as she lay on the green;
She had heard of a pleasure, and something she guessed
By the towzing and tumbling and touching her breast:
She saw the men eager, but was at a loss,
What they meant by their sighing and kissing so close;
By their praying and whining,
And clasping and twining,
And panting and wishing,
And sighing and kissing,
And sighing and kissing so close.

Ah she cried, ah for a languishing maid
In a country of Christians to die without aid!
Not a Whig, or a Tory, or trimmer at least,
Or a Protestant parson or Catholic priest,
To instruct a young virgin that is at a loss
What they meant by their sighing and kissing so close;
By their praying and whining,
And clasping and twining,
And panting and wishing,
And sighing and kissing,
And sighing and kissing so close.

Cupid in shape of a swain did appear,
He saw the sad wound, and in pity drew near,
Then show'd her his arrow, and bid her not fear,
For the pain was no more than a maiden may bear;
When the balm was infus'd, she was not at a loss
What they meant by their sighing and kissing so close;
By their praying and whining,
And clasping and twining,
And panting and wishing,
And sighing and kissing,
And sighing and kissing so close.

To the Memory of Mr Oldham

Farewell, too little and too lately known,
Whom I began to think and call my own;
For sure our souls were near allied, and thine
Cast in the same poetic mould with mine.
One common note on either lyre did strike,
And knaves and fools we both abhorred alike:
To the same goal did both our studies drive,

The last set out the soonest did arrive.
Thus Nisus fell upon the slippery place,
While his young friend performed and won the race.
O early ripe! to thy abundant store
What could advancing age have added more?
It might (what Nature never gives the young)
Have taught the numbers of thy native tongue.
But Satire needs not those, and Wit will shine
Through the harsh cadence of a rugged line.
A noble error, and but seldom made,
When poets are by too much force betrayed.
Thy generous fruits, though gathered ere their prime
Still showed a quickness; and maturing time
But mellows what we write to the dull sweets of Rhyme.
Once more, hail and farewell; farewell, thou young,
But ah too short, Marcellus of our tongue;
Thy brows with ivy, and with laurels bound;
But Fate and gloomy Night encompass thee around.

JOHN WILMOT, EARL OF ROCHESTER

A Satire Against Reason and Mankind

Were I, who to my cost already am
One of those strange, prodigious Creatures Man,
A spirit free to choose for my own share
What case of Flesh and Blood I'd please to wear,
I'd be a Dog, a Monkey or a Bear,
Or anything but that vain Animal
Who is so proud of being Rational.
The Senses are too gross, and he'll contrive
A sixth, to contradict the other five;
And before certain Instinct, will prefer
Reason, which fifty times for one does err.
Reason, an Ignis fatuus in the Mind,
Which leaves the Light of Nature (Sense) behind;
Pathless and dangerous, wandering ways it takes
Through Error's fenny Boggs and thorny Brakes;
Whilst the misguided Follower climbs with Pain
Mountains of Whimseys, heaped in his own Brain:
Stumbling from thought to thought, falls headlong down
Into Doubt's boundless Sea, where like to drown
Books bear him up a while, and make him try
To swim with Bladders of Philosophy;
In hopes still to'ertake the escaping Light
The Vapour dances in his dazzled Sight
Till spent, it leaves him to eternal night.

Then old Age and Experience hand in hand
Lead him to Death, and make him understand,
After a search so painful and so long,
That all his Life he has been in the wrong:
Huddled in Dirt this reasoning Engine lies
Who was so Proud, so Witty, and so Wise.

A Song of a Young Lady to Her Ancient Lover

Ancient person, for whom I
All the flattering youth defy,
Long be it ere thou grow old,
Aching, shaking, crazy, cold;
   But still continue as thou art,
   Ancient person of my heart.

On thy wither'd lips and dry,
Which like barren furrows lie,
Brooding kisses I will pour
Shall thy youthful heat restore
(Such kind showers in autumn fall,
and a second spring recall);
   Nor from thee will ever part,
   Ancient person of my heart.

Thy nobler part, which but to name
In our sex would be counted shame,
By age's frozen grasp possess'd,
From his ice shall be releas'd,
And sooth'd by my reviving hand,
In former warmth and vigour stand.
All a lover's wish can reach
For thy joy my love shall teach,
And for thy pleasure shall improve
All that art can add to love.
   Yet still I love thee without art,
   Ancient person of my heart.

THOMAS TRAHERNE

Shadows in the Water

In unexperienc'd Infancy
Many a sweet Mistake doth ly:
Mistake, tho false, intending tru;
A *Seeming* somwhat more than *View;*
 That doth instruct the Mind
 In Things that ly behind,
And many Secrets to us show
Which afterwards we com to know.

Thus did I by the Water's brink
Another World beneath me think;
And while the lofty spacious Skies
Reversed there abus'd mine Eys,
 I fancy'd other Feet
 Came mine to touch or meet;
As by som Puddle I did play
Another World within it lay.

Beneath the Water Peeple drown'd,
Yet with another Hev'n crown'd,
In spacious Regions seem'd to go
As freely moving to and fro:
 In bright and open Space
 I saw their very face;
Eys, Hands, and Feet they had like mine;
Another Sun did with them shine.

'Twas strange that Peeple there should walk,
And yet I could not hear them talk:
That throu a little watry Chink,
Which one dry Ox or Horse might drink,
 We other Worlds should see,
 Yet not admitted be;
And other Confines there behold
Of Light and Darkness, Heat and Cold.

I call'd them oft, but call'd in vain;
No Speeches we could entertain:
Yet did I there expect to find
Som other World, to pleas my Mind.
 I plainly saw by these
 A new *Antipodes*,
Whom, tho they were so plainly seen,
A Film kept off that stood between.

By walking Men's reversed Feet
I chanc'd another World to meet;
Tho it did not to View exceed
A Phantasm, 'tis a World indeed,
    Where Skies beneath us shine,
    And Earth by Art divine
Another face presents below,
Where Peeple's feet against Ours go.

Within the Regions of the Air,
Compass'd about with Hev'ns fair,
Great Tracts of Land there may be found
Enricht with Fields and fertil Ground;
    Where many num'rous Hosts,
    In those far distant Coasts,
For other great and glorious Ends,
Inhabit, my yet unknown Friends.

O ye that stand upon the Brink,
Whom I so near me, throu the Chink,
With Wonder see: What Faces there,
Whose Feet, whose Bodies, do ye wear?
    I my Companions see
    In You, another Me.
They seemed Others, but are We;
Our second Selvs those Shadows be.

Look how far off those lower Skies
Extend themselves! scarce with mine Eys
I can them reach. O ye my Friends,
What *Secret* borders on those Ends?
    Are lofty Hevens hurl'd
    'Bout your inferior World?
Are ye the Representatives
Of other Peopl's distant Lives?

Of all the Play-mates which I knew
That here I do the Image view
In other Selvs; what can it mean?
But that below the purling Stream
    Som unknown Joys there be
    Laid up in Store for me;
To which I shall, when that thin Skin
Is broken, be admitted in.

EDWARD TAYLOR

Upon a Spider Catching a Fly

Thou sorrow, venom Elfe:
  Is this thy play,
To spin a web out of thyselfe
  To Catch a Fly?
    For why?

I saw a pettish wasp
  Fall foule therein:
Whom yet thy whorle pins did not hasp
  Lest he should fling
    His sting.

But as afraid, remote
  Didst stand hereat,
And with thy little fingers stroke
  And gently tap
    His back.

Thus gently him didst treate
  Lest he should pet,
And in a froppish, aspish heate
  Should greatly fret
    Thy net.

Whereas the silly Fly,
  Caught by its leg,
Thou by the throate took'st hastily,
  And 'hinde the head
    Bite Dead.

This goes to pot, that not
  Nature doth call.
Strive not above what strength hath got,
  Lest in the brawle
    Thou fall.

This Fray seems thus to us:
  Hells Spider gets
His intrails spun to whip Cords thus,
  And wove to nets,
    And sets.

To tangle Adams race
  In's stratagems
To their Destructions, Spoil'd, made base
  By venom things,
    Damn'd Sins.

But mighty, Gracious Lord,
  Communicate
Thy Grace to break the Cord; afford
  Us Glorys Gate
    And State.

We'll Nightingaile sing like,
  When pearcht on high
In Glories Cage, thy glory, bright:
  Yea, thankfully,
    For joy.

LADY MARY CHUDLEIGH

To the Ladies

Wife and servant are the same,
But only differ in the name:
For when that fatal knot is tied,
Which nothing, nothing can divide,
When she the word *Obey* has said,
And man by law supreme has made,
Then all that's kind is laid aside,
And nothing left but state and pride.
Fierce as an eastern prince he grows,
And all his innate rigour shows:
Then but to look, to laugh, or speak,
Will the nuptial contract break.
Like mutes, she signs alone must make,
And never any freedom take,
But still be governed by a nod,
And fear her husband as her god:
Him still must serve, him still obey,
And nothing act, and nothing say,
But what her haughty lord thinks fit,
Who, with the power, has all the wit.
Then shun, oh! shun that wretched state,
And all the fawning flatt'rers hate.
Value yourselves, and men despise:
You must be proud, if you'll be wise.

ANNE FINCH, COUNTESS OF WINCHILSEA

'Give me there (since Heaven has shown)'

Give me there (since Heaven has shown
It was not Good to be alone)
A *Partner* suited to my Mind,
Solitary, pleas'd and kind;
Who, partially, may something see
Preferr'd to all the World in me;
Slighting, by my humble Side,
Fame and Splendor, Wealth and Pride.
When but Two the Earth possest,
'Twas their happiest Days, and best;
They by Bus'ness, nor by Wars,
They by no Domestick Cares,
From each other e'er were drawn,
But in some Grove, or flow'ry Lawn,
Spent the swiftly flying Time,
Spent their own, and Nature's Prime,
In Love; that only Passion giv'n
To perfect Man, whilst Friends with Heaven.
Rage, and Jealousie, and Hate,
Transports of his fallen State,
(When by *Satan's* Wiles betray'd)
Fly those Windings, and that Shade!

A Nocturnal Reverie

In such a night, when every louder wind
Is to its distant cavern safe confined;
And only gently zephyr fans his wings,
And lonely Philomel, still waking, sings;
Or from some tree, famed for the owl's delight,
She, holloaing clear, directs the wanderers right:
In such a night, when passing clouds give place,
Or thinly veil the heaven's mysterious face;
When in some river, overhung with green,
The waving moon and trembling leaves are seen;
When freshened grass now bears itself upright,
And makes cool banks to pleasing rest invite,
Whence springs the woodbind, and the bramble-rose,
And where the sleepy cowslip sheltered grows;
Whilst now a paler hue the foxglove takes,
Yet chequers still with red the dusky brakes:
When scattered glow-worms, but in twilight fine,
Show trivial beauties watch their hour to shine;

Whilst Salisbury stands the test of every light,
In perfect charms and perfect virtue bright.
When odours, which declined repelling day,
Thro' temperate air uninterrupted stray;
When darkened groves their softest shadows wear
And falling waters we distinctly hear;
When through the gloom more venerable shows
Some ancient fabric, awful in repose,
While sunburnt hills their swarthy looks conceal,
And swelling haycocks thicken up the vale:
When the loosed horse now, as his pasture leads,
Comes slowly grazing through the adjoining meads.
Whose stealing pace, and lengthened shade we fear,
Till torn-up forage in his teeth we hear:
When nibbling sheep at large pursue their food,
And unmolested kine re-chew the cud;
When curlews cry beneath the village walls,
And to her straggling brood the partridge calls;
Their short-lived jubilee the creatures keep,
Which but endures, while tyrant man does sleep:
When a sedate content the spirit feels,
And no fierce light disturbs, whilst it reveals;
But silent musings urge the mind to seek
Something, too high for syllables to speak;
Till the free soul to a composedness charmed,
Finding the elements of rage disarmed,
O'er all below a solemn quiet grown,
Joys in the inferior world, and thinks it like her own:
In such a night let me abroad remain,
Till morning breaks, and all's confused again;
Our cares, our toils, our clamours are renewed,
Our pleasures, seldom reached, again pursued.

MATTHEW PRIOR

To a Child of Quality

Five Years Old, 1704. The Author then Forty

Lords, knights, and squires, the numerous band
  That wear the fair Miss Mary's fetters,
Were summoned by her high command
  To show their passion by their letters.

My pen amongst the rest I took,
  Lest those bright eyes, that cannot read,
Should dart their kindling fires, and look
  The power they have to be obeyed.

Nor quality, nor reputation,
   Forbid me yet my flame to tell;
Dear Five-years-old befriends my passion,
   And I may write till she can spell.

For, while she makes her silkworms beds
   With all the tender things I swear;
Whilst all the house my passion reads,
   In papers round her baby's hair;

She may receive and own my flame,
   For, though the strictest prudes should know it,
She'll pass for a most virtuous dame,
   And I for an unhappy poet.

Then too, alas! when she shall tear
   The lines some younger rival sends,
She'll give me leave to write, I fear,
   And we shall still continue friends.

For, as our different ages move,
   'Tis so ordained (would Fate but mend it!)
That I shall be past making love
   When she begins to comprehend it.

Answer to Chloe Jealous

Dear Chloe, how blubbered is that pretty face!
Thy cheek all on fire, and thy hair all uncurled.
Prithee, quit this caprice; and (as old Falstaff says)
Let us e'en talk a little like folks of this world.

How canst thou presume thou has leave to destroy
The beauties which Venus but lent to they keeping?
Those looks were designed to inspire love and joy:
More ordinary eyes may serve people for weeping.

To be vexed at a trifle or two that I writ
Your judgement at once and my passion you wrong:
You take that for fact which will scarce be found wit:
'Od's life! must one swear to the truth of a song?

What I speak, my fair Chloe, and what I write, shows
The difference there is betwixt Nature and Art:
I court others in verse, but I love thee in prose;
And they have my whimsies, but thou hast my heart.

The God of us verse-men, you know, child, the sun,
How after his journeys he sets up his rest:

If at morning o'er Earth 'tis his fancy to run,
At night he reclines on his Thetis's breast.

So when I am wearied with wandering all day,
To thee, my delight, in the evening I come;
No matter what beauties I saw in my way,
They were but my visits, but thou art my home.

Then finish, dear Chloe, this pastoral war,
And let us like Horace and Lydia agree:
For thou are a girl as much brighter than her
As he was a poet sublimer than me.

WILLIAM CONGREVE

'False though she be to me and love'

False though she be to me and love,
I'll ne'er pursue revenge;
For still the charmer I approve
Though I deplore her change.

In hours of bliss we oft have met:
They could not always last;
And though the present I regret,
I'm grateful for the past.

ISAAC WATTS

Crucifixion to the World by the Cross of Christ

When I survey the wond'rous cross
On which the Prince of Glory died,
My richest gain I count but loss,
And pour contempt on all my pride.

Forbid it, Lord, that I should boast
Save in the death of Christ my God;
All the vain things that charm me most,
I sacrifice them to his blood.

See from his head, his hands, his feet,
Sorrow and love flow mingled down;
Did e'er such love and sorrow meet?
Or thorns compose so rich a crown?

His dying crimson like a robe
Spreads o'er his body on the tree;
Then am I dead to all the globe,
And all the globe is dead to me.

Were the whole realm of nature mine,
That were a present far too small;
Love so amazing, so divine,
Demands my soul, my life, my all.

The Sluggard

Tis the voice of the Sluggard; I heard him complain,
'You have wak'd me too soon; I must slumber again.'
As the door on its hinges, so he on his bed,
Turns his sides, and his shoulders, and his heavy head.

'A little more sleep, and a little more slumber,'
Thus he wastes half his days, and his hours without
number,
And when he gets up, he sits folding his hands,
Or walks about sant'ring, or trifling he stands.

I pass'd by his garden, and saw the wild brier,
The thorn and the thistle grow broader and higher;
The clothes than hang on him are turning to rags;
And his money still wastes, till he starves, or he begs.

I made him a visit, still hoping to find
He had took better care for improving his mind:
He told me his dreams, talk'd of eating and drinking;
But he scarce reads his Bible, and never loves thinking.

Said I then to my heart, 'Here's a lesson for me,
That man's but a picture of what I might be.
But thanks to my friends for their care in my breeding,
Who taught me betimes to love working and reading.'

JONATHAN SWIFT

A Description of the Morning

Now hardly here and there a hackney-coach
Appearing, showed the ruddy morn's approach.
Now Betty from her master's bed had flown,
And softly stole to discompose her own.
The slipshod prentice from his master's door

Had pared the dirt, and sprinkled round the floor.
Now Moll had whirled her mop with dext'rous airs,
Prepared to scrub the entry and the stairs.
The youth with broomy stumps began to trace
The kennel[1]-edge, where wheels had worn the place.
The small-coal man was heard with cadence deep,
Till drowned in shriller notes of chimney-sweep.
Duns at his lordship's gate began to meet,
And Brickdust Moll had screamed through half the street.
The turnkey now his flock returning sees,
Duly let out a-nights to steal for fees.
The watchful bailiffs take their silent stands,
And schoolboys lag with satchels in their hands.

[1]gutter

Verses on the Death of Dr Swift

The Time is not remote, when I
Must by the Course of Nature dye:
When I foresee my special Friends,
Will try to find their private Ends:
Tho' it is hardly understood,
Which way my Death can do them good;
Yet, thus methinks, I hear 'em speak;
See, how the Dean begins to break:
Poor Gentleman, he droops apace,
You plainly find it in his Face:
That old Vertigo in his Head,
Will never leave him, till he's dead:
Besides, his Memory decays,
He recollects not what he says;
He cannot call his Friends to Mind;
Forgets the Place where last he din'd:
Plyes you with Stories o'er and o'er,
He told them fifty Times before.
How does he fancy we can sit,
To hear his out-of-fashion'd Wit?
But he takes up with younger Fokes,
Who for his Wine will bear his Jokes:
Faith, he must make his Stories shorter,
Or change his Comrades once a Quarter:
In half the Time, he talks them round;
There must another Sett be found.

For Poetry, he's past his Prime,
He takes an Hour to find a Rhime:
His Fire is out, his Wit decay'd,

His Fancy sunk, his Muse a Jade.
I'd have him throw away his Pen;
But there's no talking to some Men.

And, then their Tenderness appears,
By adding largely to my Years:
'He's older that he would be reckon'd,
And well remembers *Charles* the Second.

'He hardly drinks a Pint of Wine;
And that, I doubt, is no good Sign.
His Stomach too begins to fail:
Last Year we thought him strong and hale;
But now, he's quite another Thing;
I wish he may hold out till Spring.'

* * *

My female Friends, whose tender Hearts
Have better learn'd to act their Parts,
Receive the News in doleful Dumps,
The Dean is dead (and what is Trumps?)
The Lord have Mercy on his Soul
(Ladies I'll venture for the Vole)
Six Deans they say must bear the Pall,
(I wish I knew what King to call.)
Madam, your Husband will attend
The Funeral of so good a friend.
No Madam, 'tis a shocking Sight,
And he's engag'd Tomorrow Night!
My Lady Club wou'd take it ill
If he shou'd fail her at Quadrill.
He lov'd the Dean. (I led a Heart.)
But, dearest Friends, they say, must part.
His Time was come, he ran his Race;
We hope he's in a better Place.

JOSEPH ADDISON

'The spacious Firmament on high'

The spacious Firmament on high,
With all the blue Ethereal Sky,
And spangled Heavens, a shining Frame,
Their great Original proclaim,
Th' unweary'd Sun, from Day to Day,
Does his Creator's Power display;
And publishes, to every Land,
The Work of an Almighty Hand.

Soon as the Evening Shades prevail,
The Moon takes up the wond'rous Tale;
And Nightly, to the list'ning Earth,
Repeats the Story of her Birth:
Whilst all the Stars, that round her burn,
And all the Planets, in their turn,
Confirm the Tidings as they roll,
And spread the Truth from Pole to Pole.

What tho', in solemn Silence, all
Meet round the dark Terrestrial Ball;
What tho', no real Voice, nor Sound,
Admidst their radiant Orbs be found:
In Reason's Ear they all rejoice,
And utter forth a glorious Voice;
For ever Singing as they Shine,
The Hand that made us is Divine.

JOHN GAY

Sweet William's Farewell to Black-Eyed Susan

All in the Downs the fleet was moored,
  The streamers waving in the wind,
When black-eyed Susan came aboard.
  'Oh! where shall I my true love find?
Tell me, ye jovial sailors, tell me true,
If my sweet William sails among the crew.'

William, who, high upon the yard,
  Rocked with the billow to and fro,
Soon as her well-known voice he heard,
  He sighed and cast his eyes below:
The cord slides swiftly through his glowing hands,
And (quick as lightning) on the deck he stands.

So the sweet lark, high-poised in air,
  Shuts close his pinions to his breast
(If, chance, his mate's shrill call he hear)
  And drops at once into her nest.
The noblest captain in the British fleet
Might envy William's lip those kisses sweet.

'O Susan, Susan, lovely dear,
  My vows shall ever true remain;
Let me kiss off that falling tear,
  We only part to meet again.

Change, as ye list, ye winds; my heart shall be
The faithful compass that still points to thee.

'Believe not what the landmen say,
Who tempt with doubts thy constant mind:
They'll tell thee, sailors, when away,
In ev'ry port a mistress find.
Yes, yes, believe them when they tell thee so,
For thou art present weresoe'er I go.

'If to far India's coast we sail,
They eyes are seen in di'monds bright,
Thy breath is Africk's spicy gale,
Thy skin is ivory, so white.
Thus ev'ry beauteous object that I view
Wakes in my soul some charm of lovely Sue.

'Though battle call me from thy arms,
Let not my pretty Susan mourn;
Though cannons roar, yet safe from harms
William shall to his dear return.
Love turns aside the balls that round me fly,
Lest precious tears should drop from Susan's eye.'

The boatswain gave the dreadful word,
The sails their swelling bosom spread,
No longer must she stay aboard:
They kissed, she sighed, he hung his head.
Her less'ning boat unwilling rows to land:
'Adieu!' she cries; and waves her lily hand.

My Own Epitaph

Life is a jest, and all things show it;
I thought so once, but now I know it.

The Dangers of Foot-ball

Where Covent-Garden's famous temple stands,
That boasts the work of Jones' immortal hands;
Columns with plain magnificence appear,
And graceful porches lead along the square:
Here oft' my course I bend, when lo! from far
I spy the furies of the foot-ball war:
The 'prentice quits his shop, to join the crew,
Encreasing crouds the flying game pursue.
Thus, as you roll the ball o'er snowy ground,

The gath'ring globe augments with ev'ry round.
But whither shall I run? the throng draws nigh,
The ball now skims the street, now soars on high;
The dext'rous glazier strong returns the bound,
And gingling sashes on the pent-house sound.

'A fox may steal your hens, sir'

A fox may steal your hens, sir,
A whore your health and pence, sir,
Your daughter rob your chest, sir,
Your wife may steal your rest, sir,
  A thief your goods and plate.

But this is all but picking,
With rest, pence, chest and chicken;
It ever was decreed, sir,
If lawyer's hand is fee'd, sir,
  He steals your whole estate.

Macheath and Polly

Mac. Were I laid on Greenland's coast,
  And in my arms embraced my lass,
Warm amidst eternal frost,
  Too soon the half-year's night would pass.
Polly Were I sold on Indian soil,
  Soon as the burning day was closed,
I could mock the sultry toil,
  When on my charmer's breast reposed.
Mac. And I would love you all the day,
Polly Every night would kiss and play,
Mac. If with me you'd fondly stray
Polly Over the hills and far away.

ALEXANDER POPE

Lines Written in Windsor Forest

All hail, once pleasing, once inspiring shade!
Scene of my youthful loves and happier hours!
Where the kind Muses met me as I stray'd,
  And gently press'd my hand, and said 'Be ours! –

Take all thou e'er shalt have, a constant Muse:
At Court thou may'st be liked, but nothing gain:
Stock thou may'st buy and sell, but always lose,
And love the brightest eyes, but love in vain.'

The Triumph of Dullness

TO DR JONATHAN SWIFT

In vain, in vain – the all-composing Hour
Resistless falls: the Muse obeys the Pow'r.
She comes! she comes! the sable Throne behold
Of Night primaeval and of Chaos old!
Before her, Fancy's gilded clouds decay,
And all its varying Rain-bows die away.
Wit shoots in vain its momentary fires,
The meteor drops, and in a flash expires.
As one by one, at dread Medea's strain,
The sick'ning stars fade off th' ethereal plain;
As Argus' eyes by Hermes' wand opprest,
Clos'd one by one to everlasting rest;
Thus at her felt approach, and secret might,
Art after Art goes out, and all is Night.
See skulking Truth to her old cavern fled,
Mountains of Casuistry heap'd o'er her head!
Philosophy, that lean'd on Heav'n before,
Shrinks to her second cause, and is no more.
Physic of Metaphysic begs defence,
And Metaphysic calls for aid on Sense!
See Mystery to Mathematics fly!
In vain! they gaze, turn giddy, rave, and die.
Religion blushing veils her sacred fires,
And unawares Morality expires.
For public Flame, nor private, dares to shine;
Nor human Spark is left, nor Glimpse divine!
Lo! thy dread Empire, CHAOS! is restor'd;
Light dies before thy uncreating word;
Thy hand, great Anarch! lets the curtain fall,
And universal Darkness buries All.

from *The Rape of the Lock*

Close by those meads, for ever crown'd with flow'rs,
Where Thames with pride surveys his rising tow'rs,
There stands a structure of majestic frame,
Which from the neighb'ring Hampton takes its name.
Here Britain's statesmen oft the fall foredoom

Of foreign tyrants, and of nymphs at home;
Here thou, great ANNA! whom three realms obey,
Dost sometimes counsel take – and sometimes Tea.
Hither the heroes and the nymphs resort,
To taste awhile the pleasures of a court;
In various talk th' instructive hours they past,
Who gave the ball, or paid the visit last:
One speaks the glory of the British Queen,
And one describes a charming Indian screen;
A third interprets motions, looks, and eyes;
At ev'ry word a reputation dies.
Snuff, or the fan, supply each pause of chat,
With singing, laughing, ogling, and all that.
Mean while, declining from the noon of day,
The sun obliquely shoots his burning ray;
The hungry Judges soon the sentence sign,
And wretches hang that jury-men may dine;
The merchant from th' Exchange returns in peace,
And the long labours of the Toilet cease.
Belinda now, whom thirst of fame invites,
Burns to encounter two adventrous Knights,
At Ombre singly to decide their doom;
And swells her breast with conquests yet to come.
Strait the three bands prepare in arms to join,
Each band the number of the sacred nine.
Soon as she spread her hand, th' aërial guard
Descend, and sit on each important card:
First Ariel perch'd upon a Matadore,
Then each, according to the rank they bore;
For Sylphs, yet mindful of their ancient race,
Are, as when women, wondrous fond of place.
Behold, four Kings in majesty rever'd,
With hoary whiskers and a forky beard;
And four fair Queens whose hands sustain a flow'r,
Th' expressive emblem of their softer pow'r;
Four Knaves in garbs succinct, a trusty band,
Caps on their heads, and halberts in their hand;
And particolour'd troops, a shining train,
Draw forth to combat on the velvet plain.
The skilful Nymph reviews her force with care:
Let Spades be trumps! she said, and trumps they were.
Now move to war her sable Matadores,
In show like leaders of the swarthy Moors.
Spadillio first, unconquerable Lord!
Led off two captive trumps, and swept the board.
As many more Manillio forc'd to yield,
And march'd a victor from the verdant field.
Him Basto follow'd, but his fate more hard
Gain'd but one trump and one Plebeian card.

With his broad sabre next, a chief in years,
The hoary Majesty of Spades appears,
Puts forth one manly leg, to sight reveal'd,
The rest, his many-colour'd robe conceal'd.
The rebel Knave, who dares his prince engage,
Proves the just victim of his royal rage.
Ev'n mighty Pam[1], that Kings and Queens o'erthrew
And mow'd down armies in the fights of Lu[2],
Sad chance of war! now destitute of aid,
Falls undistinguish'd by the victor Spade!
Thus far both armies to Belinda yield;
Now to the Baron fate inclines the field.
His warlike Amazon her host invades,
Th' imperial consort of the crown of Spades.
The Club's black Tyrant first her victim dy'd,
Spite of his haughty mien, and barb'rous pride:
What boots the regal circle on his head,
His giant limbs, in state unwieldy spread;
That long behind he trails his pompous robe,
And, of all monarchs, only grasps the globe?
The Baron now his Diamonds pours apace;
Th'embroidered King who shows but half his face,
And his refulgent Queen, with pow'rs combin'd,
Of broken troops an easy conquest find.
Clubs, Diamonds, Hearts, in wild disorder seen,
With throngs promiscuous strow the level green.
Thus when dispers'd a routed army runs,
Of Asia's troops, and Afric's sable sons,
With like confusion different nations fly,
Of various habit, and of various dye,
The pierc'd battalions dis-united fall,
In heaps on heaps; one fate o'erwhelms them all.
The Knave of Diamonds tries his wily arts,
And wins (oh shameful chance!) the Queen of Hearts.
At this, the blood the virgin's cheek forsook,
A livid paleness spreads o'er all her look;
She sees, and trembles at th' approaching ill,
Just in the jaws of ruin, and Codille.
And now, (as oft in some distemper'd State)
On one nice Trick depends the gen'ral fate.
An Ace of Hearts steps forth: The King unseen
Lurk'd in her hand, and mourn'd his captive Queen:
He springs to vengeance with an eager pace,
And falls like thunder on the prostrate Ace.
The nymph exulting fills with shouts the sky;
The walls, the woods, and long canals reply.
Oh thoughless mortals! ever blind to fate,
Too soon dejected, and too soon elate.
Sudden, these honours shall be snatch'd away,

And curs'd for ever this victorious day.
  For lo! the board with cups and spoons is crown'd,
The berries crackle, and the mill turns round;
On shining Altars of Japan they raise
The silver lamp; the fiery spirits blaze:
From silver spouts the grateful liquors glide,
While China's earth receives the smoaking tyde:
At once they gratify their scent and taste,
And frequent cups prolong the rich repaste.
Strait hover round the Fair her airy band;
Some, as she sipp'd, the fuming liquor fann'd,
Some o'er her lap their careful plumes display'd,
Trembling, and conscious of the rich brocade.
Coffee, (which makes the politician wise,
And see thro' all things with his half-shut eyes)
Sent up in vapours to the Baron's brain
New stratagems, the radiant Lock to gain.
Ah cease, rash youth! desist ere 'tis too late,
Fear the just Gods, and think of Scylla's Fate!
Chang'd to a bird, and sent to flit in air,
She dearly pays for Nisus' injur'd hair!
  But when to mischief mortals bend their will,
How soon they find fit instruments of ill!
Just then, Clarissa drew with tempting grace
A two-edg'd weapon from her shining case:
So Ladies in Romance assist their Knight,
Present the spear, and arm him for the fight.
He takes the gift with rev'rence, and extends
The little engine on his finger's ends;
This just behind Belinda's neck he spread,
As o'er the fragrant steams she bends her head.
Swift to the Lock a thousand Sprites repair,
A thousand wings, by turns, blow back the hair;
And thrice they twitch'd the diamond in her ear;
Thrice she look'd back, and thrice the foe drew near.
Just in that instant, anxious Ariel sought
The close recesses of the Virgin's thought;
As on the nosegay in her breast reclin'd,
He watch'd th' Idëas rising in her mind,
Sudden he view'd, in spite of all her art,
An earthly Lover lurking at her heart.
Amaz'd, confus'd, he found his pow'r expir'd,
Resign'd to fate, and with a sigh retir'd.
  The Peer now spreads the glitt'ring Forfex wide,
T' inclose the Lock; now joins it, to divide.
Ev'n then, before the fatal engine clos'd,
A wretched Sylph too fondly interpos'd;
Fate urg'd the sheers, and cut the Sylph in twain,
(But airy substance soon unites again)

The meeting points the sacred hair dissever
From the fair head, for ever, and for ever!
  Then flash'd the living lightning from her eyes,
And screams of horror rend th' affrighted skies.
Not louder shrieks to pitying heav'n are cast,
When husbands, or when lapdogs breathe their last,
Or when rich China vessels, fall'n from high,
In glitt'ring dust, and painted fragments lie!
  Let wreaths of triumph now my temples twine,
(The Victor cry'd) the glorious Prize is mine!
While fish in streams, or birds delight in air,
Or in a coach and six the British Fair,
As long as Atalantis shall be read,
Or the small pillow grace a Lady's bed,
While visits shall be paid on solemn days,
When num'rous wax-lights in bright order blaze,
While nymphs take treats, or assignations give,
So long my honour, name, and praise shall live!
What Time would spare, from steel receives its date,
And monuments, like men, submit to fate!
Steel could the labour of the Gods destroy,
And strike to dust th' imperial tow'rs of Troy;
Steel could the works of mortal pride confound,
And hew triumphal arches to the ground.
What wonder then, fair nymph! thy hairs should feel
The conqu'ring force of unresisted steel?

[1]Jack of Clubs [2]or Loo, a card game

A Little Learning

A little learning is a dangerous thing;
Drink deep, or taste not the Pierian spring:
There shallow draughts intoxicate the brain,
And drinking largely sobers us again.
Fired at first sight with what the Muse imparts,
In fearless youth we tempt the heights of Arts;
While from the bounded level of our mind
Short views we take, nor see the lengths behind,
But, more advanced, behold with strange surprise
New distant scenes of endless science rise!
So pleased at first the towering Alps we try,
Mount o'er the vales, and seem to tread the sky;
The eternal snows appear already past,
And the first clouds and mountains seem the last:
But those attained, we tremble to survey
The growing labours of the lengthened way;

The increasing prospect tires our wandering eyes,
Hills peep o'er hills, and Alps on Alps arise!

Epigram Engraved on the Collar of a Dog which I gave to his Royal Highness

I am his Highness' dog at Kew;
Pray tell me, sir, whose dog are you?

HENRY CAREY

Sally in our Alley

Of all the girls that are so smart
There's none like pretty Sally;
She is the darling of my heart,
And she lives in our alley.
There is no lady in the land
Is half so sweet as Sally;
She is the darling of my heart,
And she lives in our alley.

Her father he makes cabbage-nets,
And through the streets does cry 'em;
Her mother she sells laces long
To such as please to buy 'em:
But sure such folks could ne'er beget
So sweet a girl as Sally!
She is the darling of my heart,
And she lives in our alley.

When she is by, I leave my work,
I love her so sincerely;
My master comes like any Turk,
And bangs me most severely:
But let him bang his bellyful,
I'll bear it all for Sally;
She is the darling of my heart,
And she lives in our alley.

Of all the days that's in the week
I dearly love but one day –
And that's the day that comes betwixt
A Saturday and Monday;
For then I'm drest all in my best
To walk abroad with Sally;

She is the darling of my heart,
  And she lives in our alley.

My master carries me to church,
  And often am I blamed
Because I leave him in the lurch
  As soon as text is named;
I leave the church in sermon-time
  And slink away to Sally;
She is the darling of my heart,
  And she lives in our alley.

When Christmas comes about again,
  O, then I shall have money;
I'll hoard it up, and box and all
  I'll give it to my honey:
And would it were ten thousand pounds,
  I'd give it all to Sally,
She is the darling of my heart,
  And she lives in our alley.

My master and the neighbours all,
  Make game of me and Sally,
And, but for her, I'd better be
  A slave and row a galley;
But when my seven long years are out,
  O, then I'll marry Sally;
O, then we'll wed, and then we'll bed –
  But not in our alley!

CHARLES WESLEY

Wrestling Jacob

Come, O Thou Traveller unknown,
  Whom still I hold, but cannot see,
My Company before is gone,
  And I am left alone with Thee,
With Thee all Night I mean to stay,
And wrestle till the Break of Day.

I need not tell Thee who I am,
  My Misery, or Sin declare,
Thyself hast call'd me by my Name,
  Look on thy Hands, and read it there,
But who, I ask Thee, who art Thou,
Tell me thy Name, and tell me now?

In vain Thou strugglest to get free,
  I never will unloose my Hold:
Art Thou the Man that died for me?
  The Secret of thy Love unfold;
Wrestling I will not let Thee go,
Till I thy Name, thy Nature know.

Wilt Thou not yet to me reveal
  Thy new, unutterable Name?
Tell me, I still beseech Thee, tell,
  To know it Now resolv'd I am;
Wrestling I will not let Thee go,
Till I thy Name, thy Nature know.

'Tis all in vain to hold thy Tongue,
  Or touch the Hollow of my Thigh:
Though every Sinew be unstrung,
  Out of my Arms Thou shall not fly;
Wrestling I will not let Thee go,
Till I thy Name, thy Nature know.

What tho' my shrinking Flesh complain,
  And murmur to contend so long,
I rise superior to my Pain,
  When I am weak then I am strong,
And when my All of Strength shall fail,
I shall with the GOD-man prevail.

My Strength is gone, my Nature dies,
  I sink beneath thy weighty Hand,
Faint to revive, and fall to rise;
  I fall, and yet by Faith I stand,
I stand, and will not let Thee go,
Till I thy Name, thy Nature know.

Yield to me Now —— for I am weak;
  But confident in Self-despair:
Speak to my Heart, in Blessings speak,
  Be conquer'd by my Instant Prayer,
Speak, or Thou never hence shalt move,
And tell me, if thy Name is LOVE.

'Tis Love, 'tis Love! Thou diedst for Me,
  I hear thy Whisper in my Heart.
The Morning breaks, the Shadows flee:
  Pure UNIVERSAL LOVE Thou art,
To me, to All thy Bowels move,
Thy Nature, and thy Name is LOVE.

My Prayer hath Power with GOD; the Grace
  Unspeakable I now receive,

Thro' Faith I see Thee Face to Face,
  I see Thee Face to Face, and live:
In vain I have not wept, and strove,
Thy Nature, and thy Name is LOVE.

I know Thee, Saviour, who Thou art,
  JESUS the feeble Sinner's Friend;
Nor wilt Thou with the Night depart,
  But stay, and love me to the End;
Thy Mercies never shall remove,
Thy Nature, and thy Name is LOVE.

The Sun of Righteousness on Me
  Hath rose with Healing in his Wings,
Wither'd my Nature's Strength; from Thee
  My Soul its Life and Succour brings,
My Help is all laid up above;
Thy Nature, and thy Name is LOVE.

Contented now upon my Thigh
  I halt, till Life's short Journey end;
All Helplessness, all Weakness I,
  On Thee alone for Strength depend,
Nor have I Power, from Thee, to move;
Thy Nature, and thy Name is LOVE.

Lame as I am, I take the Prey,
  Hell, Earth, and Sin with Ease o'ercome;
I leap for Joy, pursue my Way,
  And as a bounding Hart fly home,
Thro' all Eternity to prove
Thy Nature, and thy Name Is LOVE.

In Temptation

Jesu, lover of my soul,
  Let me to thy bosom fly,
While the nearer waters roll,
  While the tempest still is high.
Hide me, O my Saviour, hide,
  Till the storm of life is past:
Safe into the haven guide;
  O receive my soul at last.

Other refuge have I none,
  Hangs my helpless soul on thee.
Leave, ah leave me not alone,
  Still support and comfort me.

All my trust on thee is stayed,
  All my help from thee I bring;
Cover my defenceless head
  With the shadow of thy wing.

Wilt thou not regard my call?
  Wilt thou not accept my prayer?
Lo, I sink, I faint, I fall!
  Lo, on thee I cast my care.
Reach me out thy gracious hand!
  While I of thy strength receive,
Hoping against hope I stand,
  Dying, and behold I live!

Thou, O Christ, art all I want;
  More than all in thee I find.
Rise the fallen, cheer the faint,
  Heal the sick, and lead the blind.
Just and holy is thy name;
  I am all unrighteousness:
False and full of sin I am,
  Thou art full of truth and grace.

Plenteous grace with thee is found,
  Grace to cover all my sin:
Let the healing streams abound,
  Make and keep me pure within.
Thou of life the fountain art:
  Freely let me take of thee,
Spring thou up within my heart,
  Rise to all eternity!

SAMUEL JOHNSON

A Short Song of Congratulation

Long-expected one-and-twenty,
Lingering year at last is flown:
Pomp and pleasure, pride and plenty,
Great Sir John, are all your own.

Loosened from the minor's tether,
Free to mortgage or to sell,
Wild as wind, and light as feather,
Bid the slaves of thrift farewell.

Call the Betties, Kates, and Jennies,
Every name that laughs at care;

Lavish of your grandsire's guineas,
Show the spirit of an heir.

All that prey on vice and folly
Joy to see their quarry fly;
Here the gamester light and jolly,
There the lender grave and sly.

Wealth, Sir John, was made to wander,
Let it wander as it will;
See the jockey, see the pander,
Bid them come and take their fill.

When the bonny blade carouses,
Pockets full, and spirits high,
What are acres? What are houses?
Only dirt, or wet or dry.

If the guardian or the mother
Tell the woes of wilful waste,
Scorn their counsel, scorn their pother:
You can hang or drown at last!

London

By numbers here from shame or censure free,
All crimes are safe, but hated poverty.
This, only this, the rigid law pursues,
This, only this, provokes the snarling muse.
The sober trader at a tattered cloak,
Wakes from his dream, and labours for a joke;
With brisker air the silken courtiers gaze,
And turn the varied taunt a thousand ways.
Of all the griefs that harrass the distressed,
Sure the most bitter is a scornful jest;
Fate never wounds more deep the gen'rous heart,
Than when a blockhead's insult points the dart.
Has heaven reserved, in pity to the poor,
No pathless waste, or undiscovered shore;
No secret island in the boundless main?
No peaceful desert yet unclaimed by Spain?
Quick let us rise, the happy seats explore,
And bear oppression's insolence no more.
This mournful truth is ev'rywhere confessed,
SLOW RISES WORTH, BY POVERTY DEPRESSED:
But here more slow, where all are slaves to gold,
Where looks are merchandise, and smiles are sold;
Where won by bribes, by flatteries implored,
The groom retails the favours of his lord.

RICHARD JAGO

The Iron Industry in Birmingham

Here, in huge cauldrons, the rough mass they stow,
Till, by the potent heat, the purer ore
Is liquefied, and leaves the dross afloat.
Then, cautious, from the glowing pond they lead
The fiery stream along the channelled floor;
Where, in the mazy moulds of figured sand,
Anon it hardens and, in ingots rude,
Is to the forge conveyed; whose weighty strokes,
Incessant aided by the rapid stream,
Spread out the ductile ore, now tapering
In lengthened masses, ready to obey
The workman's will, and take its destined form.
   Soon o'er thy furrowed pavement, Bremicham!
Ride the loose bars obstrep'rous; to the sons
Of languid sense and frame too delicate,
Harsh noise perchance, but harmony to thine.
   Instant innumerable hands prepare
To shape and mould the malleable ore.
Their heavy sides th' inflated bellows heave,
Tugged by the pulleyed line, and, with their blast
Continuous, the sleeping embers rouse
And kindle into life. Straight the rough mass,
Plunged in the blazing hearth, its heat contracts,
And glows transparent. Now, Cyclopean chief!
Quick on the anvil lay the burning bar,
And, with thy lusty fellows, on its sides
Impress the weighty stroke. See, how they strain
The swelling nerve, and lift the sinewy arm
In measured time; while, with their clatt'ring blows,
From street to street the propagated sound
Increasing echoes, and, on ev'ry side,
The tortured metal spreads a radiant show'r.
   'Tis noise and hurry all! The throngèd street,
The close-piled warehouse, and the busy shop!
With nimble stroke the tinkling hammers move;
While slow and weighty the vast sledge descends,
In solemn bass responsive, or apart,
Or socially conjoined in tuneful peal.
The rough file grates; yet useful is its touch,
As sharp corrosives to the scirrhous[1] flesh,
Or, to the stubborn temper, keen rebuke.
   How the coarse metal brightens into fame,
Shaped by their plastic hands! what ornament!
What various use! See there the glitt'ring knife

Of tempered edge! The scissors' double shaft,
Useless apart, in social union joined,
Each aiding each! Emblem how beautiful
Of happy nuptial leagues! The button round,
Plain, or embossed, or bright with steely rays!
Or oblong buckle, on the laquered shoe,
With polished lustre, bending elegant
Its shapely rim. But how shall I recount
The thronging merchandise? From gaudy signs,
The littered counter, and the show-glass trim,
Seals, rings, twees,[2] bodkins, crowd into my verse,
Too scanty to contain their num'rous tribes.
  Nor this alone thy praise! With secret art,
Thy sons a compound form of various grains,
And to the fire's dissolvent pow'r commit
The precious mixture; oft, with sleepless eye,
Watching the doubtful process, if perchance
A purer ore may bless their midnight toil;
Or wished enamel clear, or sleek japan
Meet their impatient sight. Nor skilful stroke
Is wanting of the graver's pointed steel;
Nor artful pencil, o'er the polished plate
Swift stealing, and with glowing tints well-fraught.
Thine too, of graceful form, the lettered type!
The friend of learning, and the poet's pride!
Without thee what avail his splendid aims,
And midnight labours? Painful drudgery!
And pow'rless effort! But that thought of thee
Imprints fresh vigour on his panting breast,
As thou ere long shalt on his work impress;
And, with immortal fame, his praise repay.

[1]hardened [2]etuis, cases of small instruments

MARK AKENSIDE

Hymn to Science

Science! thou fair effusive ray
From the great source of mental day,
  Free, gen'rous, and refin'd,
Descend with all thy treasures fraught,
Illumine each bewilder'd thought,
  And bless my lab'ring mind.

But first with thy resistless light,
Disperse those phantoms from my sight,

Those mimic shades of thee,
The scholiast's learning, sophist's cant,
The visionary bigot's rant,
The monk's philosophy.

Oh! let thy pow'rful charms impart
The patient head, the candid heart,
Devoted to thy sway,
Which no weak passions e'er mislead,
Which still with dauntless steps proceed
Where Reason points the way.

Give me to learn each secret cause;
Let Number's, Figure's, Motion's laws
Reveal'd before me stand;
These to great Nature's scenes apply,
And round the globe, and thro' the sky,
Disclose her working hand.

Next, to thy nobler search resign'd,
The busy, restless, human mind
Thro' ev'ry maze pursue;
Detect perception where it lies,
Catch the ideas as they rise,
And all their changes view.

Say from what simple springs began
The vast ambitious thoughts of man,
Which range beyond control,
Which seek eternity to trace,
Dive thro' th' infinity of space,
And strain to grasp the whole?

Her secret stores let Mem'ry tell,
Bid Fancy quit her fairy cell,
In all her colours dressed,
While, prompt her sallies to control,
Reason, the judge, recalls the soul
To Truth's severest test.

Then launch thro' Being's wide extent;
Let the fair scale, with just ascent,
And cautious steps be trod,
And from the dead, corporeal mass,
Thro' each progressive order pass
To Instinct, Reason, God.

There, Science! veil thy daring eye,
Nor dive too deep, nor soar too high,
In that divine abyss,
To Faith content thy beams to lend,

Her hopes t'assure, her steps befriend,
And light her way to bliss.

Then downwards take thy flight again;
Mix with the policies of men,
And social Nature's ties:
The plan, the genius of each state,
Its int'rest and its pow'rs, relate,
Its fortunes and its rise.

Thro' private life pursue thy course,
Trace ev'ry action to its source,
And means and motives weigh;
Put tempers, passions, in the scale,
Mark what degrees in each prevail,
And fix the doubtful sway.

That last, best effort of thy skill,
To form the life and rule the will,
Propitious Pow'r! impart;
Teach me to cool my passion's fires,
Make me the judge of my desires,
The master of my heart.

Raise me above the vulgar's breath,
Pursuit of fortune, fear of death,
And all in life that's mean:
Still true to Reason be my plan,
Still let my action speak the man,
Thro' every various scene.

Hail! queen of Manners, light of Truth;
Hail! charm of age, and guide of youth;
Sweet refuge of distress:
In bus'ness, thou exact, polite;
Thou giv'st retirement its delight,
Prosperity its grace.

Of wealth, pow'r, freedom, thou the cause;
Foundress of order, cities, laws;
Of arts inventress, thou!
Without thee what were humankind?
How vast their wants, their thoughts how blind,
Their joys how mean, how few!

Sun of the soul! thy beams unveil;
Let others spread the daring sail
On Fortune's faithless sea,
While undeluded, happier I
From the vain tumult timely fly,
And sit in peace with thee.

THOMAS GRAY

Elegy Written in a Country Churchyard

The curfew tolls the knell of parting day,
The lowing herd wind slowly o'er the lea,
The ploughman homeward plods his weary way,
And leaves the world to darkness and to me.

Now fades the glimmering landscape on the sight,
And all the air a solemn stillness holds,
Save where the beetle wheels his droning flight,
And drowsy tinklings lull the distant folds;

Save that from yonder ivy-mantled tower
The moping owl does to the moon complain
Of such as, wandering near her secret bower,
Molest her ancient solitary reign.

Beneath those rugged elms, that yew-tree's shade,
Where heaves the turf in many a mouldering heap,
Each in his narrow cell for ever laid,
The rude forefathers of the hamlet sleep.

The breezy call of incense-breathing morn,
The swallow twittering from the straw-built shed,
The cock's shrill clarion or the echoing horn,
No more shall rouse them from their lowly bed.

For them no more the blazing hearth shall burn,
Or busy housewife ply her evening care:
No children run to lisp their sire's return,
Or climb his knees the envied kiss to share.

Oft did the harvest to their sickle yield,
Their furrow oft the stubborn glebe has broke;
How jocund did they drive their team afield!
How bowed the woods beneath their sturdy stroke!

Let not Ambition mock their useful toil,
Their homely joys and destiny obscure;
Not Grandeur hear, with a disdainful smile,
The short and simple annals of the poor.

The boast of heraldry, the pomp of power,
And all that beauty, all that wealth e'er gave,
Awaits alike the inevitable hour.
The paths of glory lead but to the grave.

Nor you, ye Proud, impute to these the fault,
If Memory o'er their tomb no trophies raise,

Where through the long-drawn aisle and fretted vault
The pealing anthem swells the note of praise.

Can storied urn or animated bust
Back to its mansion call the fleeting breath?
Can Honour's voice provoke the silent dust,
Or Flattery soothe the dull cold ear of Death?

Perhaps in this neglected spot is laid
Some heart once pregnant with celestial fire;
Hands that the rod of empire might have swayed,
Or waked to ecstasy the living lyre.

But Knowledge to their eyes her ample page
Rich with the spoils of time did ne'er unroll;
Chill Penury repressed their noble rage,
And froze the genial current of the soul.

Full many a gem of purest ray serene
The dark unfathomed caves of ocean bear:
Full many a flower is born to blush unseen,
And waste its sweetness on the desert air.

Some village-Hampden that with dauntless breast
The little tyrant of his fields withstood;
Some mute inglorious Milton here may rest,
Some Cromwell guiltless of his country's blood.

The applause of listening senates to command,
The threats of pain and ruin to despise,
To scatter plenty o'er a smiling land,
And read their history in a nation's eyes,

Their lot forbade: nor circumscribed alone
Their growing virtues, but their crimes confined;
Forbade to wade through slaughter to a throne,
And shut the gates of mercy on mankind,

The struggling pangs of conscious truth to hide,
To quench the blushes of ingenuous shame,
Or heap the shrine of Luxury and Pride
With incense kindled at the Muse's flame.

Far from the madding crowd's ignoble strife
Their sober wishes never learned to stray;
Along the cool sequestered vale of life
They kept the noiseless tenor of their way.

Yet even these bones from insult to protect
Some frail memorial still erected nigh,
With uncouth rhymes and shapeless sculpture decked,
Implores the passing tribute of a sigh.

Their name, their years, spelt by the unlettered muse,
The place of fame and elegy supply:
And many a holy text around she strews,
That teach the rustic moralist to die.

For who to dumb Forgetfulness a prey,
This pleasing anxious being e'er resigned,
Left the warm precincts of the cheerful day,
Nor cast one longing lingering look behind?

On some found breast the parting soul relies,
Some pious drops the closing eye requires;
Even from the tomb the voice of Nature cries,
Even in our ashes live their wonted fires.

For thee who, mindful of the unhonoured dead,
Dost in these lines their artless tale relate;
If chance, by lonely Contemplation led,
Some kindred spirit shall inquire thy fate,

Haply some hoary-headed swain may say,
'Oft have we seen him at the peep of dawn
Brushing with hasty steps the dews away
To meet the sun upon the upland lawn.

'There at the foot of yonder nodding beech
That wreathes its old fantastic roots so high,
His listless length at noontide would he stretch,
And pore upon the brook that babbles by.

'Hard by yon wood, now smiling as in scorn,
Muttering his wayward fancies he would rove,
Now drooping, woeful wan, like one forlorn,
Or crazed with care, or crossed in hopeless love.

'One morn I missed him on the customed hill,
Along the heath and near his favourite tree;
Another came; nor yet beside the rill,
Nor up the lawn, nor at the wood was he;

'The next with dirges due in sad array
Slow through the church-way path we saw him borne.
Approach and read (for thou canst read) the lay,
Graved on the stone beneath yon aged thorn.'

THE EPITAPH

Here rests his head upon the lap of earth
A youth to Fortune and to Fame unknown.
Fair Science frowned not on his humble birth,
And Melancholy marked him for her own.

Large was his bounty and his soul sincere,
Heaven did a recompense as largely send:
He gave to Misery all he had, a tear,
He gained from Heaven ('twas all he wished) a friend.

No farther seek his merits to disclose,
Or draw his frailties from their dread abode,
(There they alike in trembling hope repose)
The bosom of his Father and his God.

Ode on a Distant Prospect of Eton College

Ye distant spires, ye antique towers,
That crown the watry glade,
Where grateful Science still adores
Her HENRY'S holy Shade;
And ye, that from the stately brow
Of WINDSOR'S heights th' expanse below
Of grove, of lawn, of mead survey,
Whose turf, whose shade, whose flowers among
Wanders the hoary Thames along
His silver-winding way.

Ah happy hills, ah pleasing shade,
Ah fields belov'd in vain,
Where once my careless childhood stray'd,
A stranger yet to pain!
I feel the gales, that from ye blow,
A momentary bliss bestow,
As waving fresh their gladsome wing,
My weary soul they seem to sooth,
And, redolent of joy and youth,
To breathe a second spring.

Say, Father THAMES, for thou hast seen
Full many a sprightly race
Disporting on thy margent green
The paths of pleasure trace,
Who foremost now delight to cleave
With pliant arm thy glassy wave?
The captive linnet which enthrall?
What idle progeny succeed
To chase the rolling circle's speed,
Or urge the flying ball?

While some on earnest business bent
Their murm'ring labours ply
'Gainst graver hours, that bring constraint
To sweeten liberty:

Some bold adventurers disdain
The limits of their little reign,
And unknown regions dare descry:
Still as they run they look behind,
They hear a voice in every wind,
And snatch a fearful joy.

Gay hope is theirs by fancy fed,
Less pleasing when possest;
The tear forgot as soon as shed,
The sunshine of the breast:
Theirs buxom health of rosy hue,
Wild wit, invention ever-new,
And lively chear of vigour born;
The thoughtless day, the easy night,
The spirits pure, the slumbers light,
That fly th' approach of morn.

Alas, regardless of their doom,
The little victims play!
No sense have they of ills to come,
Nor care beyond to-day:
Yet see how all around 'em wait
The Ministers of human fate,
And black Misfortune's baleful train!
Ah, shew them where in ambush stand
To seize their prey the murth'rous band!
Ah, tell them, they are men!

These shall the fury Passions tear,
The vulturs of the mind,
Disdainful Anger, pallid Fear,
And Shame that sculks behind;
Or pineing Love shall waste their youth,
Or Jealousy with rankling tooth,
That inly gnaws the secret heart,
And Envy wan, and faded Care,
Grim-visag'd comfortless Despair,
And Sorrow's piercing dart.

Ambition this shall tempt to rise,
Then whirl the wretch from high,
To bitter Scorn a sacrifice,
And grinning Infamy.
The stings of Falshood those shall try.
And hard Unkindness' alter'd eye,
That mocks the tear it forc'd to flow;
And keen Remorse with blood defil'd,
And moody Madness laughing wild
Amid severest woe.

Lo, in the vale of years beneath
A griesly troop are seen,
The painful family of Death,
More hideous than their Queen:
This racks the joints, this fires the veins,
That every labouring sinew strains,
Those in the deeper vitals rage:
Lo, Poverty, to fill the band,
That numbs the soul with icy hand,
And slow-consuming Age.

To each his suff'rings; all are men,
Condemn'd alike to groan,
The tender for another's pain;
Th' unfeeling for his own.
Yet ah! why should they know their fate?
Since sorrow never comes too late,
And happiness too swiftly flies.
Thought would destroy their paradise.
No more; where ignorance is bliss,
'Tis folly to be wise.

On the Death of a Favourite Cat, Drowned in a Tub of Gold Fishes

'Twas on a lofty vase's side,
Where China's gayest art had dyed
The azure flowers that blow;
Demurest of the tabby kind,
The pensive Selima, reclined,
Gazed on the lake below.

Her conscious tail her joy declared:
The fair round face, the snowy beard,
The velvet of her paws,
Her coat that with the tortoise vies,
Her ears of jet, and emerald eyes–
She saw; and purred applause.

Still had she gazed; but midst the tide
Two angel forms were seen to glide,
The genii of the stream:
Their scaly armour's Tyrian hue
Through richest purple to the view
Betrayed a golden gleam.

The hapless nymph with wonder saw:
A whisker first, and then a claw,
With many an ardent wish,
She stretched, in vain, to reach the prize,
What female heart can gold despise?
What cat's averse to fish?

Presumptuous maid! with looks intent
Again she stretched, again she bent,
Nor knew the gulf between.
(Malignant Fate sat by, and smiled.)
The slippery verge her feet beguiled
She tumbled headlong in.

Eight times emerging from the flood
She mewed to every watery god,
Some speedy aid to send.
No Dolphin came, no Nereid stirred:
Nor cruel Tom, nor Susan heard–
A favourite has no friend!

From hence ye beauties undeceived,
Know, one false step is ne'er retrieved,
And be with caution bold:
Not all that tempts your wandering eyes
And heedless hearts is lawful prize,
Nor all, that glisters, gold.

WILLIAM JULIUS MICKLE

There's nae Luck about the House

And are ye sure the news is true?
And are ye sure he's weel?
Is this a time to think o' wark?
Mak haste, lay by your wheel;
Is this the time to spin a thread
When Colin's at the door?
Reach me my cloak, I'll to the quay
And see him come ashore.
For there's nae luck about the house,
There's nae luck at a',
There's little pleasure in the house
When our gudeman's awa.

And gie to me my bigonet[1],
  My bishop's satin gown;
For I maun tell the bailie's wife
  That Colin's come to town.
My Turkey slippers maun gae on,
  My stockings pearly blue;
It's a' to pleasure my gudeman,
  For he's baith leel and true.
    For there's nae luck &c.

Rise, lass, and mak a clean fireside,
  Put on the muckle pot,
Gie little Kate her button gown,
  And Jock his Sunday coat;
And mak their shoon as black as slaes,
  Their hose as white as snaw,
It's a' to please my ain gudeman,
  For he's been lang awa.
    For there's nae, &c.

There's twa fat hens upo' the bauk[2]
  Been fed this month and mair,
Mak haste and thraw their necks about,
  That Colin weel may fare;
And mak the table neat and clean,
  Let everything look braw,
For wha can tell how Colin fared
  When he was far awa?
    Ah, there's nae, &c.

Sae true his heart, sae smooth his speech,
  His breath like cauler air,
His very foot has music in't
  As he comes up the stair!
And shall I see his face again,
  And shall I hear him speak?
I'm downright dizzy wi' the thought,
  In troth I'm like to greet.
    For there's nae, &c.

If Colin's weel, and weel content,
  I hae nae mair to crave–
And gin I live to keep him sae,
  I'm blest aboon the lave.
And shall I see his face again,
  And shall I hear him speak?
I'm downright dizzy wi' the thought,
  In troth I'm like to greet.
    For there's nae, &c.

[1]bonnet [2]cross-beam

OLIVER GOLDSMITH

Edmund Burke

Here lies our good Edmund, whose genius was such,
We scarcely can praise it or blame it too much;
Who, born for the universe, narrowed his mind,
And to party gave up what was meant for mankind;
Though fraught with all learning, kept straining his throat
To persuade Tommy Townshend to lend him a vote;
Who, too deep for his hearers, still went on refining,
And thought of convincing, while they thought of dining;
Though equal to all things, for all things unfit;
Too nice for a statesman, too proud for a wit;
For a patriot, too cool; for a drudge, disobedient;
And too fond of the *right* to pursue the *expedient*.
In short, 'twas his fate, unemployed or in place, sir,
To eat mutton cold and cut blocks with a razor.

The Deserted Village

Sweet Auburn, loveliest village of the plain,
Where health and plenty cheared the labouring swain,
Where smiling spring its earliest visit paid,
And parting summer's lingering blooms delayed,
Dear lovely bowers of innocence and ease,
Seats of my youth, when every sport could please,
How often have I loitered o'er thy green,
Where humble happiness endeared each scene!
How often have I paused on every charm,
The sheltered cot, the cultivated farm,
The never-failing brook, the busy mill,
The decent church that topt the neighbouring hill,
The hawthorn bush, with seats beneath the shade,
For talking age and whispering lovers made!
How often have I blest the coming day,
When toil remitting lent its turn to play,
And all the village train, from labour free
Led up their sports beneath the spreading tree,
While many a pastime circled in the shade,
The young contending as the old surveyed;
And many a gambol frolicked o'er the ground,
And slights of art and feats of strength went round;
And still as each repeated pleasure tired,
Succeeding sports the mirthful band inspired;
The dancing pair that simply sought renown
By holding out to tire each other down;

The swain mistrustless of his smutted face,
While secret laughter tittered round the place;
The bashful virgin's side-long looks of love,
The matron's glance that would those looks reprove!
These were thy charms, sweet village; sports like these,
With sweet succession, taught even toil to please;
These round thy bowers their chearful influence shed,
These were thy charms – But all these charms are fled.
Sweet smiling village, loveliest of the lawn,
Thy sports are fled, and all thy charms withdrawn;
Amidst thy bowers the tyrant's hand is seen,
And desolation saddens all thy green:
One only master grasps the whole domain,
And half a tillage stints thy smiling plain;
No more thy glassy brook reflects the day,
But choaked with sedges, works its weedy way;
Along thy glades, a solitary guest,
The hollow-sounding bittern guards its nest;
Amidst thy desert walks the lapwing flies,
And tires their ecchoes with unvaried cries.
Sunk are thy bowers, in shapeless ruin all,
And the long grass o'ertops the mouldering wall;
And, trembling, shrinking from the spoiler's hand,
Far, far away, they children leave the land.
Ill fares the land, to hastening ills a prey,
Where wealth accumulates, and men decay:
Princes and lords may flourish, or may fade;
A breath can make them, as a breath has made;
But a bold peasantry, their country's pride,
When once destroyed, can never be supplied.
A time there was, ere England's griefs began,
When every rood of ground maintained its man;
For him light labour spread her wholesome store,
Just gave what life required, but gave no more:
His best companions, innocence and health;
And his best riches, ignorance of wealth.
But times are altered; trade's unfeeling train
Usurp the land and dispossess the swain;
Along the lawn, where scattered hamlets rose,
Unwieldy wealth, and cumbrous pomp repose;
And every want to oppulence allied,
And every pang that folly pays to pride.
Those gentle hours that plenty bade to bloom,
Those calm desires that asked but little room,
Those healthful sports that graced the peaceful scene,
Lived in each look, and brightened all the green;
These, far departing seek a kinder shore,
And rural mirth and manners are no more.
Sweet Auburn! parent of the blissful hour,

Thy glades forlorn confess the tyrant's power.
Here as I take my solitary rounds,
Amidst thy tangling walks, and ruined grounds,
And, many a year elapsed, return to view
Where once the cottage stood, the hawthorn grew,
Remembrance wakes with all her busy train,
Swells at my breast, and turns the past to pain.
  In all my wanderings round this world of care,
In all my griefs – and God has given my share –
I still had hopes, my lastest hours to crown,
Amidst these humble bowers to lay me down;
To husband out life's taper at the close,
And keep the flame from wasting by repose.
I still had hopes, for pride attends us still,
Amidst the swains to shew my book-learned skill,
Around my fire an evening groupe to draw,
And tell of all I felt, and all I saw;
And, as an hare whom hounds and horns pursue,
Pants to the place from whence at first she flew,
I still had hopes, my long vexations past,
Here to return – and die at home at last.
  O blest retirement, friend to life's decline,
Retreats from care that never must be mine,
How happy he who crowns, in shades like these,
A youth of labour with an age of ease;
Who quits a world where strong temptations try,
And, since 'tis hard to combat, learns to fly!
For him no wretches, born to work and weep,
Explore the mine, or tempt the dangerous deep;
No surly porter stands in guilty state
To spurn imploring famine from the gate,
But on he moves to meet his latter end,
Angels around befriending virtue's friend;
Bends to the grave with unperceived decay,
While resignation gently slopes the way;
And, all his prospects brightening to the last,
His Heaven commences ere the world be past!
  Sweet was the sound, when oft at evening's close,
Up yonder hill the village murmur rose;
There, as I past with careless steps and slow,
The mingling notes came soften'd from below;
The swain responsive as the milk-maid sung,
The sober herd that lowed to meet their young,
The noisy geese that gabbled o'er the pool,
The playful children just let loose from school,
The watch-dog's voice that bayed the whispering wind,
And the loud laugh that spoke the vacant mind,
These all in sweet confusion sought the shade,
And filled each pause the nightingale had made.

But now the sounds of population fail,
No chearful murmurs fluctuate in the gale,
No busy steps the grass-grown foot-way tread,
For all the bloomy flush of life is fled.
All but yon widowed, solitary thing
That feebly bends beside the plashy spring;
She, wretched matron, forced in age, for bread,
To strip the brook with mantling cresses spread,
To pick her wintry faggot from the thorn,
To seek her nightly shed, and weep till morn;
She only left of all the harmless train,
The sad historian of the pensive plain.

Near yonder copse, where once the garden smiled,
And still where many a garden-flower grows wild;
There, where a few torn shrubs the place disclose,
The village preacher's modest mansion rose.
A man he was, to all the country dear,
And passing rich with forty pounds a year;
Remote from towns he ran his godly race,
Nor e'er had changed, nor wished to change his place;
Unpractised he to fawn, or seek for power,
By doctrines fashioned to the varying hour;
Far other aims his heart had learned to prize,
More skilled to raise the wretched than to rise.
His house was known to all the vagrant train,
He chid their wanderings, but relieved their pain;
The long-remembered beggar was his guest,
Whose beard descending swept his aged breast;
The ruined spendthrift, now no longer proud,
Claim'd kindred there, and had his claims allowed;
The broken soldier, kindly bade to stay,
Sate by his fire, and talked the night away;
Wept o'er his wounds, or, tales of sorrow done,
Shouldered his crutch, and shewed how fields were won.
Pleased with his guests, the good man learned to glow,
And quite forgot their vices in their woe;
Careless their merits, or their faults to scan,
His pity gave ere charity began.

Thus to relieve the wretched was his pride,
And even his failings leaned to Virtue's side;
But in his duty prompt at every call,
He watched and wept, he prayed and felt, for all.
And, as a bird each fond endearment tries,
To tempt its new-fledged offspring to the skies;
He tried each art, reproved each dull delay,
Allured to brighter worlds, and led the way.

Beside the bed where parting life was layed,
And sorrow, guilt, and pain, by turns, dismayed
The reverend champion stood. At his control,

Despair and anguish fled the struggling soul;
Comfort came down the trembling wretch to raise,
And his last faultering accents whispered praise.
At church, with meek and unaffected grace,
His looks adorned the venerable place;
Truth from his lips prevailed with double sway,
And fools, who came to scoff, remained to pray.
The service past, around the pious man,
With steady zeal, each honest rustic ran;
Even children followed, with endearing wile,
And plucked his gown, to share the good man's smile.
His ready smile a parent's warmth exprest,
Their welfare pleased him, and their cares distrest;
To them his heart, his love, his griefs were given,
But all his serious thoughts had rest in Heaven.
As some tall cliff that lifts its awful form,
Swells from the vale, and midway leaves the storm,
Tho' round its breast the rolling clouds are spread,
Eternal sunshine settles on its head.
Beside yon straggling fence that skirts the way,
With blossomed furze unprofitably gay,
There, in his noisy mansion, skill'd to rule,
The village master taught his little school;
A man severe he was, and stern to view,
I knew him well, and every truant knew;
Well had the boding tremblers learned to trace
The day's disasters in his morning face;
Full well they laughed, with counterfeited glee,
At all his jokes, for many a joke had he:
Full well the busy whisper circling round,
Conveyed the dismal tidings when he frowned;
Yet he was kind, or if severe in aught,
The love he bore to learning was in fault;
The village all declared how much he knew;
'Twas certain he could write, and cypher too;
Lands he could measure, terms and tides presage,
And even the story ran that he could gauge.
In arguing too, the parson owned his skill,
For even tho' vanquished, he could argue still;
While words of learned length and thundering sound,
Amazed the gazing rustics ranged around;
And still they gazed, and still the wonder grew,
That one small head could carry all he knew.
But past is all his fame. The very spot
Where many a time he triumphed, is forgot.
Near yonder thorn, that lifts its head on high,
Where once the sign-post caught the passing eye,
Low lies that house where nut-brown draughts inspired,
Where grey-beard mirth and smiling toil retired,

Where village statesmen talked with looks profound,
And news much older than their ale went round.
Imagination fondly stoops to trace
The parlour splendours of that festive place;
The white-washed wall, the nicely sanded floor,
The varnished clock that clicked behind the door;
The chest contrived a double debt to pay,
A bed by night, a chest of drawers by day;
The pictures placed for ornament and use,
The twelve good rules, the royal game of goose;
The hearth, except when winter chill'd the day,
With aspen boughs, and flowers, and fennel gay,
While broken tea-cups, wisely kept for shew,
Ranged o'er the chimney, glistened in a row.
Vain transitory splendours! Could not all
Reprieve the tottering mansion from its fall!
Obscure it sinks, nor shall it more impart
An hour's importance to the poor man's heart;
Thither no more the peasant shall repair
To sweet oblivion of his daily care;
No more the farmer's news, the barber's tale,
No more the woodman's ballad shall prevail;
No more the smith his dusky brow shall clear,
Relax his ponderous strength, and lean to hear;
The host himself no longer shall be found
Careful to see the mantling bliss go round;
Nor the coy maid, half willing to be prest,
Shall kiss the cup to pass it to the rest.
Yes! let the rich deride, the proud disdain,
These simple blessings of the lowly train;
To me more dear, congenial to my heart,
One native charm, than all the gloss of art;
Spontaneous joys, where Nature has its play,
The soul adopts, and owns their first-born sway;
Lightly they frolic o'er the vacant mind,
Unenvied, unmolested, unconfined.
But the long pomp, the midnight masquerade,
With all the freaks of wanton wealth arrayed,
In these, ere triflers half their wish obtain,
The toiling pleasure sickens into pain;
And even while fashion's brightest arts decoy,
The heart distrusting asks, if this be joy.
Ye friends to truth, ye statesmen, who survey
The rich man's joys encrease, the poor's decay,
'Tis yours to judge, how wide the limits stand
Between a splendid and a happy land.
Proud swells the tide with loads of freighted ore,
And shouting Folly hails them from her shore;
Hoards even beyond the miser's wish abound,

And rich men flock from all the world around.
Yet count our gains. This wealth is but a name
That leaves our useful products still the same.
Not so the loss. The man of wealth and pride
Takes up a space that many poor supplied;
Space for his lake, his park's extended bounds,
Space for his horses, equipage, and hounds;
The robe that wraps his limbs in silken sloth,
Has robbed the neighbouring fields of half their growth;
His seat, where solitary sports are seen,
Indignant spurns the cottage from the green;
Around the world each needful product flies,
For all the luxuries the world supplies.
While thus the land, adorned for pleasure, all
In barren splendour feebly waits the fall.
   As some fair female unadorned and plain,
Secure to please while youth confirms her reign,
Slights every borrowed charm that dress supplies,
Nor shares with art the triumph of her eyes.
But when those charms are past, for charms are frail,
When time advances, and when lovers fail,
She then shines forth, sollicitous to bless,
In all the glaring impotence of dress.
Thus fares the land, by luxury betrayed;
In nature's simplest charms at first arrayed;
But verging to decline, its splendours rise,
Its vistas strike, its palaces surprize;
While, scourged by famine from the smiling land,
The mournful peasant leads his humble band;
And while he sinks, without one arm to save,
The country blooms – a garden, and a grave.
   Where then, ah where, shall poverty reside,
To scape the pressure of contiguous pride?
If to some common's fenceless limits strayed,
He drives his flock to pick the scanty blade,
Those fenceless fields the sons of wealth divide,
And ev'n the bare-worn common is denied.
   If to the city sped – What waits him there?
To see profusion that he must not share;
To see ten thousand baneful arts combined
To pamper luxury, and thin mankind;
To see those joys the sons of pleasure know,
Extorted from his fellow-creature's woe.
Here, while the courtier glitters in brocade,
There the pale artist plies the sickly trade;
Here, while the proud their long-drawn pomps display,
There the black gibbet glooms beside the way.
The dome where Pleasure holds her midnight reign,
Here, richly deckt, admits the gorgeous train;

Tumultuous grandeur crowds the blazing square,
The rattling chariots clash, the torches glare.
Sure scenes like these no troubles e'er annoy!
Sure these denote one universal joy!
Are these thy serious thoughts? – Ah, turn thine eyes
Where the poor houseless shivering female lies.
She once, perhaps, in village plenty blest,
Has wept at tales of innocence distrest;
Her modest looks the cottage might adorn,
Sweet as the primrose peeps beneath the thorn;
Now lost to all; her friends, her virtue fled,
Near her betrayer's door she lays her head,
And, pinch'd with cold, and shrinking from the shower,
With heavy heart deplores that luckless hour
When idly first, ambitious of the town,
She left her wheel and robes of country brown.
  Do thine, sweet Auburn, thine, the loveliest train,
Do thy fair tribes participate her pain?
Even now, perhaps, by cold and hunger led,
At proud men's doors they ask a little bread!
  Ah, no. To distant climes, a dreary scene,
Where half the convex world intrudes between,
Through torrid tracts with fainting steps they go,
Where wild Altama murmurs to their woe.
Far different there from all that charm'd before,
The various terrors of that horrid shore;
Those blazing suns that dart a downward ray,
And fiercely shed intolerable day;
Those matted woods where birds forget to sing,
But silent bats in drowsy clusters cling;
Those poisonous fields with rank luxuriance crowned,
Where the dark scorpion gathers death around;
Where at each step the stranger fears to wake
The rattling terrors of the vengeful snake;
Where crouching tigers wait their hapless prey.
And savage men, more murderous still than they;
While oft in whirls the mad tornado flies,
Mingling the ravaged landscape with the skies.
Far different these from every former scene,
The cooling brook, the grassy vested green,
The breezy covert of the warbling grove,
That only shelter'd thefts of harmless love.
  Good Heaven! what sorrows gloom'd that parting day,
That called them from their native walks away;
When the poor exiles, every pleasure past,
Hung round their bowers, and fondly looked their last,
And took a long farewell, and wished in vain
For seats like these beyond the western main;
And shuddering still to face the distant deep,

Returned and wept, and still returned to weep.
The good old sire the first prepared to go
To new found worlds, and wept for others woe.
But for himself, in conscious virtue brave,
He only wished for worlds beyond the grave.
His lovely daughter, lovelier in her tears,
The fond companion of his helpless years,
Silent went next, neglectful of her charms,
And left a lover's for a father's arms.
With louder plaints the mother spoke her woes,
And blest the cot where every pleasure rose;
And kist her thoughtless babes with many a tear,
And claspt them close, in sorrow doubly dear;
Whilst her fond husband strove to lend relief
In all the silent manliness of grief.
O luxury! thou curst by Heaven's decree,
How ill exchanged are things like these for thee!
How do thy potions, with insidious joy,
Diffuse their pleasures only to destroy!
Kingdoms, by thee, to sickly greatness grown,
Boast of a florid vigour not their own;
At every draught more large and large they grow,
A bloated mass of rank unwieldy woe;
Till sapped their strength, and every part unsound,
Down, down they sink, and spread a ruin round.
Even now the devastation is begun,
And half the business of destruction done;
Even now, methinks, as pondering here I stand,
I see the rural virtues leave the land:
Down where yon anchoring vessel spreads the sail,
That idly waiting flaps with every gale,
Downward they move, a melancholy band,
Pass from the shore, and darken all the strand.
Contented toil, and hospitable care,
And kind connubial tenderness, are there;
And piety with wishes placed above,
And steady loyalty, and faithful love.
And thou, sweet Poetry, thou loveliest maid,
Still first to fly where sensual joys invade;
Unfit in these degenerate times of shame,
To catch the heart, or strike for honest fame;
Dear charming nymph, neglected and decried,
My shame in crowds, my solitary pride;
Thou source of all my bliss, and all my woe,
That found'st me poor at first, and keep'st me so;
Thou guide by which the nobler arts excell,
Thou nurse of every virtue, fare thee well!
Farewell, and O where'er thy voice be tried,
On Torno's cliffs, or Pambamarca's side,

Whether were equinoctial fervours glow,
Or winter wraps the polar world in snow,
Still let thy voice, prevailing over time,
Redress the rigours of the inclement clime;
Aid slighted truth with thy persuasive strain,
Teach erring man to spurn the rage of gain;
Teach him, that states of native strength possest,
Tho' very poor, may still be very blest;
That trade's proud empire hastes to swift decay,
As ocean sweeps the labour'd mole away;
While self-dependent power can time defy,
As rocks resist the billows and the sky.

Elegy – On the Death of a Mad Dog

Good people all, of every sort,
  Give ear unto my song;
And if you find it wond'rous short, –
  It cannot hold you long.

In Islington there was a man,
  Of whom the world might say,
That still a godly race he ran, –
  Whene'er he went to pray.

A kind and gentle heart he had,
  To comfort friends and foes;
The naked every day he clad, –
  When he put on his clothes.

And in that town a dog was found,
  As many dogs there be,
Both mongrel, puppy, whelp and hound,
  And curs of low degree.

This dog and man at first were friends;
  But when a pique began,
The dog, to gain some private ends,
  Went mad, and bit the man.

Around from all the neighbouring streets
  The wondering neighbours ran,
And swore the dog had lost his wits,
  To bite so good a man.

The wound it seemed both sore and sad
  To every Christian eye;
And while they swore the dog was mad,
  They swore the man would die.

But soon a wonder came to light
That showed the rogues they lied;
The man recovered of the bite,
The dog it was that died.

JAMES GRAINGER

Slaves

Yet, planter, let humanity prevail.–
Perhaps thy negro, in his native land,
Possessed large fertile plains, and slaves, and herds:
Perhaps, whene'er he deigned to walk abroad,
The richest silks, from where the Indus rolls,
His limbs invested in their gorgeous pleats:
Perhaps he wails his wife, his children, left
To struggle with adversity: perhaps
Fortune, in battle for his country fought,
Gave him a captive to his deadliest foe:
Perhaps, incautious, in his native fields
(On pleasurable scenes his mind intent)
All as he wandered, from the neighbouring grove,
Fell ambush dragged him to the hated main.–
Were they even sold for crimes; ye polished say!
Ye to whom Learning opes her amplest page!
Ye, whom the knowledge of a living God
Should lead to virtue! are ye free from crimes?
Ah pity, then, these uninstructed swains;
And still let mercy soften the decrees
Of rigid justice, with her lenient hand.
Oh, did the tender Muse possess the power,
Which monarchs have, and monarchs oft abuse:
'Twould be the fond ambition of her soul
To quell tyrannic sway; knock off the chains
Of heart-debasing slavery; give to man,
Of every colour and of every clime,
Freedom, which stamps him image of his God.
Then laws, Oppression's scourge, fair Virtue's prop,
Offspring of Wisdom! should impartial reign,
To knit the whole in well-accorded strife:
Servants, not slaves; of choice, and not compelled;
The blacks should cultivate the Cane-land isles.

JOHN FREETH

Bunker's Hill, or the Soldier's Lamentation

I am a jolly soldier,
Enlisted years ago,
To serve my king and country,
Against the common foe.
But when across th' Atlantic
My orders were to go,
I grieved to think that English hearts
Should draw their swords on those
Who fought and conquered by their side,
When Frenchmen were their foes.

In drubbing French and Spaniards
A soldier takes delight,
But troops cooped up in Boston,
Are in so sad a plight,
That many think their stomachs more
Inclined to eat than fight,
And like us would be loth to stir;
For ev'ry vet'ran knows,
We fought and conquered side by side,
When Frenchmen were our foes.

'Twas on the seventeenth of June,
I can't forget the day,
The flower of our army
For Charles-Town sailed away.
The town was soon in ashes laid,
When bombs began to play:
But oh! the cruel scene to paint,
It makes my blood run chill;
Pray heaven grant I never more
May climb up Bunker's Hill.

America to frighten
The tools of power strove,
But ministers are cheated,
Their schemes abortive prove.
The men they told us would not fight
Are to the combat drove,
And to our gallant officers,
It proved a bitter pill,
For numbers dropped before they reached
The top of Bunker's Hill.

I should not be amazed to hear
Wolfe's ghost had left the shades,
To check that shameful bloody work,
Which England's crown degrades.
The lads, who scorn to turn their backs
On Gallia's best brigades,
Undaunted stood, but frankly own
They better had lain still,
Than such a dear-bought victory gain,
As that of Bunker's Hill.

Did they, who bloody measures crave,
Our toil and danger share,
Not one to face the rifle-men
A second time would dare.
Ye Britons who your country love,
Be this your ardent pray'r:
To Britain and her colonies,
May peace be soon restored,
And knaves of high and low degree.
Be *destined to the cord.*

Botany Bay

Away with all whimsical bubbles of air,
Which only excite a momentary stare;
Attention to plans of utility pay,
Weigh anchor and steer towards Botany Bay.

Let no one think much of a trifling expense,
Who knows what may happen a hundred years hence;
The loss of America what can repay?
New colonies seek for at Botany Bay.

O'er Neptune's domain how extensive the scope!
Of quickly returning how distant the hope!
The Cape must be doubled, and then bear away
Two thousand good leagues to reach Botany Bay.

Of those *precious* souls which for nobody care,
It seems a large cargo the kingdom can spare;
To ship a few hundreds off make no delay,
They cannot too soon go to Botany Bay.

They go of an island to take special charge,
Much warmer than Britain, and ten times as large;
No Custom-house duty, no freightage to pay,
And tax-free they'll live when at Botany Bay.

This garden of Eden, this new promised land,
The time to set sail for is almost at hand;
Ye worst of land-lubbers, make ready for sea,
There's room for you all about Botany Bay.

As scores of each sex to this place must proceed,
In twenty years time – only think of the breed;
Major Semple, should Fortune much kindness display,
May live to be king over Botany Bay.

For a general good, make a general sweep,
The beauty of life is good order to keep;
With night-prowling hateful disturbers away,
And send the whole tribe into Botany Bay.

Ye chiefs who go out on this naval exploit,
The work to accomplish, and set matters right;
To Ireland be kind, call at Cork on your way,
And take a few White Boys to Botany Bay.

Commercial arrangements give prospect of joy,
Fair and firm may be kept ev'ry national tie;
And mutual confidence those who betray,
Be sent to the bottom of Botany Bay.

ISAAC BICKERSTAFFE

The Recruiting Sergeant

What a charming thing's a battle!
Trumpets sounding, drums a-beating;
Crack, crick, crack, the cannons rattle,
Every heart with joy elating.
With what pleasure are we spying,
From the front and from the rear,
Round us in the smoky air,
Heads and limbs and bullets flying!
Then the groans of soldiers dying,
Just like sparrows as it were:
At each pop,
Hundreds drop,
While the muskets prittle prattle.
Killed and wounded
Lie confounded:
What a charming thing's a battle!
But the pleasant joke of all
Is when to close attack we fall,
Like mad bulls each other butting,

Shooting, stabbing, maiming, cutting;
Horse and foot
All go to't,
Kill's the word, both men and cattle,
Then to plunder:
Blood and thunder,
What a charming thing's a battle!

RICHARD BRINSLEY SHERIDAN

Song

Here's to the maiden of bashful fifteen;
  Here's to the widow of fifty;
Here's to the flaunting extravagant quean,
  And here's to the housewife that's thrifty.

CHORUS
Let the toast pass,–
Drink to the lass,
I'll warrant she'll prove an excuse for the glass.

Here's to the charmer whose dimples we prize;
  Now to the maid who has none, sir:
Here's to the girl with a pair of blue eyes,
  And here's to the nymph with but *one*, sir.

Here's to the maid with a bosom of snow;
  Now to her that's as brown as a berry:
Here's to the wife with a face full of woe,
  And now to the girl that is merry.

For let 'em be clumsy, or let 'em be slim,
  Young or ancient, I care not a feather;
So fill a pint bumper quite up to the brim,
  And let us e'en toast them together.

JOEL BARLOW

The Husking

The days grow short; but though the falling sun
To the glad swain proclaims his day's work done,
Night's pleasing shades his various tasks prolong,
And yield new subjects to my various song.

For now, the corn-house filled, the harvest home,
The invited neighbours to the *Husking* come;
A frolic scene, where work, and mirth, and play,
Unite their charms to chase the hours away.

Where the huge heap lies centred in the hall,
The lamp suspended from the cheerful wall,
Brown corn-fed nymphs and strong hard-handed beaus,
Alternate ranged, extend in circling rows,
Assume their seats, the solid mass attack;
The dry husks rustle, and the corn-cobs crack;
The song, the laugh, alternate notes resound
And the sweet cider trips in silence round.

The laws of husking every wight can tell –
And sure no laws he ever keeps so well:
For each red ear a general kiss he gains,
With each smut ear she smuts the luckless swains;
But when to some sweet maid a prize is cast,
Red as her lips and taper as her waist,
She walks the round, and culls one favored beau,
Who leaps, the luscious tribute to bestow.
Various the sports are as the wit and brains
Of well-pleased lasses and contending swains;
Till the vast mound of corn is swept away,
And he that gets the last ear wins the day.

Meanwhile the housewife urges all her care,
The well-earned feast to hasten and prepare.
The sifted meal already waits her hand,
The milk is strained, the bowls in order stand,
The fire flames high; and, as a pool that takes
The headlong stream that o'er the mill-dam breaks,
Foams, roars, and rages, with incessant toils,
So the vexed cauldron rages, roars, and boils.

First with clean salt she seasons well the food,
Then strews the flour and thickens all the flood.
Long o'er the simmering fire she lets it stand –
To stir it well demands a stronger hand:
The husband takes his turn, and round and round
The ladle flies, at last the toil is crown'd;
When to their boards the thronging huskers pour,
And take their seats as at the corn before.

I leave them to their feast. There still belong
More useful matters to my faithful song;
For rules there are, though ne'er unfolded yet,
Nice rules and wise, how pudding should be eat.

JOANNA BAILLIE

Hay Making

Upon the grass no longer hangs the dew;
Forth hies the mower, with his glittering scythe,
In snowy shirt bedight, and all unbraced,
He moves athwart the mead with sidling bend,
And lays the grass in many a swathey line:
In every field, in every lawn and meadow,
The rousing voice of industry is heard;
The haycock rises, and the frequent rake
Sweeps on the fragrant hay in heavy wreaths.
The old and young, the weak and strong, are there,
And, as they can, help on the cheerful work.
The father jeers his awkward half-grown lad,
Who trails his tawdry armful o'er the field,
Nor does he fear the jeering to repay.
The village oracle, and simple maid,
Jest in their turns and raise the ready laugh;
All are companions in the general glee;
Authority, hard-favoured, frowns not there.
Some, more advanced, raise up the lofty rick,
Whilst on its top doth stand the parish toast,
In loose attire, and swelling ruddy cheek.
With taunts and harmless mockery she receives
The tossed-up heaps from fork of simple youth,
Who, staring on her, takes his arm away,
While half the load falls back upon himself.
Loud is her laugh, her voice is heard afar:
The mower busied on the distant lawn,
The carter trudging on his dusty way,
The shrill sound know, their bonnets toss in air,
And roar across the field to catch her notice:
She waves her arm to them, and shakes her head,
And then renews her work with double spirit.
Thus do they jest and laugh away their toil
Till the bright sun, now past his middle course,
Shoots down his fiercest beams which none may brave.
The stoutest arm feels listless, and the swart
And brawny-shouldered clown begins to fail,
But to the weary, lo! there comes relief!
A troop of welcome children o'er the lawn
With slow and wary steps approach: some bear
In baskets oaten cakes or barley scones,
And gusty cheese and stoups of milk or whey.
Beneath the branches of a spreading tree,
Or by the shady side of the tall rick,

They spread their homely fare, and seated round,
Taste every pleasure that a feast can give.

JAMES HOGG

o

A Boy's Song

Where the pools are bright and deep,
Where the grey trout lies asleep,
Up the river and over the lea,
That's the way for Billy and me.

Where the blackbird sings the latest,
Where the hawthorn blooms the sweetest,
Where the nestlings chirp and fleet,
That's the way for Billy and me.

Where the mowers mow the cleanest,
Where the hay lies thick and greenest,
There to track the homeward bee,
That's the way for Billy and me.

Where the hazel bank is steepest,
Where the shadow falls the deepest,
Where the clustering nuts fall free,
That's the way for Billy and me.

Why the boys should drive away
Little sweet maidens from the play,
Or love to banter and fight so well,
That's the thing I never could tell.

But this I know, I love to play
Through the meadow, among the hay;
Up the water and over the lea,
That's the way for Billy and me.

CHRISTOPHER SMART

o

'For I will consider my Cat Jeoffry'

For I will consider my Cat Jeoffry.
For he is the servant of the Living God, duly and daily serving him.
For at the first glance of the glory of God in the East he worships in his way.
For this is done by wreathing his body seven times round with elegant quickness.
For then he leaps up to catch the musk, which is the blessing of God upon his prayer.

For he rolls upon prank to work it in.
For having done duty and received blessing he begins to consider himself.
For this he performs in ten degrees.
For first he looks upon his fore-paws to see if they are clean.
For secondly he kicks up behind to clear away there.
For thirdly he works it upon stretch with fore-paws extended.
For fourthly he sharpens his paws by wood.
For fifthly he washes himself.
For sixthly he rolls upon wash.
For seventhly he fleas himself, that he may not be interrupted upon the beat.
For eighthly he rubs himself against a post.
For ninthly he looks up for his instructions.
For tenthly he goes in quest of food.
For having consider'd God and himself he will consider his neighbour.
For if he meets another cat he will kiss her in kindness.
For when he takes his prey he plays with it to give it a chance.
For one mouse in seven escapes by his dallying.
For when his day's work is done his business more properly begins.
For he keeps the Lord's watch in the night against the adversary.
For he counteracts the powers of darkness by his electrical skin and glaring eyes.
For he counteracts the Devil, who is death, by brisking about the life.
For in his morning orisons he loves the sun and the sun loves him.
For he is of the tribe of Tiger.
For the Cherub Cat is a term of the Angel Tiger.
For he has the subtlety and hissing of a serpent which in goodness he suppresses.
For he will not do destruction, if he is well-fed neither will he spit without provocation.
For he purrs in thankfulness, when God tells him he's a good Cat.
For he is an instrument for the children to learn benevolence upon.
For every house is incompleat without him and a blessing is lacking in the spirit.
For the Lord commanded Moses concerning the cats at the departure of the
  Children of Israel from Egypt.
For every family had one cat at least in the bag.
For the English Cats are the best in Europe.
For he is the cleanest in the use of his fore-paws of any quadrupede.
For the dexterity of his defence is an instance of the love of God to him exceedingly.
For he is the quickest to his mark of any creature.
For he is tenacious of his point.
For he is a mixture of gravity and waggery.
For he knows that God is his Saviour.
For there is nothing sweeter than his peace even at rest.
For there is nothing brisker than his life when in motion.
For he is of the Lord's poor and so indeed is he called by benevolence perpetually
  – Poor Jeoffry! poor Jeoffry! the rat has bit thy throat.
For I bless the name of the Lord Jesus that Jeoffry is better.
For the divine spirit comes about his body to sustain it in compleat cat.
For his tongue is exceeding pure so that it has in purity what it wants in musick.
For he is docile and can learn certain things.
For he can set up with gravity which is patience upon approbation.
For he can fetch and carry, which is patience in employment.

For he can jump over a stick which is patience upon proof positive.
For he can spraggle upon waggle at the word of command.
For he can jump from an eminence into his master's bosom.
For he can catch the cork and toss it again.
For he is hated by the hypocrite and miser.
For the former is afraid of detection.
For the latter refuses the charge.
For he camels his back to bear the first notion of business.
For he is good to think on, if a man would express himself neatly.
For he was made a great figure in Egypt for his signal services.
For he killed the Icneumon-rat very pernicious by land.
For his ears are so acute that they sting again.
For from this proceeds the passing quickness of his attention.
For by stroaking of him I have found out electricity.
For I perceived God's light about him both wax and fire.
For the Electrical fire is the spiritual substance, which God sends from heaven to
  sustain the bodies both of man and beast.
For God has blessed him in the variety of his movements.
For, tho he cannot fly, he is an excellent clamberer.
For his motions upon the face of the earth are more than any other quadrupede.
For he can tread to all the measures upon the musick.
For he can swim for life.
For he can creep.

THOMAS CHATTERTON

o

'If wishing for the mystic joys of love'

If wishing for the mystic joys of love
Is by eternal justice deemed a fault,
Tell me, ye Powers, what woman's innocent.
O how extensive is the power of God!
Conceived in sin, we sin by God's decree
And for such forced iniquity are damned,
For who can say his nautre is his own!
Who formed the mind and who instilled the soul,
Who gave us passions which we must obey
But the eternal justice of the God?
And for such forced iniquity we're damned.

WILLIAM COWPER

Light Shining out of Darkness

God moves in a mysterious way,
His wonders to perform;
He plants his footsteps in the sea,
And rides upon the storm.

Deep in unfathomable mines
Of never failing skill
He treasures up his bright designs,
And works his sovereign will.

Ye fearful saints, fresh courage take,
The clouds ye so much dread
Are big with mercy, and shall break
In blessings on your head.

Judge not the Lord by feeble sense,
But trust him for his grace;
Behind a frowning providence,
He hides a smiling face.

His purposes will ripen fast,
Unfolding every hour;
The bud may have a bitter taste,
But sweet will be the flower.

Blind unbelief is sure to err,
And scan his work in vain;
God is his own interpreter,
And he will make it plain.

The Winter Walk at Noon

But let the months go round, a few short months,
And all shall be restor'd. These naked shoots,
Barren as lances, among which the wind
Makes wintry music, sighing as it goes,
Shall put their graceful foliage on again,
And, more aspiring, and with ampler spread,
Shall boast new charms, and more than they have lost.
Then, each in its peculiar honours clad,
Shall publish, even to the distant eye,
Its family and tribe. Laburnum, rich
In streaming gold; syringa, iv'ry pure:
The scentless and the scented rose; this red
And of an humbler growth, the other tall,

And throwing up into the darkest gloom
Of neighb'ring cypress, or more sable yew,
Her silver globes, light as the foamy surf
That the wind severs from the broken wave
The lilac, various in array, now white,
Now sanguine, and her beauteous head now set
With purple spikes pyramidal, as if,
Studious of ornament, yet unresolv'd
Which hue she most approv'd, she chose them all;
Copious of flow'rs the woodbine, pale and wan,
But well compensating her sickly looks
With never-cloying odours, early and late;
Hypericum, all bloom, so thick a swarm
Of flow'rs, like flies clothing her slender rods,
That scarce a leaf appears, mezereon, too,
Though leafless, well attir'd, and thick beset
With blushing wreaths, investing ev'ry spray;
Althæa with the purple eye; the broom,
Yellow and bright, as bullion unalloy'd,
Her blossoms; and, luxuriant above all,
The jasmine, throwing wide her elegant sweets,
The deep dark green of whose unvarnish'd leaf
Makes more conspicuous, and illumines more
The bright profusion of her scatter'd stars. –
These have been, and these shall be in their day;
And all this uniform, uncolour'd scene,
Shall be dismantled of its fleecy load,
And flush into variety again.

On the Loss of the 'Royal George'

Written When the News Arrived

Toll for the brave –
The brave! that are no more:
All sunk beneath the wave,
Fast by their native shore.
Eight hundred of the brave,
Whose courage well was tried,
Had made the vessel heel
And laid her on her side;
A land-breeze shook the shrouds,
And she was overset;
Down went the Royal George,
With all her crew complete.

Toll for the brave –
Brave Kempenfelt is gone,
His last sea-fight is fought,
His work of glory done.
It was not in the battle,
No tempest gave the shock,
She sprang no fatal leak,
She ran upon no rock;
His sword was in the sheath,
His fingers held the pen,
When Kempenfelt went down
With twice four hundred men.

Weigh the vessel up,
Once dreaded by our foes,
And mingle with your cup
The tears that England owes;
Her timbers yet are sound,
And she may float again,
Full charg'd with England's thunder,
And plough the distant main;
But Kempenfelt is gone,
His victories are o'er;
And he and his eight hundred
Must plough the wave no more.

Lines Written During a Period of Insanity

Hatred and vengeance, my eternal portion,
Scarce can endure delay of execution,
Wait, with impatient readiness, to seize my
Soul in a moment.

Damn'd below Judas: more abhorr'd than he was,
Who for a few pence sold his holy Master.
Twice betrayed Jesus me, the last delinquent,
Deems the profanest.

Man disavows, and Deity disowns me:
Hell might afford my miseries a shelter;
Therefore hell keeps her ever hungry mouths all
Bolted against me.

Hard lot! encompass'd with a thousand dangers;
Weary, faint, trembling with a thousand terrors;
I'm called, if vanquish'd, to receive a sentence
Worse than Abiram's.

Him the vindictive rod of angry justice
Sent quick and howling to the centre headlong;
I, fed with judgment, in a fleshly tomb, am
Buried above ground.

Verses Supposed to Be Written by Alexander Selkirk, During His Solitary Abode in the Island of Juan Fernandez

I am monarch of all I survey,
My right there is none to dispute;
From the centre all round to the sea,
I am lord of the fowl and the brute.
O Solitude! where are the charms
That sages have seen in thy face?
Better dwell in the midst of alarms,
Than reign in this horrible place.

I am out of humanity's reach,
I must finish my journey alone,
Never hear the sweet music of speech;
I start at the sound of my own.
The beasts, that roam over the plain,
My form with indifference see;
They are so unacquainted with man,
Their tameness is shocking to me.

Society, friendship, and love,
Divinely bestow'd upon man,
Oh, had I the wings of a dove,
How soon would I taste you again!
My sorrows I then might assuage
In the ways of religion and truth,
Might learn from the wisdom of age,
And be cheer'd by the sallies of youth.

Religion! what treasure untold
Resides in that heavenly word!
More precious than silver and gold,
Or all that this earth can afford.
But the sound of the church-going bell
These valleys and rocks never heard,
Never sigh'd at the sound of a knell,
Or smil'd when a sabbath appear'd.

Ye winds, that have made me your sport,
  Convey to this desolate shore
Some cordial endearing report
  Of a land I shall visit no more.
My friends, do they now and then send
  A wish or a thought after me?
Oh, tell me I yet have a friend,
  Though a friend I am never to see.

How fleet is a glance of the mind!
  Compar'd with the speed of its flight,
The tempest itself lags behind,
  And the swift-wing'd arrows of light.
When I think of my own native land,
  In a moment I seem to be there;
But alas! recollection at hand
  Soon hurries me back to despair.

But the sea-fowl is gone to her nest,
  The beast is laid down in his lair,
Even here is a season of rest,
  And I to my cabin repair.
There's mercy in every place;
  And mercy, encouraging thought!
Gives even affliction a grace,
  And reconciles man to his lot.

PHILIP FRENEAU

The Indian Burying Ground

In spite of all the learned have said,
  I still my old opinion keep;
The posture, that we give the dead,
  Points out the soul's eternal sleep.

Not so the ancients of these lands –
  The Indian, when from life released,
Again is seated with his friends,
  And shares again the joyous feast.

His imaged birds, and painted bowl,
  And venison, for a journey dressed,
Bespeak the nature of the soul,
  Activity, that knows no rest.

His bow, for action ready bent,
  And arrows, with a head of stone,

Can only mean that life is spent,
  And not the old ideas gone.

Thou, stranger, that shalt come this way,
  No fraud upon the dead commit –
Observe the swelling turf, and say
  They do not lie, but here they sit.

Here still a lofty rock remains,
  On which the curious eye may trace
(Now wasted, half by wearing rains)
  The fancies of a ruder race.

Here still an aged elm aspires,
  Beneath whose far-projecting shade
(And which the shepherd still admires)
  The children of the forest played!

There oft a restless Indian queen
  (Pale Shebah, with her braided hair)
And many a barbarous form is seen
  To chide the man that lingers there.

By midnight moons, o'er moistening dews;
  In habit for the chase arrayed,
The hunter still the deer pursues,
  The hunter and the deer, a shade!

And long shall timorous fancy see
  The painted chief, and pointed spear,
And Reason's self shall bow the knee
  To shadows and delusions here.

GEORGE CRABBE

Rural Life

I grant indeed that fields and flocks have charms
For him that grazes or for him that farms;
But when amid such pleasing scenes I trace
The poor laborious natives of the place,
And see the mid-day sun, with fervid ray,
On their bare heads and dewy temples play;
While some, with feebler heads and fainter hearts,
Deplore their fortune, yet sustain their parts:
Then shall I dare these real ills to hide
In tinsel trappings of poetic pride?
  No; cast by Fortune on a frowning coast,
Which neither groves nor happy valleys boast;

Where other cares than those the Muse relates,
And other shepherds dwell with other mates;
By such examples taught, I paint the Cot,
As Truth will paint it, and as Bards will not:
Nor you, ye poor, of lettered scorn complain,
To you the smoothest song is smooth in vain;
O'ercome by labour, and bowed down by time,
Feel you the barren flattery of a rhyme?
Can poets soothe you, when you pine for bread,
By winding myrtles round your ruined shed?
Can their light tales your weighty griefs o'erpower,
Or glad with airy mirth the toilsome hour?
    Lo! where the heath, with withering brake grown o'er,
Lends the light turf that warms the neighbouring poor;
From thence a length of burning sand appears,
Where the thin harvest waves its withered ears;
Rank weeds, that every art and care defy,
Reign o'er the land, and rob the blighted rye:
There thistles stretch their prickly arms afar,
And to the ragged infant threaten war;
There poppies nodding, mock the hope of toil;
There the blue bugloss paints the sterile soil;
Hardy and high, above the slender sheaf,
The slimy mallow waves her silky leaf;
O'er the young shoot the charlock throws a shade,
And clasping tares cling round the sickly blade;
With mingled tints the rocky coasts abound,
And a sad splendour vainly shines around.
    So looks the nymph whom wretched arts adorn,
Betrayed by man, then left for man to scorn;
Whose cheek in vain assumes the mimic rose,
While her sad eyes the troubled breast disclose;
Whose outward splendour is but folly's dress,
Exposing most, when most it gilds distress.

His Late Wife's Wedding-Ring

The ring so worn, as you behold,
So thin, so pale, is yet of gold:
The passion such it was to prove;
Worn with life's cares, love yet was love.

Peter Grimes; the Outcast

Thus by himself compelled to live each day,
To wait for certain hours the tide's delay;

At the same times the same dull views to see,
The bounding marsh-bank and the blighted tree;
The water only, when the tides were high,
When low, the mud half-covered and half-dry;
The sun-burnt tar that blisters on the planks,
And bank-side stakes in their uneven ranks;
Heaps of entangled weeds that slowly float,
As the tide rolls by the impeded boat.
  When tides were neap, and, in the sultry day,
Through the tall bounding mud-banks made their way,
Which on each side rose swelling, and below
The dark warm flood ran silently and slow;
There anchoring, Peter chose from man to hide,
There hang his head, and view the lazy tide
In its hot slimy channel slowly glide;
Where the small eels that left the deeper way
For the warm shore, within the shallows play;
Where gaping mussels, left upon the mud,
Slope their slow passage to the fallen flood; –
Here dull and hopeless he'd lie down and trace
How sidelong crabs had scrawled their crooked race;
Or sadly listen to the tuneless cry
Of fishing gull or clanging golden-eye;
What time the sea-birds to the marsh would come,
And the loud bittern, from the bull-rush home,
Gave from the salt-ditch side the bellowing boom:
He nursed the feelings these dull scenes produce,
And loved to stop beside the opening sluice;
Where the small stream, confined in narrow bound,
Ran with a dull, unvaried, saddening sound;
Where all, presented to the eye or ear,
Oppressed the soul with misery, grief, and fear.

WILLIAM BLAKE

The Clod and the Pebble

'Love seeketh not itself to please,
Nor for itself hath any care,
But for another gives its ease,
And builds a Heaven in Hell's despair.'

So sung a little Clod of Clay
Trodden with the cattle's feet,
But a Pebble of the brook
Warbled out these metres meet:

'Love seeketh only self to please,
To bind another to its delight,
Joys in another's loss of ease,
And builds a Hell in Heaven's despite.'

The Sick Rose

O rose, thou art sick!
The invisible worm
That flies in the night,
In the howling storm,

Has found out thy bed
Of crimson joy,
And his dark secret love
Does thy life destroy.

The Tiger

Tiger! Tiger! burning bright
In the forests of the night,
What immortal hand or eye
Could frame thy fearful symmetry?

In what distant deeps or skies
Burned the fire of thine eyes?
On what wings dare he aspire?
What the hand dare seize the fire?

And what shoulder, and what art,
Could twist the sinews of thy heart?
And when thy heart began to beat,
What dread hand? And what dread feet?

What the hammer? What the chain?
In what furnace was thy brain?
What the anvil? What dread grasp
Dare its deadly terrors clasp?

When the stars threw down their spears,
And watered heaven with their tears,
Did he smile his work to see?
Did he who made the Lamb make thee?

Tiger! Tiger! burning bright
In the forests of the night,
What immortal hand or eye
Dare frame thy fearful symmetry?

London

I wander thro' each charter'd street,
Near where the charter'd Thames does flow,
And mark in every face I meet
Marks of weakness, marks of woe.

In every cry of every Man,
In every Infant's cry of fear,
In every voice, in every ban,
The mind-forg'd manacles I hear.

How the Chimney-sweeper's cry
Every black'ning Church appalls;
And the hapless Soldier's sigh
Runs in blood down Palace walls.

But most thro' midnight streets I hear
How the youthful Harlot's curse
Blasts the new born Infant's tear,
And blights with plagues the Marriage hearse.

Infant Sorrow

My mother groan'd! my father wept.
Into the dangerous world I leapt:
Helpless, naked, piping loud:
Like a fiend hid in a cloud.

Struggling in my father's hands,
Striving against my swadling bands,
Bound and weary I thought best
To sulk upon my mother's breast.

A Poison Tree

I was angry with my friend:
I told my wrath, my wrath did end.
I was angry with my foe:
I told it not, my wrath did grow.

And I water'd it in fears,
Night and morning with my tears;
And I sunned it with smiles,
And with soft deceitful wiles.

And it grew both day and night,
Till it bore an apple bright;
And my foe beheld it shine,
And he knew that it was mine,

And into my garden stole
When the night had veil'd the pole:
In the morning glad I see
My foe outstretch'd beneath the tree.

Auguries of Innocence

To see a World in a Grain of Sand
And a Heaven in a Wild Flower,
Hold Infinity in the palm of your hand
And Eternity in an hour.
A Robin Red breast in a Cage
Puts all Heaven in a Rage.
A dove house fill'd with doves and Pigeons
Shudders Hell thro' all its regions.
A dog starv'd at his Master's Gate
Predicts the ruin of the State.
A Horse misus'd upon the Road
Calls to Heaven for Human blood.
Each outcry of the hunted Hare
A fibre from the Brain does tear.
A Skylark wounded in the wing,
A Cherubim does cease to sing.
The Game Cock clip'd and arm'd for fight
Does the Rising Sun affright.
Every Wolf's and Lion's howl
Raises from Hell a Human Soul.
The wild deer, wand'ring here and there,
Keeps the Human Soul from Care.
The Lamb misus'd breeds Public strife
And yet forgives the Butcher's Knife.
The Bat that flits at close of Eve
Has left the Brain that won't Believe.
The Owl that calls upon the Night
Speaks the Unbeliever's fright.
He who shall hurt the little Wren
Shall never be belov'd by Men.
He who the Ox to wrath has mov'd
Shall never be by Woman lov'd.
The wanton Boy that kills the Fly
Shall feel the Spider's enmity.
He who torments the Chafer's sprite
Weaves a Bower in endless Night.

The Catterpiller on the Leaf
Repeats to thee thy Mother's grief.
Kill not the Moth nor Butterfly,
For the Last Judgment draweth nigh.
He who shall train the Horse to War
Shall never pass the Polar Bar.
The Begger's Dog and Widow's Cat,
Feed them and thou wilt grow fat.
The Gnat that sings his Summer's song
Poison gets from Slander's tongue.
The poison of the Snake and Newt
Is the sweat of Envy's Foot.
The Poison of the Honey Bee
Is the Artist's Jealousy.
The Prince's Robes and Beggar's Rags
Are Toadstools on the Miser's Bags.
A truth that's told with bad intent
Beats all the Lies you can invent.
It is right it should be so;
Man was made for Joy and Woe;
And when this we rightly know
Thro' the World we safely go.
Joy and Woe are woven fine,
A Clothing for the Soul divine;
Under every grief and pine
Runs a joy with silken twine.
The Babe is more than swadling Bands;
Throughout all these Human Lands
Tools were made, and Born were hands,
Every Farmer Understands.
Every Tear from Every Eye
Becomes a Babe in Eternity;
This is caught by Females bright
And return'd to its own delight.
The Bleat, the Bark, Bellow and Roar
Are Waves that Beat on Heaven's Shore.
The Babe that weeps the Rod beneath
Writes Revenge in realms of death.
The Beggar's Rags, fluttering in Air,
Does to Rags the Heavens tear.
The Soldier, arm'd with Sword and Gun,
Palsied strikes the Summer's Sun.
The poor Man's Farthing is worth more
Than all the Gold on Afric's Shore.
One Mite wrung from the Labrer's hands
Shall buy and sell the Miser's Lands:
Or, if protected from on high,
Does that whole Nation sell and buy.
He who mocks the Infant's Faith

Shall be mock'd in Age and Death.
He who shall teach the Child to Doubt
The rotting Grave shall ne'er get out.
He who respects the Infant's faith
Triumphs over Hell and Death.
The Child's Toys and the Old Man's Reasons
Are the Fruits of the Two seasons.
The Questioner, who sits so sly,
Shall never know how to Reply.
He who replies to words of Doubt
Doth put the Light of Knowledge out.
The Strongest Poison ever known
Came from Caesar's Laurel Crown.
Nought can deform the Human Race
Like to the Armour's iron brace.
When Gold and Gems adorn the Plow
To peaceful Arts shall Envy Bow.
A Riddle or the Cricket's Cry
Is to Doubt a fit Reply.
The Emmet's Inch and Eagle's Mile
Make Lame Philosophy to smile.
He who Doubts from what he sees
Will ne'er Believe, do what you Please.
If the Sun and Moon should doubt,
They'd immediately Go out.
To be in a Passion you Good may do,
But no Good if a Passion is in you.
The Whore and Gambler, by the State
Licenc'd, build that Nation's Fate.
The Harlot's cry from Street to Street
Shall weave Old England's winding Sheet.
The Winner's Shout, the Loser's Curse,
Dance before dead England's Hearse.
Every Night and every Morn
Some to Misery are Born.
Every Morn and every Night
Some are Born to sweet delight.
Some are Born to sweet delight,
Some are Born to Endless Night.
We are led to Believe a Lie
When we see [With *del.*] not Thro' the Eye
Which was Born in a Night to perish in a Night
When the Soul Slept in Beams of Light.
God Appears and God is Light
To those poor Souls who dwell in Night,
But does a Human Form Display
To those who Dwell in Realms of day.

My Pretty Rose Tree

A flower was offered to me,
Such a flower as May never bore;
But I said 'I've a Pretty Rose-tree,'
And I passed the sweet flower o'er.

Then I went to my Pretty Rose-tree,
To tend her by day and by night;
But my Rose turned away with jealousy,
And her thorns were my only delight.

The Chimney Sweeper

When my mother died I was very young,
And my Father sold me while yet my tongue
Could scarcely cry ''weep! 'weep! 'weep! 'weep!'
So your chimneys I sweep, and in soot I sleep.

There's little Tom Dacre, who cried when his head,
That curl'd like a lamb's back, was shav'd: so I said
'Hush, Tom! never mind it, for when your head's bare
'You know that the soot cannot spoil your white hair.'

And so he was quiet, and that very night
As Tom was a-sleeping, he had such a sight!
That thousands of sweepers, Dick, Joe, Ned, and Jack,
Were all of them lock'd up in coffins of black.

And by came an Angel who had a bright key,
And he open'd the coffins and set them all free;
Then down a green plain leaping, laughing, they run,
And wash in a river, and shine in the Sun.

Then naked and white, all their bags left behind,
They rise upon clouds and sport in the wind;
And the Angel told Tom, if he'd be a good boy,
He'd have God for his father, and never want joy.

And so Tom awoke; and we rose in the dark,
And got with our bags and our brushes to work.
Tho' the morning was cold, Tom was happy and warm;
So if all do their duty they need not fear harm.

Infant Joy

'I have no name:
'I am but two days old.'
What shall I call thee?
'I happy am,
'Joy is my name.'
Sweet joy befall thee!

Pretty joy!
Sweet joy but two days old,
Sweet joy I call thee:
Thou dost smile,
I sing the while,
Sweet joy befall thee!

The School Boy

I love to rise in a summer morn
When the birds sing on every tree;
The distant huntsman winds his horn,
And the sky-lark sings with me.
O! what sweet company.

But to go to school in a summer morn,
O! it drives all joy away;
Under a cruel eye outworn,
The little ones spend the day
In sighing and dismay.

Ah! then at times I drooping sit,
And spend many an anxious hour,
Nor in my book can I take delight,
Nor sit in learning's bower,
Worn thro' with the dreary shower.

How can the bird that is born for joy
Sit in a cage and sing?
How can a child, when fears annoy,
But droop his tender wing,
And forget his youthful spring?

O! father and mother, if buds are nip'd
And blossoms blown away,
And if the tender plants are strip'd
Of their joy in the springing day,
By sorrow and care's dismay,

How shall the summer arise in joy,
Or the summer fruits appear?
Or how shall we gather what griefs destroy,
Or bless the mellowing year,
When the blasts of winter appear?

The Divine Image

To Mercy, Pity, Peace, and Love
All pray in their distress;
And to these virtues of delight
Return their thankfulness.

For Mercy, Pity, Peace, and Love
Is God, our father dear,
And Mercy, Pity, Peace and Love,
Is Man, his child and care.

For Mercy has a human heart,
Pity a human face,
And Love, the human form divine,
And Peace, the human dress.

Then every man, of every clime,
That prays in his distress,
Prays to the human form divine,
Love, Mercy, Pity, Peace.

And all must love the human form,
In heathen, turk, or jew;
Where Mercy, Love, and Pity dwell
There God is dwelling too.

Eternity

He who bends to himself a joy
Does the wingèd life destroy;
But he who kisses the joy as it flies
Lives in eternity's sunrise.

Jerusalem

And did those feet in ancient time
Walk upon England's mountains green?
And was the holy Lamb of God
On England's pleasant pastures seen?

And did the Countenance Divine
Shine forth upon our clouded hills?
And was Jerusalem builded here
Among these dark Satanic Mills?

Bring me my Bow of burning gold!
Bring me my Arrows of desire!
Bring me my Spear! O clouds, unfold!
Bring me my Chariot of fire!

I will not cease from Mental Fight,
Nor shall my Sword sleep in my hand,
Till we have built Jerusalem
In England's green and pleasant land.

ROBERT BURNS

Robert Bruce's March to Bannockburn

Scots, wha hae wi' Wallace bled,
Scots, wham Bruce has aften led,
Welcome to your gory bed,
    Or to victory!

Now's the day, and now's the hour;
See the front o' battle lour,
See approach proud Edward's power –
    Chains and slavery!

Wha will be a traitor knave?
Wha can fill a coward's grave?
Wha sae base as be a slave? –
    Let him turn, and flee!

Wha for Scotland's King and Law
Freedom's sword will strongly draw,
Freeman stand or freeman fa',
    Let him follow me!

By Oppression's woes and pains,
By your sons in servile chains,
We will drain our dearest veins,
    But they shall be free!

Lay the proud usurpers low!
Tyrants fall in every foe!
Liberty's in every blow!
    Let us do, or die!

Grace at Kirkudbright

Some have meat and cannot eat,
Some cannot eat that want it:
But we have meat and we can eat,
Sae let the Lord be thankit.

A Red, Red Rose

O my luve's like a red, red rose,
That's newly sprung in June;
O my luve's like the melodie
That's sweetly played in tune.

As fair art thou, my bonie lass,
So deep in luve am I;
And I will love thee still, my dear,
Till a' the seas gang dry.

Till a' the seas gang dry, my dear,
And the rocks melt wi' the sun:
I will love thee still, my dear,
While the sands o' life shall run.

And fare thee weel, my only luve!
And fare thee weel, a while!
And I will come again, my luve,
Though it were ten thousand mile!

For A' That

Is there, for honest poverty
That hings his head, and a' that;
The coward-slave, we pass him by,
We dare be poor for a' that!
For a' that, and a' that,
Our toils obscure, and a' that,
The rank is but the guinea's stamp,
The man's the gowd[1] for a' that.

What though on hamely fare we dine,
Wear hoddin[2] grey, and a' that.
Gie fools their silks, and knaves their wine,
A man's a man for a' that.
For a' that, and a' that,
Their tinsel show, and a' that;

The honest man, though e'er sae poor,
Is king o' men for a' that.

Ye see yon birkie[3] ca'd a lord,
Wha struts, and stares, and a' that,
Though hundreds worship at his word,
He's but a coof[4] for a ' that.
For a' that, and a' that,
His ribband, star and a' that,
The man of independent mind,
He looks and laughs at a' that.

A prince can mak a belted knight,
A marquis, duke, and a' that;
But an honest man's aboon his might,
Gude faith he mauna fa' that!
For a' that, and a' that,
Their dignities, and a' that,
The pith o' sense, and pride o' worth
Are higher rank than a' that.

Then let us pray that come it may,
As come it will for a' that,
That sense and worth, o'er a' the earth
Shall bear the gree[5], and a' that.
For a' that, and a' that,
It's coming yet for a' that,
That man to man the warld o'er,
Shall brothers be for a' that.

[1]gold [2]homespun cloth [3]dandy [4]fool [5]come off best

To a Mouse, On Turning her up in her Nest, with the Plough, November, 1785

Wee, sleeket, cowran, tim'rous beastie,
O, what a panic's in thy breastie!
Thou need na start awa sae hasty,
Wi' bickering brattle![1]
I wad be laith to rin an' chase thee,
Wi' murd'ring pattle![2]

I'm truly sorry man's dominion
Has broken Nature's social union,
An' justifies that ill opinion,
Which makes thee startle,
At me, thy poor, earth-born companion,
An' fellow-mortal!

I doubt na whyles, but thou may thieve;
What then? poor beastie, thou maun live!
A daimen-icker[3] in a thrave[4]
'S a sma' request:
I'll get a blessin wi' the lave,[5]
An' never miss 't!

Thy wee-bit housie, too, in ruin!
It's silly wa's the win's are strewin!
An' naething, now, to big[6] a new ane,
O' foggage green!
An' bleak December's winds ensuin,
Baith snell[7] an' keen!

Thou saw the fields laid bare an' wast,
An' weary winter comin fast,
An' cozie here, beneath the blast,
Thou thought to dwell,
Till crash! the cruel coulter past
Out through thy cell.

That wee-bit heap o' leaves an' stibble,
Has cost thee monie a weary nibble!
Now thou's turned out, for a' they trouble,
But[8] house or hald,[9]
To thole the winter's sleety dribble,
An' cranreuch[10] cauld!

But mousie, thou art no thy-lane,
In proving foresight may be vain:
The best laid schemes o' mice an' men
Gang aft agley,
An' lea'e us nought but grief an' pain,
For promised joy!

Still, thou art blest, compared wi' me!
The present only toucheth thee:
But Och! I backward cast my e'e
On prospects drear!
An' forward, though I canna see,
I guess an' fear!

[1]scurrying haste [2]spade [3]odd ear of corn [4]two stooks
[5]remainder [6]build [7]bitter [8]without [9]refuge [10]frost

Green Grow the Rashes

Green grow the rashes O,
  Green grow the rashes O;
The sweetest hours that e'er I spend,
  Are spent amang the lasses O!

There's nought but care on ev'ry han',
  In ev'ry hour that passes O;
What signifies the life o' man,
  An' 'twere na for the lasses O.

The warly[1] race may riches chase,
  An' riches still may fly them O;
An' tho' at last they catch them fast,
  Their hearts can ne'er enjoy them O.

But gie me a canny hour at e'en,
  My arms about my dearie O;
An' warly cares, an' warly men,
  May a' gae tapsalteerie[2] O!

For you sae douce,[3] ye sneer at this,
  Ye're nought but senseless asses O:
The wisest man the warl' saw,
  He dearly loved the lasses O.

Auld nature swears, the lovely dears
  Her noblest work she classes O;
Her prentice han's he tried on man,
  An' then she made the lasses O.

[1]worldly [2]topsy-turvey [3]grave, sober

Auld Lang Syne

Should auld acquaintance be forgot,
  And never brought to min'?
Should auld acquaintance be forgot,
  And auld lang syne?

  For auld lang syne, my dear.
    For auld lang syne,
  We'll tak a cup o' kindness yet,
    For auld lang syne.

We twa hae run about the braes,
  And pu'd the gowans[1] fine;
But we've wandered mony a weary foot
  Sin' auld lang syne.

We twa hae paidled i' the burn,
  From morning sun till dine;
But seas between us braid hae roared
  Sin' auld lang syne.

And there's a hand, my trusty fiere[2],
  And gie's a hand o' thine;
And we'll tak a right guid-willie waught[3],
  For auld lang syne.

And surely ye'll be your pint-stowp,
  And surely I'll be mine;
And we'll tak a cup o' kindness yet
  For auld lang syne.

[1]daisies [2]comrade [3] draught

EBENEZER ELLIOTT

How Different!

Poor weaver, with the hopeless brow,
  And bare wo-whitened head;
Thou art a pauper all allow,
  All see thou begg'st thy bread;
And yet thou dost not plunder slaves,
  Then tell them they are free;
Nor hast thou joined with tax-fed knaves,
  To Corn-Bill mine and me.

What borough dost thou represent?
  Who bidd'st thou toil and pay?
Why sitt'st not though in pauperment,
  If baser beggars may?
Where are they hounds, thy palaced w——e,
  To feed on mine and me?
Thy reverend pimp, thy coach and four,
  Thy thieves in livery?

No house hast thou, no food, no fire:
  None bow to thee alas!
A beggar? yet nor Lord, nor Squire!
  Say, how comes this to pass?
While you proud pauper, dead to shame,
  Is fed by mine and me?
And yet behind the rascal's name
  The scoundrel writes M.P.!

CHARLES LAMB

The Old Familiar Faces

I have had playmates, I have had companions,
In my days of childhood, in my joyful school-days,
All, all are gone, the old familiar faces.

I have been laughing, I have been carousing,
Drinking late, sitting late, with my bosom cronies,
All, all are gone, the old familiar faces.

I loved a love once, fairest among women:
Closed are her doors on me, I must not see her –
All, all are gone, the old familiar faces.

I have a friend, a kinder friend has no man;
Like an ingrate, I left my friend abruptly;
Left him, to muse on the old familiar faces.

Ghost-like I paced round the haunts of my childhood,
Earth seemed a desert I was bound to traverse,
Seeking to find the old familiar faces.

Friend of my bosom, thou more than a brother,
Why wert not thou born in my father's dwelling?
So might we talk of the old familiar faces –

How some they have died, and some they have left me,
And some are taken from me; all are departed;
All, all are gone, the old familiar faces.

MARY and CHARLES LAMB

Parental Recollections

A child's a plaything for an hour;
   Its pretty tricks we try
For that or for a longer space;
   Then tire, and lay it by.

But I knew one that to itself
   All seasons could control;
That would have mocked the sense of pain
   Out of a grievèd soul.

Thou straggler into loving arms,
  Young climber up of knees,
When I forget thy thousand ways,
  Then life and all shall cease.

THOMAS MOORE

'They may rail at this life'

They may rail at this life – from the hour I began it,
  I've found it a life full of kindness and bliss;
And until they can show me some happier planet,
  More social and bright, I'll content me with this.
As long as the world has such lips and such eyes,
  As before me this moment enraptured I see,
They may say what they will of the orbs in the skies,
  But this earth is the planet for you, love, and me.

In Mercury's star, where each minute can bring them
  New sunshine and wit from the fountain on high,
Though the nymphs may have livelier poets to sing them,
  They've none, even there, more enamoured than I.
And as long as this harp can be wakened to love,
  And that eye its divine inspiration shall be,
They may talk as they will of their Edens above,
  But this earth is the planet for you, love, and me.

In that star of the west, by whose shadowy splendor
  At twilight so often we've roamed through the dew,
There are maidens, perhaps, who have bosoms as tender,
  And look, in their twilights, as lovely as you.
But though they were even more bright than the queen
  Of that isle they inhabit in heaven's blue sea,
As I never those fair young celestials have seen,
  Why, – this earth is the planet for you, love, and me.

As for those chilly orbs on the verge of creation,
  Where sunshine and smiles must be equally rare,
Did they want a supply of cold hearts for that station,
  Heaven knows we have plenty on earth we could spare.
Oh! think what a world we should have of it here,
  If the haters of peace, of affection, and glee,
Were to fly up to Saturn's comfortless sphere,
  And leave earth to such spirits as you, love, and me.

'Oft, in the stilly night'

Oft, in the stilly night,
Ere Slumber's chain has bound me,
Fond Memory brings the light
Of other days around me;
The smiles, the tears,
Of boyhood's years,
The words of love then spoken;
The eyes that shone,
Now dimm'd and gone,
The cheerful hearts now broken!
Thus, in the stilly night,
Ere Slumber's chain has bound me,
Sad Memory brings the light
Of other days around me.

When I remember all
The friends so link'd together,
I've seen around me fall,
Like leaves in wintry weather;
I feel like one,
Who treads alone
Some banquet-hall deserted,
Whose lights are fled,
Whose garlands dead,
And all but he departed!
Thus, in the stilly night,
Ere Slumber's chain has bound me.
Sad Memory brings the light
Of other days around me.

The Minstrel Boy

The Minstrel Boy to the war is gone,
In the ranks of death you'll find him;
His father's sword he has girded on,
And his wild harp slung behind him. –
'Land of song!' said the warrior-bard,
'Though all the world betrays thee,
One sword, at least, thy rights shall guard,
One faithful harp shall praise thee!'

The Minstrel fell! – but the foeman's chain
Could not bring his proud soul under;
The harp he loved ne'er spoke again,
For he tore its chords asunder;

And said, 'No chains shall sully thee,
Thou soul of love and bravery!
Thy songs were made for the pure and free,
They shall never sound in slavery.'

LEIGH HUNT

Rondeau

Jenny kissed me when we met,
Jumping from the chair she sat in;
Time, you thief, who love to get
Sweets into your list, put that in!
Say I'm weary, say I'm sad,
Say that health and wealth have missed me,
Say I'm growing old, but add,
Jenny kissed me.

JOHN CLARE

I Am

I am: yet what I am none cares or knows
My friends forsake me like a memory lost,
I am the self-consumer of my woes –
They rise and vanish in oblivious host,
Like shadows in love's frenzied stifled throes: –
And yet I am, and live – like vapours tost

Into the nothingness of scorn and noise,
Into the living sea of waking dreams,
Where there is neither sense of life or joys,
But the vast shipwreck of my life's esteems;
Even the dearest, that I love the best,
Are strange – nay, rather stranger than the rest.

I long for scenes, where man hath never trod,
A place where woman never smiled or wept –
There to abide with my Creator, God,
And sleep as I in childhood sweetly slept,
Untroubling, and untroubled where I lie,
The grass below – above the vaulted sky.

Summer Evening

The frog, half fearful, jumps across the path,
And little mouse that leaves its hole at eve
Nimbles with timid dread beneath the swath;
My rustling steps awhile their joys deceive,
Till past – and then the cricket sings more strong,
And grasshoppers in merry moods still wear
The short night weary with their fretting song.
Up from behind the mole-hill jumps the hare,
Cheat of his chosen bed, and from the bank
The yellow-hammer flutters in short fears
From off its nest hid in the grasses rank,
And drops again when no more noise it hears.
Thus nature's human link and endless thrall,
Proud man, still seems the enemy of all.

Harvest

Harvest approaches with its bustling day
The wheat tans brown and barley bleaches grey
In yellow garb the oat land intervenes
And tawney glooms the valley thronged with beans
Silent the village grows, wood wandering dreams
Seem not so lovely as its quiet seems
Doors are shut up as on a winters day
And not a child about them lies at play
The dust that winnows neath the breezes feet
Is all that stirs about the silent street
Fancy might think that desert spreading fear
Had whisperd terrors into quiets ear
Or plundering armys past the place had come
And drove the lost inhabitants from home
The fields now claim them where a motley crew
Of old and young their daily tasks pursue
The barleys beard is grey and wheat is brown
And wakens toil betimes to leave the town
The reapers leave their beds before the sun
And gleaners follow when home toils are done
To pick the littered ear the reaper leaves
And glean in open fields among the sheaves.

'Love lives beyond'

Love lives beyond
The tomb, the earth, which fades like dew!
I love the fond,
The faithful, and the true.

Love lives in sleep,
The happiness of healthy dreams;
Eve's dews may weep,
But love delightful seems.

'Tis seen in flowers,
And in the morning's pearly dew;
In earth's green hours,
And in the heaven's eternal blue.

'Tis heard in spring
When light and sunbeams, warm and kind,
On angel's wing
Bring love and music to the mind.

And where is voice,
So young, so beautiful, and sweet
As nature's choice,
Where spring and lovers meet?

Love lives beyond
The tomb, the earth, the flowers, and dew.
I love the fond,
The faithful, young, and true.

Schoolboys in Winter

The schoolboys still their morning rambles take
To neighbouring village school with playing speed,
Loitering with pastime's leisure till they quake,
Oft looking up the wild-geese droves to heed,
Watching the letters which their journeys make;
Or plucking haws on which the fieldfares feed,
And hips, and sloes! and on each shallow lake
Making glib slides, where they like shadows go
Till some fresh pastimes in their minds awake.
Then off they start anew and hasty blow
Their numbed and clumpsing fingers till they glow;
Then races with their shadows wildly run
That stride huge giants o'er the shining snow
In the pale splendour of the winter sun.

JAMES CLARENCE MANGAN

Dark Rosaleen

O my Dark Rosaleen,
  Do not sigh, do not weep!
The priests are on the ocean green,
  They march along the deep.
There's wine from the royal Pope,
  Upon the ocean green;
And Spanish ale shall give you hope,
  My Dark Rosaleen!
  My own Rosaleen!
Shall glad your heart, shall give you hope,
Shall give you health, and help, and hope,
  My Dark Rosaleen!

Over hills, and thro' dales,
  Have I roamed for your sake;
All yesterday I sailed with sails
  On river and on lake.
The Erne, at its highest flood,
  I dashed across unseen,
For there was lightning in my blood,
  My Dark Rosaleen!
  My own Rosaleen!
O, there was lightning in my blood,
Red lightning lightened thro' my blood.
  My Dark Rosaleen!

All day long, in unrest,
  To and fro, do I move.
The very soul within my breast
  Is wasted for you, love!
The heart in my bosom faints
  To think of you, my Queen,
My life of life, my saint of saints,
  My Dark Rosaleen!
  My own Rosaleen!
To hear your sweet and sad complaints,
My life, my love, my saint of saints,
  My Dark Rosaleen!

Woe and pain, pain and woe,
  Are my lot, night and noon,
To see your bright face clouded so,
  Like to the mournful moon,
But yet will I rear your throne
  Again in golden sheen;

'Tis you shall reign, shall reign alone,
   My Dark Rosaleen!
   My own Rosaleen!
'Tis you shall have the golden throne,
'Tis you shall reign, and reign alone,
   My Dark Rosaleen!

Over dews, over sands,
   Will I fly, for your weal:
Your holy delicate white hands
   Shall girdle me with steel.
At home, in your emerald bowers,
   From morning's dawn till e'en,
You'll pray for me, my flower of flowers,
   My Dark Rosaleen!
   My fond Rosaleen!
You'll think of me through daylight hours,
My virgin flower, my flower of flowers,
   My Dark Rosaleen!

I could scale the blue air,
   I could plough the high hills,
O, I could kneel all night in prayer,
   To heal your many ills!
And one beamy smile from you
   Would float like light between
My toils and me, my own, my true,
   My Dark Rosaleen!
   My fond Rosaleen!
Would give me life and soul anew,
A second life, a soul anew,
   My Dark Rosaleen!

O, the Erne shall run red,
   With redundance of blood,
The earth shall rock beneath our tread,
   And flames wrap hill and wood,
And gun-peal and slogan-cry
   Wake many a glen serene,
Ere you shall fade, ere you shall die,
   My Dark Rosaleen!
   My own Rosaleen!
The Judgement Hour must first be nigh,
Ere you can fade, ere you can die,
   My Dark Rosaleen!

SAMUEL ROGERS

A Wish

Mine be a cot beside the hill;
A bee-hive's hum shall soothe my ear;
A willowy brook, that turns a mill,
With many a fall shall linger near.

The swallow oft beneath my thatch
Shall twitter from her clay-built nest;
Oft shall the pilgrim lift the latch
And share my meal, a welcome guest.

Around my ivied porch shall spring
Each fragrant flower that drinks the dew;
And Lucy at her wheel shall sing
In russet gown and apron blue.

The village church among the trees,
Where first our marriage vows were given,
With merry peals shall swell the breeze
And point with taper spire to Heaven.

WILLIAM WORDSWORTH

'Bliss was it in that dawn to be alive'

Bliss was it in that dawn to be alive,
But to be young was very Heaven! O times,
In which the meagre, stale, forbidding ways
Of custom, law, and statute, took at once
The attraction of a country in romance!
When Reason seemed the most to assert her rights
When most intent on making of herself
A prime enchantress – to assist the work,
Which then was going forward in her name!
Not favoured spots alone, but the whole Earth,
The beauty wore of promise – that which sets
(As at some moments might not be unfelt
Among the bowers of Paradise itself)
The budding rose above the rose full blown.
What temper at the prospect did not wake
To happiness unthought of? The inert
Were roused, and lively natures rapt away!
They who had fed their childhood upon dreams,
The play-fellows of fancy, who had made

All powers of swiftness, subtilty, and strength
Their ministers, – who in lordly wise had stirred
Among the grandest objects of the sense,
And dealt with whatsoever they found there
As if they had within some lurking right
To wield it; – they, too, who of gentle mood
Had watched all gentle motions, and to these
Had fitted their own thoughts, schemers more mild,
And in the region of their peaceful selves; –
Now was it that *both* found, the meek and lofty
Did both find, helpers to their hearts' desire,
And stuff at hand, plastic as they could wish, –
Were called upon to exercise their skill,
Not in Utopia, – subterranean fields, –
Or some secreted island, Heaven knows where!
But in the very world, which is the world
Of all of us, – the place where, in the end,
We find our happiness, or not at all!

Upon Westminster Bridge Sept. 3, 1802

Earth has not anything to show more fair:
  Dull would he be of soul who could pass by
  A sight so touching in its majesty:
This City now doth, like a garment, wear
The beauty of the morning; silent, bare,
  Ships, towers, domes, theatres, and temples lie
  Open unto the fields, and to the sky;
All bright and glittering in the smokeless air.
Never did sun more beautifully steep
  In his first splendour, valley, rock, or hill;
Ne'er saw I, never felt, a calm so deep!
  The river glideth at his own sweet will:
Dear God! the very houses seem asleep;
  And all that mighty heart is lying still!

'She was a phantom of delight'

She was a phantom of delight
When first she gleam'd upon my sight;
A lovely apparition, sent
To be a moment's ornament;
Her eyes as stars of twilight fair;
Like Twilight's, too, her dusky hair;

But all things else about her drawn
From May-time and the cheerful dawn;
A dancing shape, an image gay,
To haunt, to startle, and waylay.

I saw her upon nearer view
A spirit, yet a woman too!
Her household motions light and free,
And steps of virgin-liberty;
A countenance in which did meet
Sweet records, promises as sweet;
A creature not too bright or good
For human nature's daily food,
For transient sorrows, simple wiles,
Praise, blame, love, kisses, tears, and smiles.

And now I see with eye serene
The very pulse of the machine;
A being breathing thoughtful breath,
A traveller between life and death:
The reason firm, the temperate will,
Endurance, foresight, strength, and skill;
A perfect woman, nobly plann'd
To warn, to comfort, and command;
And yet a Spirit still, and bright
With something of an angel-light.

'Milton! thou shouldst be living at this hour'

Milton! thou shouldst be living at this hour:
England hath need of thee: she is a fen
Of stagnant waters: altar, sword, and pen,
Fireside, the heroic wealth of hall and bower,

Have forfeited their ancient English dower
Of inward happiness. We are selfish men:
O! raise us up, return to us again;
And give us manners, virtue, freedom, power.

Thy soul was like a Star, and dwelt apart:
Thou hadst a voice whose sound was like the sea,
Pure as the naked heavens, majestic, free;

So didst thou travel on life's common way
In cheerful godliness; and yet thy heart
The lowliest duties on herself did lay.

Ode to Duty

Stern Daughter of the voice of God!
O Duty! if that name thou love
Who are a light to guide, a rod
To check the erring, and reprove;
Thou who art victory and law
When empty terrors overawe;
From vain temptations dost set free,
And calm'st the weary strife of frail humanity!

There are who ask not if thine eye
Be on them; who, in love and truth
Where no misgiving is, rely
Upon the genial sense of youth:
Glad hearts! without reproach or blot,
Who do thy work, and know it not:
O! if through confidence misplaced
They fail, thy saving arms, dread Power! around them cast.

Serene will be our days and bright
And happy will our nature be
When love is an unerring light,
And joy its own security.
And they a blissful course may hold
Ev'n now, who, not unwisely bold,
Live in the spirit of this creed;
Yet find that other strength according to their need.

I, loving freedom, and untried,
No sport of every random gust,
Yet being to myself a guide,
Too blindly have reposed my trust:
And oft, when in my heart was heard
Thy timely mandate, I deferr'd
The task, in smoother walks to stray;
But thee I now would serve more strictly, if I may.

Through no disturbance of my soul
Or strong compunction in me wrought,
I supplicate for thy controul,
But in the quietness of thought:
Me this uncharter'd freedom tires;
I feel the weight of chance-desires:
My hopes no more must change their name;
I long for a repose that ever is the same.

Stern lawgiver! yet thou dost wear
The Godhead's most benignant grace;

Nor know we anything so fair
As is the smile upon thy face:
Flowers laugh before thee on their beds,
And fragrance in thy footing treads;
Thou dost preserve the Stars from wrong;
And the most ancient Heavens, through thee, are fresh and strong.

To humbler functions, awful Power!
I call thee: I myself commend
Unto my guidance from this hour;
O let my weakness have an end!
Give unto me, made lowly wise,
The spirit of self-sacrifice;
The confidence of reason give;
And in the light of Truth thy bondman let me live.

The Green Linnet

Beneath these fruit-tree boughs that shed
Their snow-white blossoms on my head,
With brightest sunshine round me spread
Of Spring's unclouded weather,
In this sequester'd nook how sweet
To sit upon my orchard-seat!
And flowers and birds once more to greet,
My last year's friends together.

One have I mark'd, the happiest guest
In all this covert of the blest:
Hail to Thee, far above the rest
In joy of voice and pinion!
Thou, Linnet! in thy green array
Presiding Spirit here to-day
Dost lead the revels of the May,
And this is thy dominion.

While birds, and butterflies, and flowers,
Make all one band of paramours,
Thou, ranging up and down the bowers
Art sole in thy employment;
A Life, a Presence like the air,
Scattering thy gladness without care,
Too blest with any one to pair,
Thyself thy own enjoyment.

Amid yon tuft of hazel trees
That twinkle to the gusty breeze,
Behold him perch'd in ecstasies
Yet seeming still to hover;

There, where the flutter of his wings
Upon his back and body flings
Shadows and sunny glimmerings,
That cover him all over.

My dazzled sight he oft deceives –
A brother of the dancing leaves;
Then flits, and from the cottage-eaves
Pours forth his song in gushes,
As if by that exulting strain
He mock'd and treated with disdain
The voiceless Form he chose to feign,
While fluttering in the bushes.

A Rainbow

My heart leaps up when I behold
  A rainbow in the sky:
So was it when my life began,
So is it now I am a man,
So be it when I shall grow old
  Or let me die!
The Child is father of the Man:
And I could wish my days to be
Bound each to each by natural piety.

Daffodils

I wandered lonely as a cloud
  That floats on high o'er vales and hills,
When all at once I saw a crowd,
  A host, of golden daffodils;
Beside the lake, beneath the trees,
Fluttering and dancing in the breeze.

Continuous as the stars that shine
  And twinkle on the Milky Way,
They stretched in never-ending line
  Along the margin of a bay:
Ten thousand saw I at a glance,
Tossing their heads in sprightly dance.

The waves beside them danced, but they
  Out-did the sparkling waves in glee:
A poet could not but be gay,
  In such a jocund company:

I gazed – and gazed – but little thought
What wealth the show to me had brought:

For oft, when on my couch I lie
  In vacant or in pensive mood,
They flash upon that inward eye
  Which is the bliss of solitude;
And then my heart with pleasure fills,
And dances with the daffodils.

Lines Composed a Few Miles Above Tintern Abbey

On revisiting the banks of the Wye during a tour

Five years have past; five summers, with the length
Of five long winters! and again I hear
These waters, rolling from their mountain-springs
With a soft inland murmur. – Once again
Do I behold these steep and lofty cliffs,
That on a wild secluded scene impress
Thoughts of more deep seclusion; and connect
The landscape with the quiet of the sky.
The day is come when I again repose
Here, under this dark sycamore, and view
These plots of cottage-ground, these orchard-tufts,
Which at this season, with their unripe fruits,
Are clad in one green hue, and lose themselves
'Mid groves and copses. Once again I see
These hedge-rows, hardly hedge-rows, little lines
Of sportive wood run wild: these pastoral farms,
Green to the very door; and wreaths of smoke
Sent up, in silence from among the trees!
With some uncertain notice, as might seem
Of vagrant dwellers in the houseless woods,
Or of some Hermit's cave, where by his fire
The Hermit sits alone.

These beauteous forms
Through a long absence, have not been to me
As is a landscape to a blind man's eye:
But oft, in lonely rooms, and 'mid the din
Of towns and cities, I have owed to them
In hours of weariness, sensations sweet,
Felt in the blood, and felt along the heart;
And passing even into my purer mind,
With tranquil restoration: – feelings too
Of unremembered pleasure: such, perhaps,
As have no slight or trivial influence
On that best portion of a good man's life.

His little, nameless, unremembered acts
Of kindness and of love. Nor less, I trust,
To them I may have owed another gift,
Of aspect more sublime; that blessed mood,
In which the burthen of the mystery,
In which the heavy and the weary weight
Of all this unintelligible world,
Is lightened:— that serene and blessed mood,
In which the affections gently lead us on, –
Until, the breath of this corporeal frame
And even the motion of our human blood
Almost suspended, we are laid asleep
In body, and become a living soul:
While with an eye made quiet by the power
Of harmony, and the deep power of joy,
We see into the life of things.

If this
Be but a vain belief, yet, oh! how oft
In darkness and amid the many shapes
Of joyless daylight; when the fretful stir
Unprofitable, and the fever of the world,
Have hung upon the beatings of my heart –
How oft, in spirit, have I turned to thee,
O sylvan Wye! thou wanderer thro' the woods,
How often has my spirit turned to thee!

Personal Talk

I am not one who much or oft delight
To season my fireside with personal talk, –
Of friends, who live within an easy walk,
Or neighbours, daily, weekly, in my sight:
And, for my chance-acquaintance, ladies bright,
Sons, mothers, maidens withering on the stalk,
These all wear out of me, like forms, with chalk
Painted on rich men's floors, for one feast-night.
Better than such discourse doth silence long,
Long, barren silence, square with my desire;
To sit without emotion, hope, or aim,
In the loved presence of my cottage-fire,
And listen to the flapping of the flame,
Or kettle whispering its faint undersong.

'The world is too much with us'

The world is too much with us; late and soon,
Getting and spending, we lay waste our powers:
Little we see in Nature that is ours;
We have given our hearts away, a sordid boon!
This Sea that bares her bosom to the moon;
The winds that will be howling at all hours,
And are up-gathered now like sleeping flowers;
For this, for everything, we are out of tune;
It moves us not. – Great God! I'd rather be
A Pagan suckled in a creed outworn;
So might I, standing on this pleasant lea,
Have glimpses that would make me less forlorn;
Have sight of Proteus rising from the sea;
Or hear old Triton blow his wreathèd horn.

SAMUEL TAYLOR COLERIDGE

The Rime of the Ancient Mariner

PART I

An ancient Mariner meeteth three Gallants bidden to a wedding-feast, and detaineth one.

It is an ancient Mariner
And he stoppeth one of three.
'By thy long grey beard and glittering eye,
Now wherefore stopp'st thou me?

The Bridegroom's doors are opened wide,
And I am next of kin;
The guests are met, the feast is set:
Mayst hear the merry din.'

He holds him with his skinny hand,
'There was a ship,' quoth he.
'Hold off! unhand me, grey-beard loon!'
Eftsoons his hand dropt he.

The Wedding-Guest is spellbound by the eye of the old seafaring man, and constrained to hear his tale.

He holds him with his glittering eye –
The Wedding-Guest stood still,
And listens like a three years' child:
The Mariner hath his will.

The Wedding-Guest sat on a stone:
He cannot choose but hear;
And thus spake on that ancient man,
The bright-eyed Mariner.

'The ship was cheered, the harbour cleared,
Merrily did we drop

The Mariner tells how the ship sailed southward with a good wind and fair weather, till it reached the Line.

Below the kirk, below the hill,
Below the lighthouse top.

The Sun came up upon the left,
Out of the sea came he!
And he shone bright, and on the right
Went down into the sea.

Higher and higher every day,
Till over the mast at noon – '
The Wedding-Guest here beat his breast,
For he heard the loud bassoon.

The Wedding-Guest heareth the bridal music; but the Mariner continueth his tale.

The bride hath paced into the hall,
Red as a rose is she;
Nodding their heads before her goes
The merry minstrelsy.

The Wedding-Guest he beat his breast,
Yet he cannot choose but hear;
And thus spake on that ancient man,
The bright-eyed Mariner.

The ship driven by a storm toward the South Pole.

'And now the STORM-BLAST came, and he
Was tyrannous and strong:
He struck with his o'ertaking wings,
And chased us south along.

With sloping masts and dipping prow,
As who pursued with yell and blow
Still treads the shadow of his foe,
And forward bends his head,
The ship drove fast, loud roared the blast,
And southward aye we fled.

And now there came both mist and snow,
And it grew wondrous cold:
And ice, mast-high, came floating by,
As green as emerald.

The land of ice, and of fearful sounds, where no living thing was to be seen.

And through the drifts the snowy clifts
Did send a dismal sheen:
Nor shapes of men nor beasts we ken –
The ice was all between.

The ice was here, the ice was there,
The ice was all around:
It cracked and growled, and roared and howled,
Like noises in a swound!

Till a great sea-bird, called the Albatross, came through the snow-fog, and was received with great joy and hospitality.

At length did cross an Albatross,
Thorough the fog it came;
As if it had been a Christian soul,
We hailed it in God's name.

It ate the food it ne'er had eat,
And round and round it flew.
The ice did split with a thunder-fit;
The helmsman steered us through!

And lo! the Albatross proveth a bird of good omen, and followeth the ship as it returned northward through fog and floating ice.

And a good south wind sprung up behind;
The Albatross did follow,
And every day, for food or play,
Came to the mariners' hollo!

In mist or cloud, on mast or shroud,
It perched for vespers nine;
Whiles all the night, through fog-smoke white,
Glimmered the white Moon-shine.'

The ancient Mariner inhospitably killeth the pious bird of good omen.

'God save thee, ancient Mariner!
From the fiends, that plague thee thus! –
Why look'st thou so?' – 'With my cross-bow
I shot the ALBATROSS.'

PART II

'The Sun now rose upon the right:
Out of the sea came he,
Still hid in mist, and on the left
Went down into the sea.

And the good south wind still blew behind,
But no sweet bird did follow,
Nor any day for food or play
Came to the mariners' hollo!

His shipmates cry out against the ancient Mariner, for killing the bird of good luck.

And I had done a hellish thing,
And it would work 'em woe:
For all averred, I had killed the bird
That made the breeze to blow.
Ah wretch! said they, the bird to slay,
That made the breeze to blow!

But when the fog cleared off, they justify the same, and thus make themselves accomplices in the crime.

Nor dim nor red, like God's own head,
The glorious Sun uprist:
Then all averred, I had killed the bird
That brought the fog and mist.
'Twas right, said they, such birds to slay,
That bring the fog and mist.

The fair breeze continues; the ship enters the Pacific Ocean, and sails northward, even till it reaches the Line.

The fair breeze blew, the white foam flew,
The furrow followed free;
We were the first that ever burst
Into that silent sea.

Down dropt the breeze, the sails dropt down,
'Twas sad as sad could be;
And we did speak only to break
The silence of the sea!

The ship hath been suddenly becalmed.

All in a hot and copper sky,
The bloody Sun, at noon,
Right up above the mast did stand,
No bigger than the Moon.

Day after day, day after day,
We stuck, nor breath nor motion;
As idle as a painted ship
Upon a painted ocean.

And the Albatross begins to be avenged.

Water, water, every where,
And all the boards did shrink;
Water, water, every where,
Nor any drop to drink.

The very deep did rot: O Christ!
That ever this should be!
Yea, slimy things did crawl with legs
Upon the slimy sea.

About, about, in reel and rout
The death-fires danced at night;
The water, like a witch's oils,
Burnt green, and blue and white.

A Spirit had followed them; one of the invisible inhabitants of this planet, neither departed souls nor angels; concerning whom the learned Jew Josephus, and the Platonic Constantinopolitan, Michael Psellus, may be consulted. They are very numerous, and there is no climate or element without one or more.

And some in dreams assurèd were
Of the Spirit that plagued us so;
Nine fathom deep he had followed us
From the land of mist and snow.

And every tongue, through utter drought,
Was withered at the root;
We could not speak, nor more than if
We had been choked with soot.

The shipmates, in their sore distress, would fain throw the whole guilt on the ancient Mariner: in sign whereof they hang the dead sea-bird round his neck.

Ah! well a-day! What evil looks
Had I from old and young!
Instead of the cross, the Albatross
About my neck was hung.'

PART III

'There passed a weary time. Each throat
Was parched, and glazed each eye.
A weary time! a weary time!
How glazed each weary eye,
When looking westward, I beheld
A something in the sky.

The ancient Mariner beholdeth a sign in the element afar off.

At first it seemed a little speck,
And then it seemed a mist;
It moved and moved, and took at last
A certain shape, I wist.

A speck, a mist, a shape, I wist!
And still it neared and neared:
As if it dodged a water-sprite,
It plunged and tacked and veered.

At its nearer approach, it seemeth him to be a ship; and at a dear ransom he freeth his speech from the bonds of thirst.

With throats unslaked, with black lips baked,
We could nor laugh nor wail;
Through utter drought all dumb we stood!
I bit my arm, I sucked the blood,
And cried, A sail! a sail!

A flash of joy;

With throats unslaked, with black lips baked,
Agape they heard me call:
Gramercy! they for joy did grin,
And all at once their breath drew in,
As they were drinking all.

And horror follows. For can it be a ship that comes onward without wind or tide?

See! see! (I cried) she tacks no more!
Hither to work us weal;
Without a breeze, without a tide,
She steadies with upright keel!

The western wave was all a-flame.
The day was well nigh done!
Almost upon the western wave
Rested the broad bright Sun;
When that strange shape drove suddenly
Betwixt us and the Sun.

It seemeth him but the skeleton of a ship.

And straight the Sun was flecked with bars,
(Heaven's Mother send us grace!)
As if through a dungeon-grate he peered
With broad and burning face.

And its ribs are seen as bars on the face of the setting Sun. The Spectre-Woman and her Death-mate, and no other on board the skeleton ship.

Alas! (thought I, and my heart beat loud)
How fast she nears and nears!
Are those *her* sails that glance in the Sun,
Like restless gossameres?

Are those *her* ribs through which the Sun
Did peer, as through a grate?
And is that Woman all her crew?
Is that a DEATH? and are there two?
Is DEATH that woman's mate?

Like vessel, like crew!

Her lips were red, *her* looks were free,
Her locks were yellow as gold:
Her skin was as white as leprosy,
The Night-mare, LIFE-IN-DEATH was she,
Who thicks man's blood with cold.

Death and Life-in-Death have diced for the ship's crew, and she (the latter) winneth the ancient Mariner.

The naked hulk alongside came,
And the twain were casting dice;
"The game is done! I've won! I've won!"
Quoth she, and whistles thrice.

No twilight within the courts of the Sun.

The Sun's rim dips; the stars rush out:
At one stride comes the dark;
With far-heard whisper, o'er the sea,
Off shot the spectre-bark.

At the rising of the Moon,

We listened and looked sideways up!
Fear at my heart, as at a cup,
My life-blood seemed to sip!
The stars were dim, and thick the night,
The steersman's face by his lamp gleamed white;
From the sails the dew did drip –
Till clomb above the eastern bar
The hornèd Moon, with one bright star
Within the nether tip.

One after another,

One after one, by the star-dogged Moon,
Too quick for groan or sigh,
Each turned his face with a ghastly pang,
And cursed me with his eye.

His shipmates drop down dead.

Four times fifty living men,
(And I heard nor sigh nor groan)
With heavy thump, a lifeless lump,
They dropped down one by one.

But Life-in-Death begins her work on the ancient Mariner.

The souls did from their bodies fly, –
They fled to bliss or woe!
And every soul, it passed me by,
Like the whizz of my cross-bow!'

PART IV

The Wedding-Guest feareth that a Spirit is talking to him;

'I fear thee, ancient Mariner!
I fear thy skinny hand!
And thou art long, and lank, and brown,
As is the ribbed sea-sand.

I fear thee and thy glittering eye,
And thy skinny hand, so brown.' –

But the ancient Mariner assureth him of his bodily life, and proceedeth to relate his horrible penance.

'Fear not, fear not, thou Wedding-Guest!
This body dropt not down.

Alone, alone, all, all alone,
Alone on a wide wide sea!
And never a saint took pity on
My soul in agony.

He despiseth the creatures of the calm,

The many men, so beautiful!
And they all dead did lie:
And a thousand thousand slimy things
Lived on; and so did I.

And envieth that *they* should live, and so many lie dead.

I looked upon the rotting sea,
And drew my eyes away;
I looked upon the rotting deck,
And there the dead men lay.

I looked to heaven, and tried to pray;
But or ever a prayer had gusht,
A wicked whisper came, and made
My heart as dry as dust.

I closed my lids, and kept them close,
And the balls like pulses beat;
For the sky and the sea, and the sea and the sky
Lay like a load on my weary eye,
And the dead were at my feet.

But the curse liveth for him in the eye of the dead men.

The cold sweat melted from their limbs,
Nor rot nor reek did they:
The look with which they looked on me
Had never passed away.

An orphan's curse would drag to hell
A spirit from on high;
But oh! more horrible than that
Is the curse in a dead man's eye!
Seven days, seven nights, I saw that curse,
And yet I could not die.

In his loneliness and fixedness he yearneth towards the journeying Moon, and the stars that still sojourn, yet still move onward; and everywhere the blue sky belongs to them, and is their appointed rest, and their native country and their own natural homes, which they enter unannounced, as lords that are certainly expected and yet there is a silent joy at their arrival.

The moving Moon went up the sky,
And no where did abide:
Softly she was going up,
And a star or two beside –

Her beams bemocked the sultry main,
Like April hoar-frost spread;
But where the ship's huge shadow lay,
The charmèd water burnt alway
A still and awful red.

By the light of the Moon he beholdeth God's creatures of the great calm.

Beyond the shadow of the ship,
I watched the water-snakes:
They moved in tracks of shining white,
And when they reared, the elfish light
Fell off in hoary flakes.

Within the shadow of the ship
I watched their rich attire:
Blue, glossy green, and velvet black,
They coiled and swam; and every track
Was a flash of golden fire.

Their beauty and their happiness.

O happy living things! no tongue
Their beauty might declare:
A spring of love gushed from my heart,

He blesseth them in his heart.

And I blessed them unaware:
Sure my kind Saint took pity on me,
And I blessed them unaware.

The self-same moment I could pray;

The spell begins to break.

And from my neck so free
The Albatross fell off, and sank
Like lead into the sea.'

PART V

'Oh sleep! it is a gentle thing,
Beloved from pole to pole!
To Mary Queen the praise be given!
She sent the gentle sleep from Heaven,
That slid into my soul.

By grace of the holy Mother, the ancient Mariner is refreshed with rain.

The silly buckets on the deck,
That had so long remained,
I dreamt that they were filled with dew;
And when I awoke, it rained.

My lips were wet, my throat was cold,
My garments all were dank;
Sure I had drunken in my dreams,
And still my body drank.

I moved, and could not feel my limbs:
I was so light – almost
I thought that I had died in sleep,
And was a blessed ghost.

He heareth sounds and seeth strange sights and commotions in the sky and the element.

And soon I heard a roaring wind:
It did not come anear;
But with its sound it shook the sails,
That were so thin and sere.

The upper air burst into life!
And a hundred fire-flags sheen,
To and fro they were hurried about!
And to and fro, and in and out,
The wan stars danced between.

And the coming wind did roar more loud,
And the sails did sigh like sedge;
And the rain poured down from one black cloud;
The Moon was at its edge.

The thick black cloud was cleft, and still
The Moon was at its side:
Like waters shot from some high crag,
The lightning fell with never a jag,
A river steep and wide.

The bodies of the ship's crew are inspired and the ship moves on;

The loud wind never reached the ship,
Yet now the ship moved on!
Beneath the lightning and the Moon
The dead men gave a groan.

They groaned, they stirred, they all uprose,
Nor spake, nor moved their eyes;
It had been strange, even in a dream,
To have seen those dead men rise.

The helmsman steered, the ship moved on;
Yet never a breeze up-blew;
The mariners all 'gan work the ropes,
Where they were wont to do;
They raised their limbs like lifeless tools –
We were a ghastly crew.

The body of my brother's son
Stood by me, knee to knee:
The body and I pulled at one rope,
But he said nought to me.'

But not by the souls of the men, nor by daemons of earth or middle air, but by a blessed troop of angelic spirits, sent down by the invocation of the guardian saint.

'I fear thee, ancient Mariner!'
'Be calm, thou Wedding-Guest!
'Twas not those souls that fled in pain,
Which to their corses came again,
But a troop of spirits blest:

For when it dawned – they dropped their arms,
And clustered round the mast;
Sweet sounds rose slowly through their mouths,
And from their bodies passed.

Around, around, flew each sweet sound,
Then darted to the Sun;
Slowly the sounds came back again,
Now mixed, now one by one.

Sometimes a-dropping from the sky
I heard the sky-lark sing;
Sometimes all little birds that are,
How they seemed to fill the sea and air
With their sweet jargoning!

And now 'twas like all instruments,
Now like a lonely flute;
And now it is an angel's song,
That makes the heavens be mute.

It ceased; yet still the sails made on
A pleasant noise till noon,
A noise like of a hidden brook
In the leafy month of June,
That to the sleeping woods all night
Singeth a quiet tune.

Till noon we quietly sailed on,
Yet never a breeze did breathe:
Slowly and smoothly went the ship,
Moved onward from beneath.

The lonesome Spirit from the South Pole carries on the ship as far as the Line, in obedience to the angelic troop, but still requireth vengeance.

Under the keel nine fathom deep,
From the land of mist and snow,
The spirit slid: and it was he
That made the ship to go.
The sails at noon left off their tune,
And the ship stood still also.

The Sun, right up above the mast,
Had fixed her to the ocean:
But in a minute she 'gan stir,

With a short uneasy motion –
Backwards and forwards half her length
With a short uneasy motion.

Then like a pawing horse let go,
She made a sudden bound:
It flung the blood into my head,
And I fell down in a swound.

The Polar Spirit's fellow-daemons, the invisible inhabitants of the element, take part in his wrong; and two of them relate, one to the other, that penance long and heavy for the ancient Mariner hath been accorded to the Polar Spirit, who returneth southward.

How long in that same fit I lay,
I have not to declare;
But ere my living life returned,
I heard and in my soul discerned
Two voices in the air.

"Is it he?" quoth one, "Is this the man?
By him who dies on cross,
With his cruel bow he laid full low
The harmless Albatross.

The spirit who bideth by himself
In the land of mist and snow,
He loved the bird that loved the man
Who shot him with his bow."

The other was a softer voice,
As soft as honey-dew:
Quoth he, "The man hath penance done,
And penance more will do." '

PART VI

First voice ' "But tell me, tell me! speak again,
Thy soft response renewing –
What makes that ship drive on so fast?
What is the ocean doing?"

Second voice "Still as a slave before his lord,
The ocean hath no blast;
His great bright eye most silently
Up to the Moon is cast –

If he may know which way to go;
For she guides him smooth or grim.
See, brother, see! how graciously
She looketh down on him."

The Mariner hath been cast into a trance; for the angelic power causeth the vessel to drive northward faster than human life could endure.

First voice "But why drives on that ship so fast,
Without or wave or wind?"

Second voice "The air is cut away before,
And closes from behind.

Fly, brother, fly! more high, more high!
Or we shall be belated:
For slow and slow that ship will go,
When the Mariner's trance is abated."

The supernatural motion is retarded; the Mariner awakes, and his penance begins anew.

I woke, and we were sailing on
As in a gentle weather:
'Twas night, calm night, the moon was high;
The dead men stood together.

All stood together on the deck,
For a charnel-dungeon fitter:
All fixed on me their stony eyes,
That in the Moon did glitter.

The pang, the curse, with which they died,
Had never passed away:
I could not draw my eyes from theirs,
Nor turn them up to pray.

The curse is finally expiated.

And now this spell was snapt: once more
I viewed the ocean green,
And looked far forth, yet little saw
Of what had else been seen –

Like one, that on a lonesome road
Doth walk in fear and dread,
And having once turned round walks on,
And turns no more his head;
Because he knows, a frightful fiend
Doth close behind him tread.

But soon there breathed a wind on me,
Nor sound nor motion made:
Its path was not upon the sea,
In ripple or in shade.

It raised my hair, it fanned my cheek
Like a meadow-gale of spring –
It mingled strangely with my fears,
Yet it felt like a welcoming.

Swiftly, swiftly flew the ship,
Yet she sailed softly too:
Sweetly, sweetly blew the breeze –
On me alone it blew.

And the ancient Mariner beholdeth his native country.

Oh! dream of joy! is this indeed
The light-house top I see?
Is this the hill? is this the kirk?
Is this mine own countree?

We drifted o'er the harbour-bar,
And I with sobs did pray –
O let me be awake, my God!
Or let me sleep alway.

The harbour-bay was clear as glass,
So smoothly it was strewn!
And on the bay the moonlight lay,
And the shadow of the Moon.

The rock shone bright, the kirk no less,
That stands above the rock:
The moonlight steeped in silentness
The steady weathercock.

And the bay was white with silent light,
Till rising from the same,
Full many shapes, that shadows were,
In crimson colours came.

The angelic spirits leave the dead bodies,

A little distance from the prow
Those crimson shadows were:
I turned my eyes upon the deck –
Oh, Christ! what saw I there!

And appear in their own forms of light.

Each corse lay flat, lifeless and flat,
And, by the holy rood!
A man all light, a seraph-man,
On every corse there stood.

This seraph-band, each waved his hand:
It was a heavenly sight!
They stood as signals to the land,
Each one a lovely light;

This seraph-band, each waved his hand,
No voice did they impart –
No voice; but oh! the silence sank
Like music on my heart.

But soon I heard the dash of oars,
I heard the Pilot's cheer;
My head was turned perforce away
And I saw a boat appear.

The Pilot and the Pilot's boy,
I heard them coming fast:
Dear Lord in Heaven! it was a joy
The dead men could not blast.

I saw a third – I heard his voice:
It is the Hermit good!

He singeth loud his godly hymns
That he makes in the wood.
He'll shrieve my soul, he'll wash away
The Albatross's blood.'

PART VII

The Hermit of the Wood,

'This Hermit good lives in that wood
Which slopes down to the sea.
How loudly his sweet voice he rears!
He loves to talk with marineres
That come from a far countree.

He kneels at morn, and noon, and eve –
He hath a cushion plump:
It is the moss that wholly hides
The rotted old oak-stump.

The skiff-boat neared: I heard them talk,
"Why, this is strange, I trow!
Where are those lights so many and fair,
That signal made but now?"

Approacheth the ship with wonder.

"Strange, by my faith!" the Hermit said –
"And they answered not our cheer!
The planks looked warped! and see those sails,
How thin they are and sere!
I never saw aught like to them,
Unless perchance it were

Brown skeletons of leaves that lag
My forest-brook along;
When the ivy-tod is heavy with snow,
And the owlet whoops to the wolf below,
That eats the she-wolf's young."

"Dear Lord! it hath a fiendish look –
(The Pilot made reply)
I am a-feared" – "Push on, push on!"
Said the Hermit cheerily.

The boat came closer to the ship,
But I nor spake nor stirred;
The boat came close beneath the ship,
And straight a sound was heard.

The ship suddenly sinketh.

Under the water it rumbled on,
Still louder and more dread:
It reached the ship, it split the bay;
The ship went down like lead.

The ancient Mariner is saved in the Pilot's boat.

Stunned by that loud and dreadful sound,
Which sky and ocean smote,
Like one that hath been seven days drowned
My body lay afloat;
But swift as dreams, myself I found
Within the Pilot's boat.

Upon the whirl, where sank the ship,
The boat spun round and round;
And all was still, save that the hill
Was telling of the sound.

I moved my lips – the Pilot shrieked
And fell down in a fit;
The holy Hermit raised his eyes,
And prayed where he did sit.

I took the oars: the Pilot's boy,
Who now doth crazy go
Laughed loud and long, and all the while
His eyes went to and fro.
"Ha! Ha!" quoth he, "full plain I see,
The Devil knows how to row."

And now, all in my own countree,
I stood on the firm land!
The Hermit stepped forth from the boat,
And scarcely he could stand.

The ancient Mariner earnestly entreateth the Hermit to shrieve him; and the penance of life falls on him.

"O shrieve me, shrieve me, holy man!"
The Hermit crossed his brow.
"Say quick," quoth he, "I bid thee say –
What manner of man art thou?"

Forthwith this frame of mine was wrenched
With a woful agony,
Which forced me to begin my tale;
And then it left me free.

And ever and anon throughout his future life an agony constraineth him to travel from land to land;

Since then, at an uncertain hour,
That agony returns:
And till my ghastly tale is told,
This heart within me burns.

I pass, like night, from land to land;
I have strange power of speech;
That moment that his face I see,
I know the man that must hear me:
To him my tale I teach.

What loud uproar bursts from that door!
The wedding-guests are there:

But in the garden-bower the bride
And bride-maids singing are:
And hark the little vesper bell,
Which biddeth me to prayer!

O Wedding-Guest! this soul hath been
Alone on a wide wide sea:
So lonely 'twas, that God himself
Scarce seemèd there to be.

O sweeter than the marriage-feast,
'Tis sweeter far to me,
To walk together to the kirk
With a goodly company! –

To walk together to the kirk
And all together pray,
While each to his great Father bends,
Old men, and babes, and loving friends
And youths and maidens gay!

And to teach, by his own example, love and reverence to all things that God made and loveth.

Farewell, farewell! but this I tell
To thee, thou Wedding-Guest!
He prayeth well, who loveth well
Both man and bird and beast.

He prayeth best, who loveth best
All things both great and small;
For the dear God who loveth us,
He made and loveth all.'

The Mariner, whose eye is bright,
Whose beard with age is hoar,
Is gone: and now the Wedding-Guest
Turned from the bridegroom's door.

He went like one that hath been stunned,
And is of sense forlorn:
A sadder and a wiser man,
He rose the morrow morn.

Kubla Khan

In Xanadu did Kubla Khan
A stately pleasure-dome decree:
Where Alph, the sacred river, ran
Through caverns measureless to man
Down to a sunless sea.
So twice five miles of fertile ground
With walls and towers were girdled round.

And there were gardens bright with sinuous rills
Where blossomed many an incense-bearing tree;
And here were forests ancient as the hills,
Enfolding sunny spots of greenery.

But, oh, that deep romantic chasm which slanted
Down the green hill athwart a cedarn cover:
A savage place, as holy and enchanted
As e'er beneath a waning moon was haunted
By woman wailing for her demon-lover.
And from the chasm, with ceaseless turmoil seething,
As if this earth in fast thick pants were breathing,
A mightly fountain momently was forced:
Amid whose swift half-intermitted burst
Huge fragments vaulted like rebounding hail,
Or chaffy grain beneath the thresher's flail:
And mid these dancing rocks at once and ever
It flung up momently the sacred river.
Five miles meandering with a mazy motion
Through wood and dale the sacred river ran,
Then reached the caverns measureless to man,
And sank in tumult to a lifeless ocean:
And 'mid this tumult Kubla heard from far
Ancestral voices prophesying war.

The shadow of the dome of pleasure
Floated midway on the waves;
Where was heard the mingled measure
From the fountain and the caves.
It was a miracle of rare device,
A sunny pleasure-dome with caves of ice.

A damsel with a dulcimer
In a vision once I saw:
It was an Abyssinian maid,
And on her dulcimer she played,
Singing of Mount Abora.
Could I revive within me
Her symphony and song,
To such a deep delight 'twould win me
That with music loud and long,
I would build that dome in air,
That sunny dome: those caves of ice:
And all who heard should see them there,
And all should cry, 'Beware . . . Beware,
His flashing eyes, his floating hair:
Weave a circle round him thrice,
And close your eyes with holy dread,
For he on honey-dew hath fed,
And drunk the milk of Paradise.'

Work without Hope

All Nature seems at work. Slugs leave their lair –
The bees are stirring – birds are on the wing –
And Winter, slumbering in the open air,
Wears on his smiling face a dream of Spring!
And I, the while, the sole unbusy thing,
Nor honey make, nor pair, nor build, nor sing.

Yet well I ken the banks where amaranths blow,
Have traced the fount whence streams of nectar flow.
Bloom, O ye amaranths! bloom for whom ye may,
For me ye bloom not! Glide, rich streams, away!
With lips unbrightened, wreathless brow, I stroll:
And would you learn the spells that drowse my soul?
Work without Hope draws nectar in a sieve,
And Hope without an object cannot live.

The Valley of Seclusion

Low was our pretty Cot: our tallest Rose
Peeped at the chamber-window. We could hear
At silent noon, and eve, and early morn,
The Sea's faint murmur. In the open air
Our Myrtles blossomed; and across the porch
Thick Jasmins twined: the little landscape round
Was green and woody, and refreshed the eye.
It was a spot which you might aptly call
The Valley of Seclusion! Once I saw
(Hallowing his Sabbath-day by quietness)
A wealthy son of Commerce saunter by,
Bristowa's citizen: methought, it calmed
His thirst of idle gold, and made him muse
With wiser feelings: for he paused, and looked
With a pleased sadness, and gazed all around,
Then eyed our Cottage, and gazed round again,
And sighed, and said, it was a Blessed Place.
And we *were* blessed. Oft with patient ear
Long-listening to the viewless sky-lark's note
(Viewless, or haply for a moment seen
Gleaming on sunny wings) in whispered tones
I've said to my Beloved, 'Such, sweet Girl!
The inobtrusive song of Happiness,
Unearthly minstrelsy! then only heard
When the Soul seeks to hear; when all is hushed,
And the Heart listens!'

But the time, when first
From that low Dell, steep up the stony Mount
I climbed with perilous toil and reached the top,
Oh! what a goodly scene! *Here* the bleak mount,
The bare bleak mountain speckled thin with sheep;
Grey clouds, that shadowing spot the sunny fields;
And river, now with bushy rocks o'er-browed,
Now winding bright and full, with naked banks;
And seats, and lawns, the Abbey and the wood,
And cots, and hamlets, and faint city-spire;
The Channel *there*, the Islands and white sails,
Dim coasts, and cloud-like hills, and shoreless Ocean –
It seemed like Omnipresence! God, methought,
Had built him there a Temple: the whole World
Seemed *imaged* in its vast circumference:
No *wish* profaned my overwhelmed heart.
Blest hour! It was a luxury, – to be!

GEORGE GORDON NOËL, LORD BYRON

The Eve of Waterloo

There was a sound of revelry by night,
And Belgium's Capital had gathered then
Her Beauty and her Chivalry, and bright
The lamps shone o'er fair women and brave men;
A thousand hearts beat happily; and when
Music arose with its voluptuous swell,
Soft eyes looked love to eyes which spake again,
And all went merry as a marriage bell;
But hush! hark! a deep sound strikes like a rising knell!

Did ye not hear it? – No; 'twas but the wind,
Or the car rattling o'er the stony street;
On with the dance! let joy be unconfined;
No sleep till morn, when Youth and Pleasure meet
To chase the glowing Hours with flying feet –
But hark! – that heavy sound breaks in once more,
As if the clouds its echo would repeat;
And nearer, clearer, deadlier than before!
Arm! Arm! it is – it is – the cannon's opening roar!

Within a windowed niche of that high hall
Sate Brunswick's fated chieftain; he did hear
That sound the first amidst the festival,
And caught its tone with Death's prophetic ear;
And when they smiled because he deemed it near,

His heart more truly knew that peal too well
Which stretched his father on a bloody bier,
And roused the vengeance blood alone could quell;
He rushed into the field, and, foremost fighting, fell.

Ah! then and there was hurrying to and fro,
And gathering tears, and tremblings of distress,
And cheeks all pale, which but an hour ago
Blushed at the praise of their own loveliness;
And there were sudden partings, such as press
The life from out young hearts, and choking sighs
Which ne'er might be repeated; who could guess
If ever more should meet those mutual eyes,
Since upon night so sweet such awful morn could rise!

And there was mounting in hot haste: the steed,
The mustering squadron, and the clattering car,
Went pouring forward with impetuous speed,
And swiftly forming in the ranks of war;
And the deep thunder peal on peal afar;
And near, the beat of the alarming drum
Roused up the soldier ere the morning star;
While thronged the citizens with terror dumb,
Or whispering, with white lips – 'The foe! They come! they come!'

And wild and high the 'Cameron's Gathering' rose!
The war-note of Lochiel, which Albyn's hills
Have heard, and heard, too, have her Saxon foes:-
How in the noon of night that pibroch thrills,
Savage and shrill! But with the breath which fills
Their mountain-pipe, so fill the mountaineers
With the fierce native daring which instils
The stirring memory of a thousand years,
And Evan's, Donald's fame rings in each clansman's ears!

And Ardennes waves above them her green leaves,
Dewy with nature's tear-drops, as they pass,
Grieving, if aught inanimate e'er grieves,
Over the unreturning brave, – alas!
Ere evening to be trodden like the grass
Which now beneath them, but above shall grow
In its next verdure, when this fiery mass
Of living valour, rolling on the foe
And burning with high hope, shall moulder cold and low.

Last noon beheld them full of lusty life,
Last eve in Beauty's circle proudly gay,
The midnight brought the signal-sound of strife,
The morn the marshalling in arms, – the day
Battle's magnificently-stern array!

The thunder-clouds close o'er it, which when rent
The earth is covered thick with other clay
Which her own clay shall cover, heaped and pent,
Rider and horse, – friend, foe, – in one red burial blent!

The Isles of Greece

The isles of Greece! the isles of Greece
  Where burning Sappho loved and sung,
Where grew the arts of war and peace,
  Where Delos rose, and Phœbus sprung!
Eternal summer gilds them yet,
But all, except their sun, is set.

The Scian and the Teian muse,
  The hero's harp, the lover's lute,
Have found the fame your shores refuse:
  Their place of birth alone is mute
To sounds which echo further west
Than your sires' 'Islands of the Blest.'

The mountains look on Marathon –
  And Marathon looks on the sea;
And musing there an hour alone,
  I dreamed that Greece might still be free;
For standing on the Persians' grave,
I could not deem myself a slave.

A king sate on the rocky brow
  Which looks o'er sea-born Salamis;
And ships, by thousands, lay below,
  And men in nations; – all were his!
He counted them at break of day –
And when the sun set, where were they?

And where are they? and where art thou,
  My country? On thy voiceless shore
The heroic lay is tuneless now –
  The heroic bosom beats no more!
And must thy lyre, so long divine,
Degenerate into hands like mine?

'Tis something in the dearth of fame,
  Though linked among a fettered race,
To feel at least a patriot's shame,
  Even as I sing, suffuse my face;
For what is left the poet here?
For Greeks a blush – for Greece a tear.

Must *we* but weep o'er days more blest?
  Must *we* but blush? – Our fathers bled.
Earth! render back from out thy breast
  A remnant of our Spartan dead!
Of the three hundred grant but three,
To make a new Thermopylæ!

What, silent still? and silent all?
  Ah! no; – the voices of the dead
Sound like a distant torrent's fall,
  And answer, 'Let one living head,
But one, arise, – we come, we come!'
'Tis but the living who are dumb.

In vain – in vain: strike other chords;
  Fill high the cup with Samian wine!
Leave battles to the Turkish hordes,
  And shed the blood of Scio's vine!
Hark! rising to the ignoble call –
How answers each bold Bacchanal!

You have the Pyrrhic dance as yet;
  Where is the Pyrrhic phalanx gone?
Of two such lessons, why forget
  The nobler and the manlier one?
You have the letters Cadmus gave –
Think ye he meant them for a slave?

Fill high the bowl with Samian wine!
  We will not think of themes like these!
It made Anacreon's song divine:
  He served – but served Polycrates –
A tyrant; but our masters then
Were still, at least, our countrymen.

The tyrant of the Chersonese
  Was freedom's best and bravest friend;
That tyrant was Miltiades!
  O that the present hour would lend
Another despot of the kind!
Such chains as his were sure to bind.

Fill high the bowl with Samian wine!
  On Suli's rock, and Parga's shore,
Exists the remnant of a line
  Such as the Doric mothers bore;
And there, perhaps, some seed is sown,
The Heracleidan blood might own.

Trust not for freedom to the Franks –
  They have a king who buys and sells;
In native swords and native ranks
  The only hope of courage dwells:
But Turkish force and Latin fraud
Would break your shield, however broad.

Fill high the bowl with Samian wine!
  Our virgins dance beneath the shade –
I see their glorious black eyes shine;
  But gazing on each glowing maid,
My own the burning tear-drop laves,
To think such breasts must suckle slaves.

Place me on Sunium's marbled steep,
  Where nothing, save the waves and I,
May hear our mutual murmurs sweep;
  There, swan-like, let me sing and die:
A land of slaves shall ne'er be mine –
Dash down yon cup of Samian wine!

Growing Old

But now at thirty years my hair is grey –
  (I wonder what it will be like at forty?
I thought of a peruke the other day –)
  My heart is not much greener; and, in short, I
Have squandered my whole summer while 'twas May,
  And feel no more the spirit to retort; I
Have spent my life, both interest and principal,
And deem not, what I deemed, my soul invincible.

No more – no more – Oh! never more on me
  The freshness of the heart can fall like dew,
Which out of all the lovely things we see
  Extracts emotions beautiful and new;
Hived in our bosoms like the bag o' the bee.
  Think'st thou the honey with those objects grew?
Alas! 'twas not in them, but in thy power
To double even the sweetness of a flower.

No more – no more – Oh! never more, my heart,
  Canst thou be my sole world, my universe!
Once all in all, but now a thing apart,
  Thou canst not be my blessing or my curse:
The illusion's gone for ever, and thou art
  Insensible, I trust, but none the worse,
And in thy stead I've got a deal of judgement,
Though Heaven knows how it ever found a lodgement.

My days of love are over; me no more
  The charms of maid, wife, and still less of widow,
Can make the fool of which they made before, –
  In short, I must not lead the life I did do;
The credulous hope of mutual minds is o'er,
  The copious use of claret is forbid too,
So for a good old-gentlemanly vice,
I think I must take up with avarice.

Ambition was my idol, which was broken
  Before the shrines of Sorrow, and of Pleasure;
And the two last have left me many a token
  O'er which reflection may be made at leisure:
Now, like Friar Bacon's Brazen Head, I've spoken,
  'Time is, Time was, Time's past': a chymic treasure
Is glittering Youth, which I have spent betimes –
My heart in passion, and my head on rhymes.

What is the end of Fame? 'tis but to fill
  A certain portion of uncertain paper:
Some liken it to climbing up a hill,
  Whose summit, like all hills, is lost in vapour;
For this men write, speak, preach, and heroes kill,
  And bards burn what they call their 'midnight taper',
To have, when the original is dust,
A name, a wretched picture and worse bust.

What are the hopes of man? Old Egypt's King
  Cheops erected the first Pyramid
And largest, thinking it was just the thing
  To keep his memory whole, and mummy hid;
But somebody or other rummaging,
  Burglariously broke his coffin's lid:
Let not a monument give you or me hopes,
Since not a pinch of dust remains of Cheops.

But I, being fond of true philosophy,
  Say very often to myself, 'Alas!
All things that have been born were born to die,
  And flesh (which Death mows down to hay) is grass;
You've passed your youth not so unpleasantly,
  And if you had it o'er again – 'twould pass –
So thank your stars that matters are no worse,
And read your Bible, sir, and mind your purse.'

'So, we'll go no more a-roving'

So, we'll go no more a-roving
  So late into the night,
Though the heart be still as loving,
  And the moon be still as bright.

For the sword outwears its sheath,
  And the soul wears out the breast,
And the heart must pause to breathe,
  And love itself have rest.

Though the night was made for loving,
  And the day returns too soon,
Yet we'll go no more a-roving
  By the light of the moon.

She Walks in Beauty

She walks in beauty, like the night
  Of cloudless climes and starry skies;
And all that's best of dark and bright
  Meet in her aspect and her eyes:
Thus mellow'd to that tender light
  Which heaven to gaudy day denies.

One shade the more, one ray the less,
  Had half impair'd the nameless grace
Which waves in every raven tress,
  Or softly lightens o'er her face;
Where thoughts serenely sweet express
  How pure, how dear their dwelling-place.

And on that cheek, and o'er that brow,
  So soft, so calm, yet eloquent,
The smiles that win, the tints that glow,
  But tell of days in goodness spent,
A mind at peace with all below,
  A heart whose love is innocent!

Remember Thee!

Remember thee! remember thee!
  Till Lethe quench life's burning stream
Remorse and shame shall cling to thee,
  And haunt thee like a feverish dream!

Remember thee! Ay, doubt it not.
  Thy husband too shall think of thee!
By neither shalt thou be forgot,
  Thou *false* to him, thou *fiend* to me!

'I would to Heaven'

I would to Heaven that I were so much clay,
  As I am blood, bone, marrow, passion, feeling –
Because at least the past were passed away,
  And for the future – (but I write this reeling,
Having got drunk exceedingly today,
  So that I seem to stand upon the ceiling)
  I say – the future is a serious matter –
  And so – for God's sake – hock and soda-water!

Lines Written Beneath a Picture

Dear object of defeated care!
  Though now of Love and thee bereft,
To reconcile me with despair
  Thine image and my tears are left.

'Tis said with Sorrow Time can cope;
  But this I feel can ne'er be true:
For by the death-blow of my Hope
  My Memory immortal grew.

'They say that Hope is happiness'

They say that Hope is happiness;
  But genuine Love must prize the past,
And Memory wakes the thoughts that bless:
  They rose the first – they set the last;

And all that Memory loves the most
  Was once our only Hope to be,
And all that Hope adored and lost
  Hath melted into Memory.

Alas! it is delusion all;
  The future cheats us from afar,
Nor can we be what we recall,
  Nor dare we think on what we are.

PERCY BYSSHE SHELLEY

Summer and Winter

It was a bright and cheerful afternoon,
Towards the end of the sunny month of June,
When the north wind congregates in crowds
The floating mountains of the silver clouds
From the horizon – and the stainless sky
Opens beyond them like eternity.
All things rejoiced beneath the sun; the weeds,
The river, and the corn-fields, and the reeds;
The willow leaves that glanced in the light breeze,
And the firm foliage of the larger trees.

It was a winter such as when birds die
In the deep forests; and the fishes lie
Stiffened in the translucent ice, which makes
Even the mud and slime of the warm lakes
A wrinkled clod as hard as brick; and when,
Among their children, comfortable men
Gather about great fires, and yet feel cold:
Alas then for the homeless beggar old!

The Moon

And, like a dying lady lean and pale,
Who totters forth, wrapp'd in a gauzy veil,
Out of her chamber, led by the insane
And feeble wanderings of her fading brain,
The moon arose up in the murky east
A white and shapeless mass.

    Art thou pale for weariness
Of climbing heaven and gazing on the earth,
    Wandering companionless
Among the stars that have a different birth,
And ever changing, like a joyless eye
That finds no object worth its constancy?

Ode to a Skylark

Hail to thee, blithe spirit!
Bird thou never wert –
That from heaven or near it
Pourest thy full heart
In profuse strains of unpremeditated art.

Higher still and higher
From the earth thou springest,
Like a cloud of fire;
The blue deep thou wingest,
And singing still dost soar, and soaring ever singest.

In the golden lightning
Of the sunken sun,
O'er which clouds are brightening,
Thou dost float and run,
Like an unbodied joy whose race is just begun.

The pale purple even
Melts around thy flight;
Like a star of heaven,
In the broad daylight
Thou art unseen, but yet I hear thy shrill delight –

Keen as are the arrows
Of that silver sphere
Whose intense lamp narrows
In the white dawn clear,
Until we hardly see, we feel that it is there.

All the earth and air
With thy voice is loud,
As, when night is bare,
From one lonely cloud
The moon rains out her beams, and heaven is overflowed.

What thou art we know not;
What is most like thee?
From rainbow clouds there flow not
Drops so bright to see,
As from thy presence showers a rain of melody:-

Like a poet hidden
In the light of thought,
Singing hymns unbidden,
Till the world is wrought
To sympathy with hopes and fears it heeded not:

Like a high-born maiden
   In a palace tower,
Soothing her love-laden
   Soul in secret hour
With music sweet as love, which overflows her bower:

Like a glow-worm golden
   In a dell of dew,
Scattering unbeholden
   Its aërial hue
Among the flowers and grass which screen it from the view:

Like a rose embowered
   In its own green leaves,
By warm winds deflowered,
   Till the scent it gives
Makes faint with too much sweet these heavy-winged thieves:

Sound of vernal showers
   On the twinkling grass,
Rain-awakened flowers –
   All that ever was
Joyous and clear and fresh – thy music doth surpass.

Teach us, sprite or bird,
   What sweet thoughts are thine:
I have never heard
   Praise of love or wine
That panted forth a flood of rapture so divine.

Chorus hymeneal,
   Or triumphal chant,
Matched with thine would be all
   But an empty vaunt –
A thing wherein we feel there is some hidden want.

What objects are the fountains
   Of thy happy strain?
What fields, or waves, or mountains?
   What shapes of sky or plain?
What love of thine own kind? what ignorance of pain?

With thy clear keen joyance
   Languor cannot be:
Shadow of annoyance
   Never came near thee:
Thou lovest, but ne'er knew love's sad satiety.

Waking or asleep,
   Thou of death must deem

Things more true and deep
Than we mortals dream,
Or how could thy notes flow in such a crystal stream?

We look before and after,
And pine for what is not:
Our sincerest laughter
With some pain is fraught;
Our sweetest songs are those that tell of saddest thought.

Yet, if we could scorn
Hate and pride and fear,
If we were things born
Not to shed a tear,
I know not how thy joy we ever should come near.

Better than all measures
Of delightful sound,
Better than all treasures
That in books are found,
Thy skill to poet were, thou scorner of the ground!

Teach me half the gladness
That thy brain must know;
Such harmonious madness
From my lips would flow,
The world should listen then, as I am listening now.

England in 1819

An old, mad, blind, despised, and dying king, –
Princes, the dregs of their dull race, who flow
Through public scorn, – mud from a muddy spring, –
Rulers who neither see, nor feel, nor know,
But leech-like to their fainting country cling,
Till they drop, blind in blood, without a blow, –
A people starved and stabbed in the untilled field, –
An army, which liberticide and prey
Makes as a two-edged sword to all who wield, –
Golden and sanguine laws which tempt and slay;
Religion Christless, Godless – a book sealed;
A Senate, – Time's worst statute unrepealed, –
Are graves, from which a glorious Phantom may
Burst, to illumine our tempestuous day.

'One word is too often profaned'

One word is too often profaned
  For me to profane it,
One feeling too falsely disdained
  For thee to disdain it;
One hope is too like despair
  For prudence to smother,
And pity from thee more dear
  Than that from another.

I can give not what men call love,
  But wilt thou accept not
The worship the heart lifts above
  And the Heavens reject not, –
The desire of the moth for the star,
  Of the night for the morrow,
The devotion to something afar
  From the sphere of our sorrow?

Stanzas Written in Dejection Near Naples

The sun is warm, the sky is clear,
The waves are dancing fast and bright,
Blue isles and snowy mountains wear
The purple noon's transparent light:
The breath of the moist earth is light
Around its unexpanded buds;
Like many a voice of one delight –
The winds', the birds', the ocean-floods' –
The City's voice itself is soft like Solitude's.

I see the Deep's untrampled floor
With green and purple sea-weeds strown;
I see the waves upon the shore
Like light dissolved in star-showers thrown:
I sit upon the sands alone;
The lightning of the noon-tide ocean
Is flashing round me, and a tone
Arises from its measured motion –
How sweet! did any heart now share in my emotion.

Alas! I have nor hope nor health,
Nor peace within nor calm around,
Nor that Content, surpassing wealth,
The sage in meditation found,
And walk'd with inward glory crown'd –
Nor fame, nor power, nor love, nor leisure;

Others I see whom these surround –
Smiling they live, and call life pleasure;
To me that cup has been dealt in another measure.

Yet now despair itself is mild
Even as the winds and waters are;
I could lie down like a tired child,
And weep away the life of care
Which I have borne, and yet must bear,
Till death like sleep might steal on me,
And I might feel in the warm air
My cheek grow cold, and hear the sea
Breathe o'er my dying brain its last monotony.

JOHN KEATS

'A thing of beauty is a joy for ever'

A thing of beauty is a joy for ever:
Its loveliness increases; it will never
Pass into nothingness; but still will keep
A bower quiet for us, and a sleep
Full of sweet dreams, and health, and quiet breathing.
Therefore, on every morrow, are we wreathing
A flowery band to bind us to the earth,
Spite of despondence, of the inhuman dearth
Of noble natures, of the gloomy days,
Of all the unhealthy and o'er-darken'd ways
Made for our searching: yes, in spite of all,
Some shape of beauty moves away the pall
From our dark spirits. Such the sun, the moon,
Trees old and young, sprouting a shady boon
For simple sheep; and such are daffodils
With the green world they live in; and clear rills
That for themseles a cooling covert make
'Gainst the hot season; the mid-forest brake,
Rich with a sprinkling of fair musk-rose blooms:
And such too is the grandeur of the dooms
We have imagined for the mighty dead;
All lovely tales that we have heard or read:
An endless fountain of immortal drink,
Pouring unto us from the heaven's brink.

Ode on Melancholy

No, no! go not to Lethe, neither twist
Wolf's-bane, tight-rooted, for its poisonous wine;
Nor suffer thy pale forehead to be kiss'd
By nightshade, ruby grape of Proserpine;
Make not your rosary of yew-berries,
Nor let the beetle, nor the death-moth be
Your mournful Psyche, nor the downy owl
A partner in your sorrow's mysteries;
For shade to shade will come too drowsily,
And drown the wakeful anguish of the soul.

But when the melancholy fit shall fall
Sudden from heaven like a weeping cloud,
That fosters the droop-headed flowers all,
And hides the green hill in an April shroud;
Then glut thy sorrow on a morning rose,
Or on the rainbow of the salt sand-wave,
Or on the wealth of globed peonies;
Or if thy mistress some rich anger shows,
Emprison her soft hand, and let her rave,
And feed deep, deep upon her peerless eyes.

She dwells with Beauty – Beauty that must die;
And Joy, whose hand is ever at his lips
Bidding adieu; and aching Pleasure nigh,
Turning to poison while the bee-mouth sips:
Ay, in the very temple of Delight
Veil'd Melancholy has her sovran shrine,
Though seen of none save him whose strenuous tongue
Can burst Joy's grape against his palate fine;
His soul shall taste the sadness of her might,
And be among her cloudy trophies hung.

Ode on a Grecian Urn

Thou still unravished bride of quietness!
Thou foster-child of Silence and slow Time,
Sylvan historian, who canst thus express
A flowry tale more sweetly than our rhyme:
What leaf-fringed legend haunts about thy shape
Of deities or mortals, or of both,
In Tempe or the dales of Arcady?
What men or gods are these? What maidens loth?
What mad pursuit? What struggle to escape?
What pipes and timbrels? What wild ecstasy?

Heard melodies are sweet, but those unheard
  Are sweeter: therefore, ye soft pipes, play on;
Not to the sensual ear, but, more endeared,
  Pipe to the spirit ditties of no tone:
Fair youth, beneath the trees, thou canst not leave
  Thy song, nor ever can those trees be bare;
    Bold Lover, never, never canst thou kiss,
Though winning near the goal – yet, do not grieve;
    She cannot fade, though thou has not thy bliss,
  For ever wilt thou love, and she be fair!

Ah, happy, happy boughs! that cannot shed
  Your leaves, nor ever bid the Spring adieu;
And, happy melodist, unwearièd,
  For ever piping songs for ever new;
More happy love! more happy, happy love!
  For ever warm and still to be enjoyed,
    For ever panting and for ever young;
All breathing human passion far above,
  That leaves a heart high sorrowful and cloyed,
    A burning forehead, and a parching tongue.

Who are these coming to the sacrifice?
  To what green altar, O mysterious priest,
Lead'st thou that heifer lowing at the skies,
  And all her silken flanks with garlands drest?
What little town by river or sea-shore,
  Or mountain-built with peaceful citadel,
    Is emptied of its folk, this pious morn?
And, little town, thy streets for evermore
  Will silent be; and not a soul to tell
    Why thou are desolate, can e'er return.

O Attic shape! Fair attitude! with brede
  Of marble men and maidens overwrought,
With forest branches and the trodden weed;
  Thou, silent form, dost tease us out of thought
As doth eternity: Cold Pastoral!
  When old age shall this generation waste,
    Thou shalt remain, in midst of other woe
  Than ours, a friend to man, to whom thou say'st,
'Beauty is truth, truth beauty, – that is all
    Ye know on earth, and all ye need to know.'

Escape from the City

To one who has been long in city pent,
'Tis very sweet to look into the fair
And open face of heaven, – to breathe a prayer
Full in the smile of the blue firmament.
Who is more happy, when, with heart's content,
Fatigued he sinks into some pleasant lair
Of wavy grass, and reads a debonair
And gentle tale of love and languishment?
Returning home at evening, with an ear
Catching the notes of Philomel, – an eye
Watching the sailing cloudlet's bright career,
He mourns that day so soon has glided by:
E'en like the passage of an angel's tear
That falls through the clear ether silently.

Ode to a Nightingale

My heart aches, and a drowsy numbness pains
My sense, as though of hemlock I had drunk,
Or emptied some dull opiate to the drains
One minute past, and Lethe-wards had sunk:
'Tis not through envy of thy happy lot,
But being too happy in thy happiness, –
That thou, light-winged Dryad of the trees,
In some melodious plot
Of beechen green, and shadows numberless,
Singest of summer in full-throated ease.

O for a draught of vintage, that hath been
Cool'd a long age in the deep-delved earth,
Tasting of Flora and the country-green,
Dance, and Provençal song, and sun-burnt mirth!
O for a beaker full of the warm South,
Full of the true, the blushful Hippocrene,
With beaded bubbles winking at the brim,
And purple-stained mouth;
That I might drink, and leave the world unseen,
And with thee fade away into the forest dim:

Fade far away, dissolve, and quite forget
What thou among the leaves hast never known,
The weariness, the fever, and the fret
Here, where men sit and hear each other groan;

Where palsy shakes a few, sad, last grey hairs,
Where youth grows pale, and spectre-thin, and dies;
Where but to think is to be full of sorrow
And leaden-eyed despairs;
Where beauty cannot keep her lustrous eyes,
Or new Love pine at them beyond to-morrow.

Away! away! for I will fly to thee,
Not charioted by Bacchus and his pards,
But on the viewless wings of Poesy,
Though the dull brain perplexes and retards:
Already with thee! tender is the night,
And haply the Queen-Moon is on her throne,
Cluster'd around by all her starry Fays;
But here there is no light,
Save what from heaven is with the breezes blown
Through verdurous glooms and winding mossy ways.

I cannot see what flowers are at my feet,
Nor what soft incense hangs upon the boughs,
But, in embalmed darkness, guess each sweet
Wherewith the seasonable month endows
The grass, the thicket, and the fruit-tree wild;
White hawthorn, and the pastoral eglantine;
Fast-fading violets cover'd up in leaves;
And mid-May's eldest child,
The coming musk-rose, full of dewy wine,
The murmurous haunt of flies on summer eves.

Darkling I listen; and for many a time
I have been half in love with easeful Death,
Call'd him soft names in many a mused rhyme,
To take into the air my quiet breath;
Now more than ever seems it rich to die,
To cease upon the midnight with no pain,
While thou art pouring forth thy soul abroad
In such an ecstasy!
Still wouldst thou sing, and I have ears in vain –
To thy high requiem become a sod.

Thou wast not born for death, immortal Bird!
No hungry generations tread thee down;
The voice I hear this passing night was heard
In ancient days by emperor and clown:
Perhaps the self-same song that found a path
Through the sad heart of Ruth, when sick for home,
She stood in tears amid the alien corn;
The same that oft-times hath
Charm'd magic casements, opening on the foam
Of perilous seas, in faery lands forlorn.

Forlorn! the very word is like a bell
  To toll me back from thee to my sole self!
Adieu! the fancy cannot cheat so well
  As she is famed to do, deceiving elf.
Adieu! adieu! thy plaintive anthem fades
  Past the near meadows, over the still stream,
    Up the hill-side; and now 'tis buried deep
        In the next valley-glades:
  Was it a vision, or a waking dream?
    Fled is that music:- do I wake or sleep?

To Autumn

Season of mists and mellow fruitfulness!
  Close bosom-friend of the maturing sun;
Conspiring with him how to load and bless
  With fruit the vines that round the thatch-eaves run;
To bend with apples the mossed cottage-trees,
  And fill all fruit with ripeness to the core;
    To swell the gourd, and plump the hazel shells
  With a sweet kernel; to set budding more,
And still more, later flowers for the bees,
Until they think warm days will never cease,
    For Summer has o'er-brimmed their clammy cells.

Who hath not seen thee oft amid thy store?
  Sometimes whoever seeks abroad may find
Thee sitting careless on a granary floor,
  Thy hair soft-lifted by the winnowing wind;
Or on a half-reaped furrow sound asleep,
  Drowsed with the fume of poppies, while thy hook
    Spares the next swath and all its twinèd flowers;
And sometimes like a gleaner thou dost keep
  Steady thy laden head across a brook;
  Or by a cider-press, with patient look,
    Thou watchest the last oozings, hours by hours.

Where are the songs of Spring? Ay, where are they?
  Think not of them, thou has thy music too,
    While barrèd clouds bloom the soft-dying day,
And touch the stubble-plains with rosy hue;
  Then in a wailful choir the small gnats mourn
  Among the river sallows, borne aloft
    Or sinking as the light wind lives or dies;
And full-grown lambs loud bleat from hilly bourn;
  Hedge-crickets sing; and now with treble soft
  The redbreast whistles from a garden-croft,
    And gathering swallows twitter in the skies.

La Belle Dame Sans Merci

'O what can ail thee, knight-at-arms,
  Alone and palely loitering?
The sedge has withered from the lake,
    And no birds sing.

'O what can ail thee, knight-at-arms,
  So haggard and so woe-begone?
The squirrel's granary is full,
    And the harvest's done.

'I see a lily on thy brow
  With anguish moist and fever dew;
And on thy cheek a fading rose
    Fast withereth too.'

'I met a lady in the meads,
  Full beautiful – a faery's child,
Her hair was long, her foot was light,
    And her eyes were wild.

'I made a garland for her head,
  And bracelets too, and fragrant zone;
She looked at me as she did love,
    And made sweet moan.

'I set her on my pacing steed
  And nothing else saw all day long,
For sideways would she lean, and sing
    A faery's song.

'She found me roots of relish sweet,
  And honey wild and manna dew,
And sure in language strange she said,
    "I love thee true!"

'She took me to her elfin grot,
  And there she wept and sighed full sore;
And there I shut her wild, wild eyes
    With kisses four.

'And there she lullèd me asleep,
  And there I dreamed – Ah! woe betide!
The latest dream I ever dreamed
    On the cold hill's side.

'I saw pale kings and princes too,
  Pale warriors, death-pale were they all;
Who cried – "La belle Dame sans Merci
    Hath thee in thrall!"

'I saw their starved lips in the gloam
With horrid warning gapèd wide,
And I awoke and found me here
On the cold hill's side.

'And this is why I sojourn here
Alone and palely loitering,
Though the sedge is withered from the lake,
And no birds sing.'

On First Looking into Chapman's Homer

Much have I travell'd in the realms of gold,
And many goodly states and kingdoms seen;
Round many western islands have I been
Which bards in fealty to Apollo hold.
Oft of one wide expanse had I been told
That deep-brow'd Homer ruled as his demesne;
Yet did I never breathe its pure serene
Till I heard Chapman speak out loud and bold:
Then felt I like some watcher of the skies
When a new planet swims into his ken;
Or like stout Cortez when with eagle eyes
He star'd at the Pacific – and all his men
Look'd at each other with a wild surmise –
Silent, upon a peak in Darien.

SIR WALTER SCOTT

Boat Song

'Hail to the chief who in triumph advances!
Honoured and blessed be the evergreen Pine!
Long may the tree, in his banner that glances,
Flourish, the shelter and grace of our line!
Heaven send it happy dew,
Earth lend it sap anew,
Gayly to bourgeon, and broadly to grow,
While every Highland glen
Sends our shout back agen,
Roderigh Vich Alpine, dhu, ho! ieroe!

'Ours is no sapling, chance-sown by the fountain,
Blooming at Beltane, in winter to fade;
When the whirlwind has stripped every leaf on the mountain,
The more shall Clan-Alpine exult in her shade.

Moored in the rifted rock,
Proof to the tempest's shock,
Firmer he roots him the ruder it blow;
Menteith and Breadalbane, then,
Echo his praise agen,
Roderigh Vich Alpine dhu, ho! ieroe!

'Proudly our pibroch has thrilled in Glen Fruin,
And Bannochar's groans to our slogan replied;
Glen Luss and Ross-dhu, they are smoking in ruin,
And the best of Loch Lomond lie dead on her side.
Widow and Saxon maid
Long shall lament our raid,
Think of Clan-Alpine with fear and with woe;
Lennox and Leven-glen
Shake when they hear agen,
Roderigh Vich Alpine dhu, ho! ieroe!

'Row, vassals, row, for the pride of the Highlands!
Stretch to your oars, for the evergreen Pine!
O! that the rose-bud that graces yon islands
Were wreathed in a garland around him to twine!
O that some seedling gem,
Worthy such noble stem,
Honoured and blessed in their shadow might grow!
Loud should Clan-Alpine then
Ring from her deepmost glen,
Roderigh Vich Alpine dhu, ho! ieroe!'

Lochinvar

O, young Lochinvar is come out of the west,
Through all the wide Border his steed was the best;
And save his good broadsword he weapons had none,
He rode all unarmed, and he rode all alone.
So faithful in love, and so dauntless in war,
There never was knight like the young Lochinvar.

He stayed not for brake, and he stopped not for stone,
He swam the Eske river where ford there was none;
But ere he alighted at Nertherby gate,
The bride had consented, the gallant came late:
For a laggard in love, and a dastard in war,
Was to wed the fair Ellen of brave Lochinvar.

So boldly he entered the Netherby Hall,
Among bride's-men, and kinsmen, and brothers, and all:
Then spoke the bride's father, his hand on his sword,

(For the poor craven bridegroom said never a word)
'O come ye in peace here, or come ye in war,
Or to dance at our bridal, young Lord Lochinvar?'

'I long wooed your daughter, my suit you denied;-
Love swells like the Solway, but ebbs like its tide –
And now am I come, with this lost love of mine,
To lead but one measure, drink one cup of wine.
There are maidens in Scotland more lovely by far,
That would gladly be bride to the young Lochinvar.'

The bride kissed the goblet: the knight took it up,
He quaffed off the wine, and he threw down the cup.
She looked down to blush, and she looked up to sigh,
With a smile on her lips, and a tear in her eye.
He took her soft hand, ere her mother could bar, –
'Now tread we a measure!' said the young Lochinvar.

So stately his form and so lovely her face,
That never a hall such a galliard did grace;
While her mother did fret, and her father did fume,
And the bridegroom stood dangling his bonnet and plume;
And the bride-maidens whispered, ''Twere better by far,
To have matched our fair cousin with young Lochinvar.'

One touch to her hand, and one word in her ear,
When they reached the hall-door, and the charger stood near;
So light to the croup the fair lady he swung,
So light to the saddle before her he sprung!
'She is won! we are gone, over bank, bush, and scaur;
They'll have fleet steeds that follow,' quoth young Lochinvar.

There was mounting 'mong Graemes of the Netherby clan;
Forsters, Fenwicks, and Musgraves, they rode and they ran:
There was racing and chasing on Cannobie Lee,
But the lost bride of Netherby ne'er did they see.
So daring in love, and so dauntless in war,
Have ye e'er heard of gallant like young Lochinvar?

The Patriot

Breathes there the man, with soul so dead,
Who never to himself hath said,
This is my own, my native land!
Whose heart hath ne'er within him burned,
As home his footsteps he hath turned,
From wandering on a foreign strand!
If such there breathe, go, mark him well;
For him no Minstrel raptures swell;

High though his titles, proud his name,
Boundless his wealth as wish can claim;
Despite those titles, power, and pelf,
The wretch, concentred all in self,
Living, shall forfeit fair renown,
And, doubly, dying, shall go down
To the vile dust, from whence he sprung,
Unwept, unhonoured, and unsung.

O Caledonia! stern and wild,
Meet nurse for a poetic child!
Land of brown heath and shaggy wood,
Land of the mountain and the flood,
Land of my sires! what mortal hand
Can e'er untie the filial band,
That knits me to thy rugged strand!
Still, as I view each well known scene,
Think what is now, and what hath been,
Seems as, to me, of all bereft,
Sole friends thy woods and streams were left;
And thus I love them better still,
Even in extremity of ill.
By Yarrow's stream still let me stray,
Though none should guide my feeble way;
Still feel the breeze down Ettricke break,
Although it chill my withered cheek;
Still lay my head by Teviot Stone,
Though there, forgotten and alone,
The Bard may draw his parting groan.

JOHN GALT

Canadian Boat-song

Listen to me, as when ye heard our father
   Sing long ago the song of other shores –
Listen to me, and then in chorus gather
   All your deep voices, as ye pull your oars:

CHORUS

Fair these broad meads – these hoary woods are grand;
But we are exiles from our fathers' land.

From the lone shieling of the misty island
   Mountains divide us, and the waste of seas –
Yet still the blood is strong, the heart is Highland,
   And we in dreams behold the Hebrides:
      Fair these broad meads, etc.

We ne'er shall tread the fancy-haunted valley,
  Where 'tween the dark hills creeps the small clear stream,
In arms around the patriarch banner rally,
  Nor see the moon on royal tombstones gleam:
    Fair these broad meads, etc.

When the bold kindred, in the time long-vanish'd,
  Conquer'd the soil and fortified the keep, –
No seer foretold the children would be banish'd,
  That a degenerate Lord might boast his sheep:
    Fair these broad meads, etc.

Come foreign rage – let Discord burst in slaughter!
  O then for clansman true, and stern claymore –
The hearts that would have given their blood like water,
  Beat heavily beyond the Atlantic roar:
    Fair these broad meads – these hoary woods are grand;
    But we are exiles from our fathers' land.

ROBERT SOUTHEY

The Battle of Blenheim

It was a summer evening,
  Old Kaspar's work was done,
And he before his cottage door
  Was sitting in the sun,
And by him sported on the green
His little grandchild Wilhelmine.

She saw her brother Peterkin
  Roll something large and round,
Which he beside the rivulet
  In playing there had found;
He came to ask what he had found,
That was so large, and smooth, and round.

Old Kaspar took it from the boy,
  Who stood expectant by;
And then the old man shook his head,
  And with a natural sigh,
'Tis some poor fellow's skull, said he,
Who fell in the great victory.

I find them in the garden,
  For there's many here about,
And often when I go to plough,
  The ploughshare turns them out;

For many thousand men, said he,
Were slain in the great victory.

Now tell us what 'twas all about,
  Young Peterkin, he cries,
And little Wilhelmine looks up
  With wonder-waiting eyes;
Now tell us all about the war,
And what they kill'd each other for.

It was the English, Kaspar cried,
  That put the French to rout;
But what they kill'd each other for,
  I could not well make out;
But every body said, quoth he,
That 'twas a famous victory.

My father lived at Blenheim then,
  Yon little stream hard by;
They burnt his dwelling to the ground
  And he was forced to fly;
So with his wife and child he fled,
Nor had he where to rest his head.

With fire and sword the country round
  Was wasted far and wide,
And many a childing mother then,
  And new-born baby died.
But things like that, you know, must be
At every famous victory.

They say it was a shocking sight
  After the field was won,
For many thousand bodies here
  Lay rotting in the sun;
But things like that, you know, must be
After a famous victory.

Great praise the Duke of Marlbro' won,
  And our good Prince Eugene. –
Why 'twas a very wicked thing!
  Said little Wilhelmine.
Nay – nay – my little girl, quoth he,
It was a famous victory.

And every body praised the Duke
  Who this great fight did win.
But what good came of it at last?
  Quoth little Peterkin.
Why that I cannot tell, said he,
But 'twas a famous victory.

REGINALD HEBER

From Greenland's Icy Mountains

From Greenland's icy mountains,
  From India's coral strand,
Where Afric's sunny fountains
  Roll down their golden sand,
From many an ancient river,
  From many a palmy plain,
They call us to deliver
  Their land from error's chain.

What though the spicy breezes
  Blow soft o'er Java's isle,
Though every prospect pleases
  And only man is vile,
In vain with lavish kindness
  The gifts of God are strown,
The heathen in his blindness
  Bows down to wood and stone.

Can we, whose souls are lighted
  With wisdom from on high,
Can we to men benighted
  The lamp of life deny?
Salvation! oh, salvation!
  The joyful sound proclaim,
Till each remotest nation
  Has learned Messiah's name.

Waft, waft, ye winds, his story,
  And you, ye waters, roll,
Till, like a sea of glory,
  It spreads from pole to pole;
Till o'er our ransomed nature
  The Lamb for sinners slain,
Redeemer, King, Creator,
  In bliss returns to reign.

GEORGE OUTRAM

On Hearing a Lady Praise a Certain Rev. Doctor's Eyes

I cannot praise the Doctor's eyes,
I never saw his glance divine;
He always shuts them when he prays
And when he preaches he shuts mine.

THOMAS LOVE PEACOCK

Rich and Poor

The poor man's sins are glaring;
In the face of ghostly warning
He is caught in the fact
Of an overt act –
Buying greens on Sunday morning.

The rich man's sins are hidden
In the pomp of wealth and station;
And escape the sight
Of the children of light,
Who are wise in their generation.

The rich man has a kitchen,
And cooks to dress his dinner;
The poor who would roast
To the baker's must post,
And thus becomes a sinner.

The rich man has a cellar,
And a ready butler by him;
The poor must steer
For his pint of beer
Where the saint can't choose but spy him.

The rich man's painted windows
Hide the concerts of the quality;
The poor can but share
A cracked fiddle in the air,
Which offends all sound morality.

The rich man is invisible
In the crowd of his gay society;
But the poor man's delight
Is a sore in the sight,
And a stench in the nose of piety.

The rich man has a carriage
Where no rude eye can flout him;
    The poor man's bane
    Is a third class train,
With the day-light all about him.

The rich man goes out yachting,
Where sanctity can't pursue him;
    The poor goes afloat
    In a fourpenny boat,
Where the bishop groans to view him.

Love and Age

I played with you 'mid cowslips blowing,
When I was six and you were four;
When garlands weaving, flower-balls throwing,
Were pleasures soon to please no more.
Through groves and meads, o'er grass and heather,
With little playmates, to and fro,
We wandered hand in hand together;
But that was sixty years ago.

You grew a lovely roseate maiden,
And still our early love was strong;
Still with no care our days were laden,
They glided joyously along;
And I did love you, very dearly,
How dearly words want power to show;
I thought your heart was touched as nearly;
But that was fifty years ago.

Then other lovers came around you,
Your beauty grew from year to year,
And many a splendid circle found you
The centre of its glittering sphere.
I saw you then, first vows forsaking,
On rank and wealth your hand bestow;
Oh, then I thought my heart was breaking, –
But that was forty years ago.

And I lived on, to wed another:
No cause she gave me to repine;
And when I heard you were a mother,
I did not wish the children mine.
My own young flock, in fair progression,
Made up a pleasant Christmas row:
My joy in them was past expression; –
But that was thirty years ago.

You grew a matron plump and comely,
You dwelt in fashion's brightest blaze;
My earthly lot was far more homely;
But I too had my festal days.
No merrier eyes have ever glistened
Around the hearth-stone's wintry glow,
Than when my youngest child was christened:-
But that was twenty years ago.

Time passed. My eldest girl was married,
And I am now a grandsire grey;
One pet of four years old I've carried
Among the wild-flowered meads to play.
In our old fields of childish pleasure,
Where now, as then, the cowslips blow,
She fills her basket's ample measure, –
And that is not ten years ago.

But though first love's impassioned blindness
Has passed away in colder light,
I still have thought of you with kindness,
And shall do, till our last good-night.
The ever-rolling silent hours
Will bring a time we shall not know,
When our young days of gathering flowers
Will be a hundred years ago.

THOMAS HOOD

Ruth

She stood breast high amid the corn,
Clasped by the golden light of morn,
Like the sweetheart of the sun,
Who many a glowing kiss had won.

On her cheek an autumn flush,
Deeply ripened; – such a blush
In the midst of brown was born,
Like red poppies grown with corn.

Round her eyes her tresses fell,
Which were blackest none could tell,
But long lashes veiled a light,
That had else been all too bright.

And her hat, with shady brim,
Made her tressy forehead dim; –
Thus she stood amid the stooks,
Praising God with sweetest looks:-

Sure, I said, heaven did not mean,
Where I reap thou shouldst but glean,
Lay thy sheaf adown and come,
Share my harvest and my home.

I Remember, I Remember

I remember, I remember,
The house where I was born,
The little window where the sun
Came peeping in at morn;
He never came a wink too soon,
Nor brought too long a day,
But now, I often wish the night
Had borne my breath away!

I remember, I remember,
The roses, red and white,
The violets, and the lily-cups,
Those flowers made of light!
The lilacs where the robin built,
And where my brother set
The laburnum on his birthday, –
The tree is living yet!

I remember, I remember,
Where I was used to swing,
And thought the air must rush as fresh
To swallows on the wing;
My spirit flew in feathers then,
That is so heavy now,
And summer pools could hardly cool
The fever on my brow!

I remember, I remember,
The fir trees dark and high;
I used to think their slender tops
Were close against the sky:
It was a childish ignorance,
But now 'tis little joy
To know I'm farther off from heaven
Than when I was a boy.

CHARLOTTE BRONTË

Speak of the North

Speak of the North! A lonely moor
Silent and dark and trackless swells,
The waves of some wild streamlet pour
Hurriedly through its ferny dells.

Profoundly still the twilight air,
Lifeless the landscape; so we deem
Till like a phantom gliding near
A stag bends down to drink the stream.

And far away a mountain zone,
A cold, white waste of snow-drifts lies,
And one star, large and soft and lone,
Silently lights the unclouded skies.

CHARLOTTE and EMILY BRONTË

The Visionary

Silent is the house: all are laid asleep:
One alone looks out o'er the snow-wreaths deep;
Watching every cloud, dreading every breeze
That whirls the wildering drift, and bends the groaning trees.

Cheerful is the hearth, soft the matted floor;
Not one shivering gust creeps through pane or door;
The little lamp burns straight, its rays shoot strong and far:
I trim it well, to be the wanderer's guiding-star.

Frown, my haughty sire! chide, my angry dame;
Set your slaves to spy; threaten me with shame:
But neither sire nor dame, nor prying serf shall know,
What angel nightly tracks that waste of frozen snow.

What I love shall come like visitant of air,
Safe in secret power from lurking human snare;
What loves me, no word of mine shall e'er betray,
Though for faith unstained my life must forfeit pay.

Burn, then, little lamp; glimmer straight and clear –
Hush! a rustling wing stirs, methinks, the air:
He for whom I wait, thus ever comes to me;
Strange Power! I trust thy might; trust thou my constancy.

ANNE BRONTË

Lines Composed in a Wood on a Windy Day

My soul is awakened, my spirit is soaring,
And carried aloft on the wings of the breeze;
For, above, and around me, the wild wind is roaring
Arousing to rapture the earth and the seas.

The long withered grass in the sunshine is glancing,
The bare trees are tossing their branches on high;
The dead leaves beneath them are merrily dancing,
The white clouds are scudding across the blue sky.

I wish I could see how the ocean is lashing
The foam of its billows to whirlwinds of spray,
I wish I could see how its proud waves are dashing
And hear the wild roar of their thunder today!

The Captive Dove

Poor restless Dove, I pity thee,
And when I hear thy plaintive moan
I'll mourn for thy captivity
And in thy woes forget mine own.

To see thee stand prepared to fly,
And flap those useless wings of thine,
And gaze into the distant sky
Would melt a harder heart than mine.

In vain! In vain! Thou canst not rise –
Thy prison roof confines thee there;
Its slender wires delude thine eyes,
And quench thy longing with despair.

O! thou wert made to wander free
In sunny mead and shady grove,
And far beyond the rolling sea
In distant climes at will to rove.

Yet hadst thou but one gentle mate
Thy little drooping heart to cheer
And share with thee thy captive state,
Thou could'st be happy even there.

Yes, even there, if listening by
One faithful dear companion stood,

While gazing on her full bright eye
Thou might'st forget thy native wood.

But thou, poor solitary dove,
Must make unheard thy joyless moan;
The heart that nature formed to love
Must pine neglected and alone.

The Arbour

I'll rest me in this sheltered bower,
And look upon the clear blue sky
That smiles upon me through the trees,
Which stand so thickly clustering by;

And view their green and glossy leaves,
All glistening in the sunshine fair;
And list the rustling of their boughs,
So softly whispering through the air.

And while my ear drinks in the sound,
My wingèd soul shall fly away;
Reviewing long departed years
As one mild, beaming, autumn day;

And soaring on to future scenes,
Like hills and woods, and valleys green,
All basking in the summer's sun,
But distant still, and dimly seen.

Oh, list! 'tis summer's very breath
That gently shakes the rustling trees –
But look! the snow is on the ground –
How can I think of scenes like these?

WILLIAM BARNES

Grammer's Shoes

I do seem to zee Grammer as she did use
Vor to show us, at Chris'mas, her weddèn shoes,
An' her flat spreadèn bonnet so big an' roun'
As a girt pewter dish a-turn'd upside down;
When we all did draw near
In a cluster to hear
O' the merry wold soul how she did use
To walk an' to dance wi' her high-heel shoes.

She'd a gown wi' girt flowers lik' hollyhocks,
An' zome stockèns o' gramfer's a-knit wi' clocks,
An' a token she kept under lock an' key, –
A small lock ov his heäir off avor 't wer grey.
An' her eyes wer red,
An' she shook her head,
When we'd all a-look'd at it, an' she did use
To lock it away wi' her weddèn shoes.

She could tell us such teäles about heavy snows,
An' o' raïns an' o' floods when the waters rose
All up into the housen, an' carr'd awoy
All the bridge wi' a man an' his little bwoy;
An' o' vog an' vrost,
An' o' vo'k a-lost,
An' o' peärties at Chris'mas, when she did use
Vor to walk hwome wi' gramfer in high-heel shoes.

Ev'ry Chris'mas she lik'd vor the bells to ring,
An' to have in the zingers to heär em zing
The wold carols she heärd many years a-gone,
While she warm'd em zome cider avore the bron';
An' she'd look an' smile
An our dancèn, while
She did tell how her friends now a-gone did use
To reely wi' her in their high-heel shoes.

Ah! an' how she did like vor to deck wi' red
Holly-berries the window an' wold clock's head,
An' the clavy wi' boughs o' some bright green leaves,
An to meäke twoast an' eäle upon Chris'mas eves;
But she's now, drough greäce,
In a better pleäce,
Though we'll never vorget her, poor soul, nor lose
Gramfer's token ov heäir, nor her weddèn shoes.

CHARLES KINGSLEY

Young and Old

When all the world is young, lad,
And all the trees are green;
And every goose a swan, lad,
And every lass a queen;
Then hey for boot and horse, lad,
And round the world away;
Young blood must have its course, lad,
And every dog his day.

When all the world is old, lad,
  And all the trees are brown;
And all the sport is stale, lad,
  And all the wheels run down;
Creep home, and take your place there,
  The spent and maimed among:
God grant you find one face there,
  You loved when all was young.

ELIZABETH BARRETT BROWNING

How Do I Love Thee?

How do I love thee? Let me count the ways.
I love thee to the depth and breadth and height
My soul can reach, when feeling out of sight
For the ends of Being and ideal Grace.
I love thee to the level of every day's
Most quiet need, by sun and candlelight.
I love thee freely, as men strive for Right;
I love thee purely, as they turn from Praise.
I love thee with the passion put to use
In my old griefs, and with my childhood's faith.
I love thee with a love I seemed to lose
With my lost saints, – I love thee with the breath,
Smiles, tears, of all my life! – and, if God choose,
I shall but love thee better after death.

'First time he kissed me, he but only kissed'

First time he kissed me, he but only kissed
The fingers of this hand wherewith I write;
And ever since, it grew more clean and white,
Slow to world-greetings, quick with its 'Oh, list,'
When the angels speak. A ring of amethyst
I could not wear here, plainer to my sight,
Than that first kiss. The second passed in height
The first, and sought the forehead, and half missed,
Half falling on the hair. O beyond meed!
That was the chrism of love, which love's own crown,
With sanctifying sweetness, did precede.
The third upon my lips was folded down
In perfect, purple state; since when, indeed,
I have been proud and said, 'My love, my own.'

The Cry of the Children

Do ye hear the children weeping, O my brothers,
    Ere the sorrow comes with years?
They are leaning their young heads against their mothers,
    And *that* cannot stop their tears.
The young lambs are bleating in the meadows,
  The young birds are chirping in the nest,
The young fawns are playing with the shadows,
  The young flowers are blowing toward the west –
But the young, young children, O my brothers,
    They are weeping bitterly!
They are weeping in the playtime of the others,
    In the country of the free.

Do you question the young children in the sorrow,
    Why their tears are falling so?
The old man may weep for his to-morrow
    Which is lost in Long Ago;
The old tree is leafless in the forest,
  The old year is ending in the frost,
The old wound, if stricken, is the sorest,
  The old hope is hardest to be lost.
But the young, young children, O my brothers,
    Do you ask them why they stand
Weeping sore before the bosoms of their mothers,
    In our happy Fatherland?

They look up with their pale and sunken faces,
    And their looks are sad to see,
For the man's hoary anguish draws and presses
    Down the cheeks of infancy.
'Your old earth,' they say, 'is very dreary;
  Our young feet,' they say, 'are very weak!
Few paces have we taken, yet are weary –
  Our grave-rest is very far to seek.
Ask the aged why they weep, and not the children;
    For the outside earth is cold;
And we young ones stand without, in our bewildering,
    And the graves are for the old.'

'True,' say the children, 'it may happen
    That we die before our time;
Little Alice died last year – her grave is shapen
    Like a snowball, in the rime.
We looked into the pit prepared to take her;
  Was no room for any work in the close clay!
From the sleep wherein she lieth none will wake her,
  Crying, "Get up, little Alice! it is day."

If you listen by that grave, in sun and shower,
With your ear down, little Alice never cries;
Could we see her face, be sure we should not know her,
For the smile has time for growing in her eyes:
And merry go her moments, lulled and stilled in
The shroud by the kirk-chime!
It is good when it happens,' say the children,
'That we die before our time.'

Alas, alas, the children! they are seeking
Death in life, as best to have;
They are binding up their hearts away from breaking,
With a cerement from the grave.
Go out, children, from the mine and from the city,
Sing out, children, as the little thrushes do;
Pluck you handfuls of the meadow cowslips pretty,
Laugh aloud, to feel your fingers let them through!
But they answer, 'Are your cowslips of the meadows
Like our weeds anear the mine?
Leave us quiet in the dark of the coal-shadows,
From your pleasures fair and fine!

'For oh,' say the children, 'we are weary,
And we cannot run or leap;
If we cared for any meadows, it were merely
To drop down in them and sleep.
Our knees tremble sorely in the stooping,
We fall upon our faces, trying to go;
And, underneath our heavy eyelids drooping,
The reddest flower would look as pale as snow;
For, all day, we drag our burden tiring
Through the coal-dark, underground –
Or, all day, we drive the wheels of iron
In the factories, round and round.

'For, all day, the wheels are droning, turning, –
Their wind comes in our faces, –
Till our hearts turn, – our head, with pulses burning,
And the walls turn in their places;
Turns the sky in the high window blank and reeling,
Turns the long light that drops adown the wall,
Turn the black flies that crawl along the ceiling,
All are turning, all the day, and we with all.
And all day, the iron wheels are droning,
And sometimes we could pray,
"O ye wheels" (breaking out in a mad moaning),
"Stop! be silent for to-day!" '

Ay! be silent! Let them hear each other breathing
For a moment, mouth to mouth!
Let them touch each other's hands, in a fresh wreathing
Of their tender human youth!
Let them feel that this cold metallic motion
Is not all the life God fashions or reveals:
Let them prove their living souls against the notion
That they live in you, or under you, O wheels! –
Still, all day, the iron wheels go onward,
Grinding life down from its mark;
And the children's souls, which God is calling sunward,
Spin on blindly in the dark.

Now tell the poor young children, O my brothers,
To look up to Him and pray;
So the blessèd One who blesseth all the others,
Will bless them another day.
They answer, 'Who is God that He should hear us,
While the rushing of the iron wheels is stirred?
When we sob aloud, the human creatures near us
Pass by, hearing not, or answer not a word.
And *we* hear not (for the wheels in their resounding)
Strangers speaking at the door,
Is it likely God, with angels singing round Him,
Hears our weeping any more?

'Two words, indeed, of praying we remember,
And at midnight's hour of harm,
"Our Father," looking upward in the chamber,
We say softly for a charm.
We know no other words, except "Our Father,"
And we think that, in some pause of angel's song,
God may pluck them with the silence sweet to gather,
And hold both within His right hand which is strong.
"Our Father!" If He heard us, He would surely
(For they call Him good and mild)
Answer, smiling down the steep world very purely,
"Come and rest with Me, My child."

'But, no!' say the children, weeping faster,
'He is speechless as a stone;
And they tell us, of His image is the master
Who commands us to work on.
Go to!' say the children, – 'up in Heaven,
Dark, wheel-like, turning clouds are all we find.
Do not mock us; grief has made us unbelieving –
We look up for God, but tears have made us blind.'
Do you hear the children weeping and disproving,
O my brothers, what ye preach?

For God's possible is taught by His world's loving,
    And the children doubt of each.

And well may the children weep before you!
    They are weary ere they run;
They have never seen the sunshine, nor the glory
    Which is brighter than the sun.
They know the grief of man, without its wisdom;
  They sink in man's despair, without its calm;
Are slaves, without the liberty in Christdom,
  Are martyrs, by the pang without the palm, –
Are worn, as if with age, yet unretrievingly
    The harvest of its memories cannot reap, –
Are orphans of the earthly love and heavenly.
    Let them weep! let them weep!

They look up, with their pale and sunken faces,
    And their look is dread to see,
For they mind you of their angels in high places,
    With eyes turned on Deity! –
'How long,' they say, 'how long, O cruel nation,
  Will you stand, to move the world, on a child's heart, –
Stifle down with a mailed heel its palpitation,
  And tread onward to your throne amid the mart?
Our blood splashes upward, O gold-heaper,
    And your purple shows your path!
But the child's sob in the silence curses deeper
    Than the strong man in his wrath.'

Grief

I tell you, hopeless grief is passionless;
That only men incredulous of despair,
Half-taught in anguish, through the midnight air
Beat upward to God's throne in loud access
Of shrieking and reproach. Full desertness,
In souls as countries, lieth silent-bare
Under the blanching, vertical eye-glare
Of the absolute Heavens. Deep-hearted man, express
Grief for thy Dead in silence like to death –
Most like a monumental statue set
In everlasting watch and moveless woe
Till itself crumble to the dust beneath.
Touch it; the marble eyelids are not wet;
If it could weep, it could arise and go.

The Best Thing in the World

What's the best thing in the world?
June-rose, by May-dew impearled;
Sweet south-wind, that means no rain;
Truth, not cruel to a friend;
Pleasure, not in haste to end;
Beauty, not self-decked and curled
Till its pride is over-plain;
Light, that never makes you wink;
Memory, that gives no pain;
Love, when, *so*, you're loved again.
What's the best thing in the world?
– Something out of it, I think.

ROBERT BROWNING

How They Brought the Good News from Ghent to Aix

I sprang to the stirrup, and Joris, and he;
I galloped, Dirck galloped, we galloped all three;
'Good speed!' cried the watch, as the gate-bolts undrew;
'Speed!' echoed the wall to us galloping through;
Behind shut the postern, the lights sank to rest,
And into the midnight we galloped abreast.

Not a word to each other: we kept the great pace
Neck by neck, stride by stride, never changing our place;
I turned in my saddle and made its girths tight,
Then shortened each stirrup, and set the pique right,
Rebuckled the cheek-strap, chained slacker the bit,
Nor galloped less steadily Roland a whit.

'Twas moonset at starting; but while we drew near
Lokeren, the cocks crew and twilight dawned clear;
At Boom, a great yellow star came out to see;
At Düffeld, 'twas morning as plain as could be;
And from Mecheln church-steeple we heard the half-chime,
So Joris broke silence with, 'Yet there is time!'

At Aerschot, up leaped of a sudden the sun,
And against him the cattle stood black every one,
To stare thro' the mist at us galloping past,
And I saw my stout galloper Roland at last,
With resolute shoulders, each butting away
The haze, as some bluff river headland its spray.

And his low head and crest, just one sharp ear bent back
For my voice, and the other pricked out on his track;
And one eye's black intelligence, – ever that glance
O'er its white edge at me, his own master, askance!
And the thick heavy spume-flakes which aye and anon
His fierce lips shook upwards in galloping on.

By Hasselt, Dirck groaned; and cried Joris, 'Stay spur!
Your Roos galloped bravely, the fault's not in her,
We'll remember at Aix' – for one heard the quick wheeze
Of her chest, saw the stretched neck and staggering knees,
And sunk tail, and horrible heave of the flank,
As down on her haunches she shuddered and sank.

So we were left galloping, Joris and I,
Past Looz and past Tongres, no cloud in the sky;
The broad sun above laughed a pitiless laugh,
'Neath our feet broke the brittle bright stubble like chaff;
Till over by Dalhem a dome-spire sprang white,
And 'Gallop,' gasped Joris, 'for Aix is in sight!'

'How they'll greet us!' – and all in a moment his roan
Rolled neck and croup over, lay dead as a stone;
And there was my Roland to bear the whole weight
Of the news which alone could save Aix from her fate,
With his nostrils like pits full of blood to the brim,
And with circles of red from his eye-sockets' rim.

Then I cast loose my buffcoat, each holster let fall,
Shook off both my jack-boots, let go belt and all,
Stood up in the stirrup, leaned, patted his ear,
Called my Roland his pet-name, my horse without peer;
Clapped my hands, laughed and sang, any noise, bad or good,
Till at length into Aix Roland galloped and stood.

And all I remember is, friends flocking round
As I sat with his head 'twixt my knees on the ground;
And no voice but was praising this Roland of mine,
As I poured down his throat our last measure of wine,
Which (the burgesses voted by common consent)
Was no more than his due who brought good news from Ghent.

Home Thoughts from Abroad

Oh, to be in England
Now that April's there,
And whoever wakes in England
Sees, some morning, unaware,
That the lowest boughs and the brushwood sheaf

Round the elm-tree bole are in tiny leaf,
While the chaffinch sings on the orchard bough
In England – now!
And after April, when May follows,
And the whitethroat builds, and all the swallows!
Hark, where my blossomed pear-tree in the hedge
Leans to the field and scatters on the clover
Blossoms and dewdrops – at the bent spray's edge –
That's the wise thrush; he sings each song twice over,
Lest you should think he never could recapture
The first fine careless rapture!
And though the fields look rough with hoary dew
All will be gay when noontide wakes anew
The buttercups, the little children's dower
– Far brighter than this gaudy melon-flower!

Home Thoughts from the Sea

Nobly, nobly Cape Saint Vincent to the North-west died away;
Sunset ran, one glorious blood-red, reeking into Cadiz Bay;
Bluish 'mid the burning water, full in face Trafalgar lay;
In the dimmest North-east distance dawned Gibraltar grand and gray;
'Here and here did England help me: how can I help England?' – say,
Whoso turns as I, this evening, turn to God to praise and pray,
While Jove's planet rises yonder, silent over Africa.

Meeting at Night

The grey sea and the long black land;
And the yellow half-moon large and low;
And the startled little waves that leap
In fiery ringlets from their sleep,
As I gain the cove with pushing prow,
And quench its speed in the slushy sand.

Then a mile of warm sea-scented beach;
Three fields to cross till a farm appears;
A tap at the pane, the quick sharp scratch
And blue spurt of a lighted match,
And a voice less loud, through its joys and fears,
Than the two hearts beating each to each!

Appearances

And so you found that poor room dull,
Dark, hardly to your taste, my dear?
Its features seemed unbeautiful:
But this I know – 'twas there, not here,
You plighted troth to me, the word
Which – ask that poor room how it heard!

And this rich room obtains your praise
Unqualified, – so bright, so fair,
So all whereat perfection stays?
Ay, but remember – here, not there,
The other word was spoken! – Ask
This rich room how you dropped the mask!

My Last Duchess

Ferrara

That's my last Duchess painted on the wall,
Looking as if she were alive. I call
That piece a wonder, now: Frà Pandolf's hands
Worked busily a day, and there she stands.
Will't please you sit and look at her? I said
'Fra Pandolf' by design, for never read
Strangers like you that pictured countenance,
The depth and passion of its earnest glance,
But to myself they turned (since none puts by
The curtain I have drawn for you, but I)
And seemed as they would ask me, if they durst,
How such a glance came there; so, not the first
Are you to turn and ask thus. Sir, 'twas not
Her husband's presence only, called that spot
Of joy into the Duchess' cheek: perhaps
Frà Pandolf chanced to say 'Her mantle laps
Over my lady's wrist too much,' or 'Paint
Must never hope to reproduce the faint
Half-flush that dies along her throat:' such stuff
Was courtesy, she thought, and cause enough
For calling up that spot of joy. She had
A heart – how shall I say? – too soon made glad,
Too easily impressed; she liked whate'er
She looked on, and her looks went everywhere.
Sir, 'twas all one! My favour at her breast,
The dropping of the daylight in the West,
The bough of cherries some officious fool
Broke in the orchard for her, the white mule
She rode with round the terrace – all and each
Would draw from her alike the approving speech,

Or blush, at least. She thanked men, – good! but thanked
Somehow – I know not how – as if she ranked
My gift of a nine-hundred-years-old name
With anybody's gift. Who'd stoop to blame
This sort of trifling? Even had you skill
In speech – (which I have not) – to make your will
Quite clear to such an one, and say, 'Just this
Or that in you disgusts me; here you miss,
Or there exceed the mark' – and if she let
Herself be lessoned so, nor plainly set
Her wits to yours, forsooth, and made excuse,
– E'en then would be some stooping; and I choose
Never to stoop. Oh sir, she smiled, no doubt,
Whene'er I passed her; but who passed without
Much the same smile? This grew; I gave commands;
Then all smiles stopped together. There she stands
As if alive. Will 't please you rise? We'll meet
The company below, then. I repeat,
The Count your master's known munificence
Is ample warrant that no just pretence
Of mine for dowry will be disallowed;
Though his fair daughter's self, as I avowed
At starting, is my object. Nay, we'll go
Together down, sir. Notice Neptune, though,
Taming a sea-horse, thought a rarity,
Which Claus of Innsbruck cast in bronze for me!

ALFRED, LORD TENNYSON

Ring Out, Wild Bells

Ring out, wild bells, to the wild sky,
  The flying cloud, the frosty light:
  The year is dying in the night;
Ring out, wild bells, and let him die.

Ring out the old, ring in the new,
  Ring, happy bells, across the snow:
  The year is going, let him go;
Ring out the false, ring in the true.

Ring out the grief that saps the mind,
  For those that here we see no more;
  Ring out the feud of rich and poor,
Ring in redress to all mankind.

Ring out a slowly dying cause,
  And ancient forms of party strife;

Ring in the nobler modes of life,
With sweeter manners, purer laws.

Ring out the want, the care, the sin,
The faithless coldness of the times;
Ring out, ring out my mournful rhymes,
But ring the fuller minstrel in.

Ring out false pride in place and blood,
The civic slander and the spite;
Ring in the love of truth and right,
Ring in the common love of good.

Ring out old shapes of foul disease;
Ring out the narrowing lust of gold;
Ring out the thousand wars of old,
Ring in the thousand years of peace.

Ring in the valiant man and free,
The larger heart, the kindlier hand;
Ring out the darkness of the land,
Ring in the Christ that is to be.

The Lotos-Eaters

'Courage!' he said, and pointed toward the land,
'This mounting wave will roll us shoreward soon.'
In the afternoon they came unto a land
In which it seemèd always afternoon.
All round the coast the languid air did swoon,
Breathing like one that hath a weary dream.
Full-faced above the valley stood the moon;
And like a downward smoke, the slender stream
Along the cliff to fall and pause and fall did seem.

A land of streams! some, like a downward smoke,
Slow-dropping veils of thinnest lawn, did go;
And some thro' wavering lights and shadows broke,
Rolling a slumbrous sheet of foam below.
They saw the gleaming river seaward flow
From the inner land: far off, three mountain-tops,
Three silent pinnacles of agèd snow,
Stood sunset flushed: and, dewed with showery drops,
Up-clomb the shadowy pine above the woven copse.

The charmèd sunset lingered low adown
In the red West: thro' mountain clefts the dale
Was seen far inland, and the yellow down
Bordered with palm, and many a winding vale
And meadow, set with slender galingale;

A land where all things always seemed the same!
And round about the keel with faces pale,
Dark faces pale against that rosy flame,
The mild-eyed melancholy Lotos-eaters came.

Branches they bore of that enchanted stem,
Laden with flower and fruit, whereof they gave
To each, but whoso did receive of them,
And taste, to him the gushing of the wave
Far far away did seem to mourn and rave
On alien shores; and if his fellow spake,
His voice was thin, as voices from the grave;
And deep-asleep he seemed, yet all awake,
And music in his ears his beating heart did make.

They sat them down upon the yellow sand,
Between the sun and moon upon the shore;
And sweet it was to dream of Fatherland,
Of child, and wife, and slave; but evermore
Most weary seemed the sea, weary the oar,
Weary the wandering fields of barren foam.
Then some one said, 'We will return no more';
And all at once they sang, 'Our island home
Is far beyond the wave; we will no longer roam.'

The Lady of Shalott

PART I

On either side the river lie
Long fields of barley and of rye,
That clothe the wold and meet the sky;
And thro' the field the road runs by
            To many-towered Camelot;
And up and down the people go,
Gazing where the lilies blow
Round an island there below,
            The island of Shalott.

Willows whiten, aspens quiver,
Little breezes dusk and shiver
Thro' the wave that runs for ever
By the island in the river
            Flowing down to Camelot.
Four grey walls, and four grey towers,
Overlook a space of flowers,
And the silent isle imbowers
            The Lady of Shalott.

By the margin, willow-veiled,
Slide the heavy barges trailed
By slow horses; and unhailed
The shallop flitteth silken-sailed
Skimming down to Camelot:
But who hath seen her wave her hand?
Or at the casement seen her stand?
Or is she known in all the land,
The Lady of Shalott?

Only reapers, reaping early
In among the bearded barley,
Hear a song that echoes cheerly
From the river winding clearly,
Down to towered Camelot:
And by the moon the reaper weary,
Piling sheaves in uplands airy,
Listening, whispers ''Tis the fairy
Lady of Shalott.'

PART II

There she weaves by night and day
A magic web with colours gay.
She has heard a whisper say,
A curse is on her if she stay
To look down to Camelot.
She knows not what the curse may be,
And so she weaveth steadily,
And little other care hath she,
The Lady of Shalott.

And moving thro' a mirror clear
That hangs before her all the year,
Shadows of the world appear.
There she sees the highway near
Winding down to Camelot:
There the river eddy whirls,
And there the surly village-churls,
And the red cloaks of market girls,
Pass onward from Shalott.

Sometimes a troop of damsels glad,
An abbot on an ambling pad,
Sometimes a curly shepherd lad,
Or long-haired page in crimson clad,
Goes by to towered Camelot;
And sometimes thro' the mirror blue
The knights come riding two and two:
She hath no loyal knight and true,
The Lady of Shalott.

But in her web she still delights
To weave the mirror's magic sights,
For often thro' the silent nights
A funeral, with plumes and lights,
    And music, went to Camelot:
Or when the moon was overhead,
Came two young lovers lately wed:
'I am half sick of shadows,' said
    The Lady of Shalott.

PART III

A bow-shot from her bower-eaves,
He rode between the barley-sheaves,
The sun came dazzling thro' the leaves,
And flamed upon the brazen greaves
    Of bold Sir Lancelot.
A red-cross knight for ever kneeled
To a lady in his shield,
That sparkled on the yellow field,
    Beside remote Shalott.

The gemmy bridle glittered free,
Like to some branch of stars we see
Hung in the golden Galaxy.
The bridle bells rang merrily
    As he rode down to Camelot:
And from his blazoned baldric slung
A mighty silver bugle hung,
And as he rode his armour rung,
    Beside remote Shalott.

All in the blue unclouded weather
Thick-jewelled shone the saddle-leather,
The helmet and the helmet-feather
Burned like one burning flame together,
    As he rode down to Camelot.
As often thro' the purple night,
Below the starry clusters bright,
Some bearded meteor, trailing light,
    Moves over still Shalott.

His broad clear brow in sunlight glowed;
On burnished hooves his war-horse trode;
From underneath his helmet flowed
His coal-black curls as on he rode,
    As he rode down to Camelot.
From the bank and from the river
He flashed into the crystal mirror,
'Tirra lirra,' by the river.
    Sang Sir Lancelot.

She left the web, she left the loom,
She made three paces thro' the room,
She saw the water-lily bloom,
She saw the helmet and the plume,
    She looked down to Camelot.
Out flew the web and floated wide;
The mirror cracked from side to side;
'The curse is come upon me,' cried
    The Lady of Shalott.

PART IV

In the stormy east-wind straining,
The pale yellow woods were waning,
The broad stream in his banks complaining,
Heavily the low sky raining
    Over towered Camelot;
Down she came and found a boat
Beneath a willow left afloat,
And round about the prow she wrote
    The Lady of Shalott.

And down the river's dim expanse –
Like some bold seër in a trance,
Seeing all his own mischance –
With a glassy countenance
    Did she look to Camelot.
And at the closing of the day
She loosed the chain, and down she lay;
The broad stream bore her far away,
    The Lady of Shalott.

Lying, robed in snowy white
That loosely flew to left and right –
The leaves upon her falling light –
Thro' the noises of the night
    She floated down to Camelot:
And as the boat-head wound along
The willowy hills and fields among,
They heard her singing her last song,
    The Lady of Shalott.

Heard a carol, mournful, holy,
Chanted loudly, chanted lowly,
Till her blood was frozen slowly,
And her eyes were darkened wholly,
    Turned to towered Camelot.
For ere she reached upon the tide
The first house by the water-side,
Singing in her song she died,
    The Lady of Shalott.

Under tower and balcony,
By garden wall and gallery,
A gleaming shape she floated by,
Dead-pale between the houses high,
Silent into Camelot.
Out upon the wharfs they came,
Knight and burgher, lord and dame,
And round the prow they read her name,
The Lady of Shalott.

Who is this? and what is here?
And in the lighted palace near
Died the sound of royal cheer;
And they crossed themselves for fear,
All the knights at Camelot:
But Lancelot mused a little space;
He said, 'She has a lovely face;
God in his mercy lend her grace,
The Lady of Shalott.'

Maud

Come into the garden, Maud,
For the black bat, night, has flown,
Come into the garden, Maud,
I am here at the gate alone;
And the woodbine spices are wafted abroad,
And the musk of the rose is blown.

For a breeze of morning moves,
And the planet of Love is on high,
Beginning to faint in the light that she loves
On a bed of daffodil sky,
To faint in the light of the sun she loves,
To faint in his light, and to die.

All night have the roses heard
The flute, violin, bassoon;
All night has the casement jessamine stirred
To the dancers dancing in tune;
Till a silence fell with the waking bird,
And a hush with the setting moon.

I said to the lily, 'There is but one
With whom she has heart to be gay.
When will the dancers leave her alone?
She is weary of dance and play.'
Now half to the setting moon are gone,
And half to the rising day;

Low on the sand and loud on the stone
  The last wheel echoes away.

I said to the rose, 'The brief night goes
  In babble and revel and wine.
O young lord-lover, what sighs are those,
  For one that will never be thine?
But mine, but mine,' so I sware to the rose,
  'For ever and ever, mine.'

And the soul of the rose went into my blood,
  As the music clashed in the hall;
And long by the garden lake I stood,
  For I heard your rivulet fall
From the lake to the meadow and on to the wood,
  Our wood, that is dearer than all;

From the meadow your walks have left so sweet
  That whenever a March-wind sighs
He sets the jewel-print of your feet
  In violets blue as your eyes,
To the woody hollows in which we meet
  And the valleys of Paradise.

The slender acacia would not shake
  One long milk-bloom on the tree;
The white lake-blossom fell into the lake
  As the pimpernel dozed on the lea;
But the rose was awake all night for your sake,
  Knowing your promise to me;
The lilies and roses were all awake,
  They sighed for the dawn and thee.

Queen rose of the rosebud garden of girls,
  Come hither, the dances are done,
In gloss of satin and glimmer of pearls,
  Queen lily and rose in one;
Shine out, little head, sunning over with curls,
  To the flowers, and be their sun.

There has fallen a splendid tear
  From the passion-flower at the gate.
She is coming, my dove, my dear;
  She is coming, my life, my fate;
The red rose cries, 'She is near, she is near';
  And the white rose weeps, 'She is late';
The larkspur listens, 'I hear, I hear';
  And the lily whispers, 'I wait.'

She is coming, my own, my sweet;
  Were it ever so airy a tread,
My heart would hear her and beat,
  Were it earth in an earthy bed;
My dust would hear her and beat,
  Had I lain for a century dead;
Would start and tremble under her feet,
  And blossom in purple and red.

The Eagle

He clasps the crag with crooked hands;
Close to the sun in lonely lands,
Ring'd with the azure world, he stands.

The wrinkled sea beneath him crawls;
He watches from his mountain walls,
And like a thunderbolt he falls.

The Charge of the Light Brigade

Half a league, half a league,
  Half a league onward,
All in the valley of Death
  Rode the six hundred.
'Forward, the Light Brigade!
Charge for the guns!' he said:
Into the valley of Death
  Rode the six hundred.

'Forward, the Light Brigade!'
Was there a man dismay'd?
Not tho' the soldier knew
  Some one had blunder'd:
Their's not to make reply,
Their's not to reason why,
Their's but to do and die:
Into the valley of Death
  Rode the six hundred.

Cannon to right of them,
Cannon to left of them,
Cannon in front of them
  Volley'd and thunder'd;
Storm'd at with shot and shell,
Boldly they rode and well,

Into the jaws of Death,
Into the mouth of Hell
  Rode the six hundred.

Flash'd all their sabres bare,
Flash'd as they turn'd in air
Sabring the gunners there,
Charging an army, while
  All the world wonder'd:
Plunged in the battery-smoke
Right thro' the line they broke;
Cossack and Russian
Reel'd from the sabre-stroke
  Shatter'd and sunder'd.
Then they rode back, but not
  Not the six hundred.

Cannon to right of them,
Cannon to left of them,
Cannon behind them
  Volley'd and thunder'd;
Storm'd at with shot and shell,
While horse and hero fell,
They that had fought so well
Came thro' the jaws of Death,
Back from the mouth of Hell,
All that was left of them,
  Left of six hundred.

When can their glory fade?
O the wild charge they made!
  All the world wonder'd.
Honour the charge they made!
Honour the Light Brigade,
  Noble six hundred!

Rizpah

Wailing, wailing, wailing, the wind over land and sea –
And Willy's voice in the wind, 'O mother, come out to me.'
Why should he call me to-night, when he knows that I cannot go?
For the downs are as bright as day, and the full moon stares at the snow.

We should be seen, my dear; they would spy us out of the town.
The loud black nights for us, and the storm rushing over the down,
When I cannot see my own hand, but am led by the creak of the chain,
And grovel and grope for my son till I find myself drenched with the rain.

Anything fallen again? nay – what was there left to fall?
I have taken them home, I have number'd the bones, I have hidden them all.
What am I saying? and what are *you*? do you come as a spy?
Falls? what falls? who knows? As the tree falls so must it lie.
Who let her in? how long has she been? you – what have you heard?
Why did you sit so quiet? you never have spoken a word.
O – to pray with me – yes – a lady – none of their spies –
But the night has crept into my heart, and begun to darken my eyes.

Ah – you, that have lived so soft, what should *you* know of the night,
The blast and the burning shame and the bitter frost and the fright?
I have done it, while you were asleep – you were only made for the day.
I have gather'd my baby together – and now you may go your way.

Nay – for it's kind of you, Madam, to sit by an old dying wife.
But say nothing hard of my boy, I have only an hour of life.
I kiss'd my boy in the prison, before he went out to die.
'They dared me to do it,' he said, and he never has told me a lie.
I whipt him for robbing an orchard once when he was but a child –
'The farmer dared me to do it,' he said: he was always so wild –
And idle – and couldn't be idle – my Willy – he never could rest.
The King should have made him a soldier, he would have been one of his best.

But he lived with a lot of wild mates, and they never would let him be good;
They swore that he dare not rob the mail, and he swore that he would;
And he took no life, but he took one purse, and when all was done
He flung it among his fellows – I'll none of it, said my son.

I came into court to the Judge and the lawyers. I told them my tale,
God's own truth – but they kill'd him, they kill'd him for robbing the mail.
They hang'd him in chains for a show – we had always borne a good name –
To be hang'd for a thief – and then put away – isn't that enough shame?

Dust to dust – low down – let us hide! but they set him so high
That all the ships of the world could stare at him, passing by.
God 'ill pardon the hell-black raven and horrible fowls of the air,
But not the black heart of the lawyer who kill'd him and hang'd him there.

And the jailer forced me away. I had bid him my last goodbye;
They had fasten'd the door of his cell. 'O mother!' I heard him cry.
I couldn't get back tho' I tried, he had something further to say,
And now I never shall know it. The jailer forced me away.

Then since I couldn't but hear that cry of my boy that was dead,
They seized me and shut me up: they fasten'd me down on my bed.
'Mother, O mother!' – he call'd in the dark to me year after year –
They beat me for that, they beat me – you know that I couldn't but hear;
And then at the last they found I had grown so stupid and still
They let me abroad again – but the creatures had worked their will.

Flesh of my flesh was gone, but bone of my bone was left –
I stole them all from the lawyers – and you, will you call it a theft? –
My baby, the bones that had suck'd me, the bones that had laughed and had
  cried –
Theirs? O no! they are mine – not theirs – they had moved in my side.
Do you think I was scared by the bones? I kiss'd 'em, I buried 'em all –
I can't dig deep, I am old – in the night by the churchyard wall.
My Will 'ill rise up whole when the trumpet of judgment 'ill sound,
But I charge you never to say that I laid him in holy ground.

They would scratch him up – they would hang him again on the cursed tree.
Sin? O yes – we are sinners, I know – let all that be,
And read me a Bible verse of the Lord's good will toward men –
'Full of compassion and mercy, the Lord' – let me hear it again;
'Full of compassion and mercy – long suffering.' Yes, O yes!
For the lawyer is born but to murder – the Saviour lives but to bless.
He'll never put on the black cap except for the worst of the worst,
And the first may be last – I have heard it in church – and the last may be first.
Suffering – O long-suffering – yes, as the Lord must know,
Year after year in the mist and the wind and the shower and the snow.

Heard, have you? what? they have told you he never repented his sin.
How do they know it? are *they* his mother? are *you* of his kin?
Heard! have you ever heard, when the storm on the downs began,
The wind that 'ill wail like a child and the sea that 'ill moan like a man?

Election, Election and Reprobation – it's all very well.
But I go to-night to my boy, and I shall not find him in Hell.
For I cared so much for my boy that the Lord has look'd into my care,
And he means me I'm sure to be happy with Willy, I know not where.

And if *he* be lost – but to save *my* soul, that is all your desire:
Do you think that I care for *my* soul if my boy be gone to the fire?
I have been with God in the dark – go, go, you may leave me alone –
You never have borne a child – you are just as hard as a stone.

Madam, I beg your pardon! I think that you mean to be kind,
But I cannot hear what you say for my Willy's voice in the wind –
The snow and the sky so bright – he used but to call in the dark,
And he calls to me now from the church and not from the gibbet – for hark!
Nay – you can hear it yourself – it is coming – shaking the walls –
Willy – the moon's in a cloud – Good night. I am going. He calls.

EDGAR ALLAN POE

Eldorado

Gaily bedight,
A gallant knight,
In sunshine and in shadow,
Had journeyed long,
Singing a song,
In search of Eldorado.

But he grew old –
This knight so bold –
And o'er his heart a shadow
Fell, as he found
No spot of ground
That looked like Eldorado.

And, as his strength
Failed him at length,
He met a pilgrim shadow –
'Shadow,' said he,
'Where can it be –
This land of Eldorado?'

'Over the Mountains
Of the Moon,
Down the Valley of the Shadow,
Ride, boldly ride,'
The shade replied,
'If you seek for Eldorado!'

RALPH WALDO EMERSON

Letters

Every day brings a ship,
Every ship brings a word;
Well for those who have no fear,
Looking seaward, well assured
That the word the vessel brings
Is the word they wish to hear.

Days

Daughters of Time, the hypocritic Days,
Muffled and dumb like barefoot dervishes,
And marching single in an endless file,
Bring diadems and faggots in their hands.
To each they offer gifts after his will,
Bread, kingdoms, stars, and sky that holds them all.
I, in my pleached garden, watched the pomp,
Forgot my morning wishes, hastily
Took a few herbs and apples, and the Day
Turned and departed silent. I, too late,
Under her solemn fillet saw the scorn.

JULIA WARD HOWE

Battle Hymn of the Republic

Mine eyes have seen the glory of the coming of the Lord;
He is trampling out the vintage where the grapes of wrath are stored;
He hath loosed the fatal lightning of his terrible swift sword:
His Truth is marching on.

I have seen him in the watch-fires of a hundred circling camps;
They have builded him an altar in the evening dews and damps;
I have read his righteous sentence by the dim and flaring lamps:
His Day is marching on.

I have read a fiery gospel, writ in burnished rows of steel:
'As you deal with my contemners, so with you my grace shall deal;'
Let the Hero born of woman crush the serpent with his heel,
Since God is marching on.

He has sounded forth the trumpet that shall never call retreat;
He is sifting out the hearts of men before his judgment-seat;
O be swift, my soul, to answer him; be jubilant, my feet!
Our God is marching on.

In the beauty of the lilies Christ was born across the sea,
With a glory in his bosom that transfigures you and me;
As he died to make men holy, let us die to make men free,
While God is marching on.

He is coming like the glory of the morning on the wave;
He is wisdom to the mighty, he is succour to the brave;
So the world shall be his footstool, and the soul of time his slave:
Our God is marching on.

EDWARD FITZGERALD

Rubáiyát of Omar Khayyám

Awake! for Morning in the Bowl of Night
Has flung the Stone that puts the Stars to Flight:
  And Lo! the Hunter of the East has caught
The Sultán's Turret in a Noose of Light.

Dreaming when Dawn's Left Hand was in the Sky
I heard a Voice within the Tavern cry,
  'Awake, my Little ones, and fill the Cup
Before Life's Liquor in its Cup be dry.'

And, as the Cock crew, those who stood before
The Tavern shouted – 'Open then the Door!
  'You know how little while we have to stay,
'And, once departed, may return no more.'

Now the New Year reviving old Desires,
The thoughtful Soul to Solitude retires,
  Where the WHITE HAND OF MOSES on the Bough
Puts out, and Jesus from the Ground suspires.

Irám indeed is gone with all its Rose,
And Jamshýd's Sev'n-ring'd Cup where no one knows;
  But still the Vine her ancient Ruby yields,
And still a Garden by the Water blows.

And David's Lips are lock't; but in divine
High piping Péhlevi, with 'Wine! Wine! Wine!
  '*Red* Wine!' – the Nightingale cries to the Rose
That yellow Cheek of her's to'incarnadine.

Come, fill the Cup, and in the Fire of Spring
The Winter Garment of Repentance fling:
  The Bird of Time has but a little way
To fly – and Lo! the Bird is on the Wing.

And look – a thousand Blossoms with the Day
Woke – and a thousand scatter'd into Clay;
  And this first Summer Month that brings the Rose
Shall take Jamshýd and Kaikobád away.

But come with old Khayyám, and leave the Lot
Of Kaikobád and Kaikhosrú forgot:
  Let Rustum lay about him as he will,
Or Hátim Tai cry Supper – heed them not.

With me along some Strip of Herbage strown
That just divides the desert from the sown,

Where name of Slave and Sultán scarce is known,
And pity Sultán Máhmúd on his Throne.

Here with a Loaf of Bread beneath the Bough,
A Flask of Wine, a Book of Verse – and Thou
Beside me singing in the Wilderness –
And Wilderness is Paradise enow.

'How sweet is mortal Sovranty!' – think some:
Others – 'How blest the Paradise to come!'
Ah, take the Cash in hand and waive the Rest;
Oh, the brave Music of a *distant* Drum!

Look to the Rose that blows about us – 'Lo,
'Laughing,' she says, 'into the World I blow:
'At once the silken Tassel of my purse
'Tear, and its Treasure on the Garden throw.'

The Worldly Hope men set their Hearts upon
Turns ashes – or it prospers; and anon,
Like Snow upon the Desert's dusty Face
Lighting a little Hour or two – is gone.

And those who husbanded the Golden Grain,
And those who flung it to the Winds like Rain,
Alike to no such aureate Earth are turn'd
As, buried once, Men want dug up again.

Think, in this batter'd Caravanserai
Whose Doorways are alternate Night and Day,
How Sultán after Sultán with his Pomp
Abode his Hour or two, and went his way.

They say the Lion and the Lizard keep
The Courts where Jamshýd gloried and drank deep:
And Bahrám, that great Hunter – the Wild Ass
Stamps o'er his Head, and he lies fast asleep.

I sometimes think that never blows so red
The Rose as where some buried Cæsar bled;
That every Hyacinth the Garden wears
Dropt in its Lap from some once lovely Head.

And this delightful Herb whose tender Green
Fledges the River's Lip on which we lean –
Ah, lean upon it lightly! for who knows
From what once lovely Lip it springs unseen!

Ah, my Belovéd, fill the Cup that clears
TO-DAY of past Regrets and future Fears –
To-morrow? – Why, To-morrow I may be
Myself with Yesterday's Sev'n Thousand Years.

Lo! some we loved, the loveliest and best
That Time and Fate of all their Vintage prest,
  Have drunk their Cup a Round or two before,
And one by one crept silently to Rest.

And we, that now make merry in the Room
They left, and Summer dresses in new Bloom,
  Ourselves must we beneath the Couch of Earth
Descend, ourselves to make a Couch – for whom?

Ah, make the most of what we yet may spend,
Before we too into the Dust descend;
  Dust into Dust, and under Dust, to lie,
Sans Wine, sans Song, sans Singer, and – sans End!

Alike for those who for TO-DAY prepare,
And those that after a TO-MORROW stare,
  A Muezzin from the Tower of Darkness cries
'Fools! your Reward is neither Here nor There!'

Why, all the Saints and Sages who discuss'd
Of the Two Worlds so learnedly, are thrust
  Like foolish Prophets forth; their Words to Scorn
Are scatter'd, and their Mouths are stopt with Dust.

Oh, come with old Khayyám, and leave the Wise
To talk; one thing is certain, that Life flies;
  One thing is certain, and the Rest is Lies;
The Flower that once has blown for ever dies.

Myself when young did eagerly frequent
Doctor and Saint, and heard great Argument
  About it and about: but evermore
Came out by the same Door as in I went.

With them the Seed of Wisdom did I sow,
And with my own hand labour'd it to grow:
  And this was all the Harvest that I reap'd –
'I came like Water, and like Wind I go.'

Into this Universe, and *why* not knowing,
Nor *whence*, like Water willy-nilly flowing:
  And out of it, as Wind along the Waste,
I know not *whither*, willy-nilly blowing.

What, without asking, hither hurried *whence?*
And, without asking, *whither* hurried hence!
  Another and another Cup to drown
The Memory of this Impertinence!

Up from Earth's Centre through the Seventh Gate
I rose, and on the Throne of Saturn sate,

And many Knots unravel'd by the Road;
But not the Knot of Human Death and Fate.

There was a Door to which I found no Key:
There was a Veil past which I could not see:
Some little Talk awhile of ME and THEE
There seemed – and then no more of THEE and ME.

Then to the rolling Heav'n itself I cried,
Asking, 'What Lamp had Destiny to guide
'Her little Children stumbling in the Dark?'
And – 'A blind Understanding!' Heav'n replied.

Then to this earthen Bowl did I adjourn
My Lip the secret Well of Life to learn:
And Lip to Lip it murmur'd – 'While you live
'Drink! – for once dead you never shall return.'

I think the Vessel, that with fugitive
Articulation answer'd, once did live,
And merry-make; and the cold Lip I kiss'd
How many Kisses might it take – and give!

For in the Market-place, one Dusk of Day,
I watch'd the Potter thumping his wet Clay:
And with its all obliterated Tongue
It murmur'd – 'Gently, Brother, gently, pray!'

Ah, fill the Cup: – what boots it to repeat
How Time is slipping underneath our Feet:
Unborn TO-MORROW, and dead YESTERDAY,
Why fret about them if TO-DAY be sweet!

One Moment in Annihilation's Waste,
One Moment, of the Well of Life to taste –
The Stars are setting and the Caravan
Starts for the Dawn of Nothing – Oh, make haste!

How long, how long, in infinite Pursuit
Of This and That endeavour and dispute?
Better be merry with the fruitful Grape
Than sadden after none, or bitter, Fruit.

You know, my Friends, how long since in my House
For a new Marriage I did make Carouse:
Divorced old barren Reason from my Bed,
And took the Daughter of the Vine to Spouse.

For 'Is' and 'IS-NOT' though *with* Rule and Line,
And 'UP-AND-DOWN' *without*, I could define,
I yet in all I only cared to know,
Was never deep in anything but – Wine.

And lately, by the Tavern Door agape,
Came stealing through the Dusk an Angel Shape
  Bearing a Vessel on his Shoulder; and
He bid me taste of it, and 'twas – the Grape!

The Grape that can with Logic absolute
The Two-and-Seventy jarring Sects confute:
  The subtle Alchemist that in a Trice
Life's leaden Metal into Gold transmute.

The mighty Mahmúd, the victorious Lord,
That all the misbelieving and black Horde
  Of Fears and Sorrows that infest the Soul
Scatters and slays with his enchanted Sword.

But leave the Wise to wrangle, and with me
The Quarrel of the Universe let be:
  And, in some corner of the Hubbub coucht,
Make Game of that which make as much of Thee.

For in and out, above, about, below,
'Tis nothing but a Magic Shadow-show,
  Play'd in a Box whose Candle is the Sun,
Round which we Phantom Figures come and go.

And if the Wine you drink, the Lip you press,
End in the Nothing all Things end in – Yes –
  Then fancy while Thou art, Thou art but what
Thou shalt be – Nothing – Thou shalt not be less.

While the Rose blows along the River Brink,
With old Khayyám the Ruby Vintage drink:
  And when the Angel with his darker Draught
Draws up to Thee – take that, and do not shrink.

'Tis all a Chequer-board of Nights and Days
Where Destiny with Men for Pieces plays:
  Hither and thither moves, and mates, and slays,
And one by one back in the Closet lays.

The Ball no Question makes of Ayes and Noes,
But Right or Left as strikes the Player goes;
  And He that toss'd Thee down into the Field,
He knows about it all – HE knows – HE knows!

The Moving Finger writes; and, having writ,
Moves on: nor all thy Piety nor Wit
  Shall lure it back to cancel half a Line,
Nor all thy Tears wash out a Word of it.

And that inverted Bowl we call The Sky,
Whereunder crawling coop't we live and die,

Lift not thy hands to *It* for help – for It
Rolls impotently on as Thou or I.

With Earth's first Clay They did the Last Man's knead,
And then of the Last Harvest sow'd the Seed:
Yea, the first Morning of Creation wrote
What the Last Dawn of Reckoning shall read.

I tell Thee this – When, starting from the Goal,
Over the shoulders of the flaming Foal
Of Heav'n Parwín and Mushtara they flung,
In my predestin'd Plot of Dust and Soul

The Vine had struck a Fibre; which about
If clings my Being – let the Súfi flout;
Of my Base Metal may be filed a Key,
That shall unlock the Door he howls without.

And this I know: whether the one True Light,
Kindle to Love, or Wrath consume me quite,
One Glimpse of It within the Tavern caught
Better than in the Temple lost outright.

Oh Thou, who didst with Pitfall and with Gin
Beset the Road I was to wander in,
Thou wilt not with Predestination round
Enmesh me, and impute my Fall to Sin?

Oh, Thou, who Man of baser Earth didst make,
And who with Eden didst devise the Snake;
For all the Sin wherewith the face of Man
Is blacken'd, Man's Forgiveness give – and take!

* * *

KÚZA-NÁMA

Listen again. One Evening at the Close
Of Ramazán, ere the better Moon arose,
In that old Potter's Shop I stood alone
With the clay Population round in Rows.

And, strange to tell, among that Earthen Lot
Some could articulate, while others not:
And suddenly one more impatient cried –
'Who *is* the Potter, pray, and who the Pot?'

Then said another – 'Surely not in vain
'My Substance from the common Earth was ta'en,
'That He who subtly wrought me into Shape
'Should stamp me back to common Earth again.'

Another said – 'Why, ne'er a peevish Boy,
'Would break the Bowl from which he drank in Joy;

'Shall He that *made* the Vessel in pure Love
'And Fansy, in an after Rage destroy!'

None answer'd this; but after Silence spake
A Vessel of a more ungainly Make:
'They sneer at me for leaning all awry;
'What! did the Hand then of the Potter shake?'

Said one – 'Folks of a surly Tapster tell,
'And daub his Visage with the Smoke of Hell;
'They talk of some strict Testing of us – Pish!
'He's a Good Fellow, and 'twill all be well.'

Then said another with a long-drawn Sigh,
'My Clay with long oblivion is gone dry:
'But, fill me with the old familiar Juice,
'Methinks I might recover by-and-bye!'

So while the Vessels one by one were speaking,
One spied the little Crescent all were seeking:
And then they jogg'd each other, 'Brother! Brother!
'Hark to the Porter's Shoulder-knot a-creaking!'

* * *

Ah, with the Grape my fading Life provide,
And wash my Body whence the Life has died,
And in a Windingsheet of Vine-leaf wrapt,
So bury me by some sweet Garden-side.

That ev'n my buried Ashes such a Snare
Of Perfume shall fling up into the Air,
As not a True Believer passing by
But shall be overtaken unaware.

Indeed the Idols I have loved so long
Have done my Credit in Men's Eye much wrong:
Have drown'd my Honour in a shallow Cup,
And sold my Reputation for a Song.

Indeed, indeed, Repentance oft before
I swore – but was I sober when I swore?
And then and then came Spring, and Rose-in-hand
My thread-bare Penitence apieces tore.

And much as Wine has play'd the Infidel,
And robb'd me of my Robe of Honour – well,
I often wonder what the Vintners buy
One half so precious as the Goods they sell.

Alas, that Spring should vanish with the Rose!
That Youth's sweet-scented Manuscript should close!

The Nightingale that in the Branches sang,
Ah, whence, and wither flown again, who knows!

Ah Love! could thou and I with Fate conspire
To grasp this sorry Scheme of Things entire,
Would not we shatter it to bits – and then
Re-mould it nearer to the Heart's Desire!

Ah, Moon of my Delight who know'st no wane,
The Moon of Heav'n is rising once again:
How oft hereafter rising shall she look
Through this same Garden after me – in vain!

And when Thyself with shining Foot shall pass
Among the Guests Star-scatter'd on the Grass,
And in thy joyous Errand reach the Spot
Where I made one – turn down an empty Glass!

TAMÁM SHUD

WALT WHITMAN

'Are you the new person drawn toward me?'

Are you the new person drawn toward me?
To begin with take warning, I am surely far different from what you suppose;
Do you suppose you will find in me your ideal?
Do you think it is so easy to have me become your lover?
Do you think the friendship of me would be unalloy'd satisfaction?
Do you think I am trusty and faithful?
Do you see no further than this façade, this smooth and tolerant manner of me?
Do you suppose yourself advancing on real ground toward a real heroic man?
Have you no thought O dreamer that it may be all maya, illusion?

'Sometimes with one I love'

Sometimes with one I love I fill myself with rage for fear I effuse unreturn'd love,
But now I think there is no unreturn'd love, the pay is certain one way or another,
(I loved a certain person ardently and my love was not return'd,
Yet out of that I have written these songs).

'A noiseless patient spider'

A noiseless patient spider,
I mark'd where on a little promontory it stood isolated,
Mark'd how to explore the vacant vast surrounding,
It launch'd forth filament, filament, filament, out of itself,
Ever unreeling them, ever tirelessly speeding them.

And you O my soul where you stand
Surrounded, detached, in measureless oceans of space,
Ceaselessly musing, venturing, throwing, seeking the spheres to connect them,
Till the bridge you will need be form'd, till the ductile anchor hold,
Till the gossamer thread you fling catch somewhere, O my soul.

'Ah poverties, wincings, and sulky retreats'

Ah poverties, wincings, and sulky retreats,
Ah you foes that in conflict have overcome me,
(For what is my life or any man's life but a conflict with foes, the old, the incessant war?)
You degradations, you tussle with passions and appetites,
You smarts from dissatisfied friendships, (ah wounds the sharpest of all!)
You toil of painful and choked articulations, you meannesses,
You shallow tongue-talks at tables, (my tongue the shallowest of any;)
You broken resolutions, you racking angers, you smother'd ennuis!
Ah think not you finally triumph, my real self has yet to come forth,
It shall yet march forth o'ermastering, till all lies beneath me,
It shall yet stand up the soldier of ultimate victory.

EMILY DICKINSON

'They say that time assuages'

They say that time assuages.
Time never did assuage.
An actual suffering strengthens,
As sinews do, with age.

Time is a test of trouble
But not a remedy.
If such it prove, it prove too
There was no malady.

'It dropped so low in my regard'

It dropped so low in my regard
I heard it hit the ground
And go to pieces on the stones
At bottom of my mind;

Yet blamed the fate that fractured less
Than I reviled myself
For entertaining plated wares
Upon my silver shelf.

'I stepped from plank to plank'

I stepped from plank to plank,
A slow and cautious way;
The stars about my head I felt,
About my feet the sea.

I knew not but the next
Would be my final inch.
This gave me that precarious gait
Some call experience.

'Drowning is not so pitiful'

Drowning is not so pitiful
As the attempt to rise.
Three times, 'tis said, a sinking man
Comes up to face the skies,
And then declines forever
To the abhorred abode,
Where hope and he part company –
For he is grasped of God.
The Maker's cordial visage,
However good to see,
Is shunned, we must admit it,
Like an adversity.

HENRY WADSWORTH LONGFELLOW

from *The Song of Hiawatha*

By the shores of Gitche Gumee,
By the shining Big-Sea-Water,
Stood the wigwam of Nokomis,
Daughter of the Moon, Nokomis.
Dark behind it rose the forest,
Rose the black and gloomy pine-trees,
Rose the firs with cones upon them;
Bright before it beat the water,
Beat the shining Big-Sea-Water.
  Thus the wrinkled, old Nokomis
Nursed the little Hiawatha,
Rocked him in his linden cradle,
Bedded soft in moss and rushes,
Safely bound with reindeer sinews;
Stilled his fretful wail by saying,
'Hush! the naked bear will get thee!'
Lulled him into slumber, singing:
'Ewa-yea! my little owlet!
Who is this, that lights the wigwam?
With his great eyes lights the wigwam?
Ewa-yea! my little owlet!'
  Many things Nokomis taught him
Of the stars that shine in heaven;
Showed him Ishkoodah, the comet,
Ishkoodah, with fiery tresses;
Showed the Death-Dance of the spirits,
Warriors with their plumes and war-clubs,
Flaring far away to northward
In the frosty nights of Winter;
Showed the broad, white road in heaven,
Pathway of the ghosts, the shadows,
Running straight across the heavens,
Crowded with the ghosts, the shadows.
  At the door on Summer evenings
Sat the little Hiawatha;
Heard the whispering of the pine-trees,
Heard the lapping of the water,
Sounds of music, words of wonder;
'Minne-wawa!' said the pine-trees,
'Mudway-aushka!' said the water.
  Saw the fire-fly, Wah-wah-taysee,
Flitting through the dusk of evening,
With the twinkle of its candle
Lighting up the brakes and bushes,

And he sang the song of children,
Sang the song Nokomis taught him:
'Wah-wah-taysee, little fire-fly,
Little, flitting, white-fire insect,
Little dancing, white-fire creature,
Light me with your little candle,
Ere upon my bed I lay me,
Ere in sleep I close my eyelids!'
   Saw the moon rise from the water,
Rippling, rounding, from the water,
Saw the flecks and shadows on it,
Whispered, 'What is that, Nokomis?'
And the good Nokomis answered:
'Once a warrior, very angry,
Seized his grandmother, and threw her
Up into the sky at midnight;
Right against the moon he threw her;
'Tis her body that you see there.'
   Saw the rainbow in the heaven,
In the eastern sky the rainbow,
Whispered, 'What is that, Nokomis?'
And the good Nokomis answered:
''Tis the heaven of flowers you see there;
All the wild-flowers of the forest,
All the lilies of the prairie,
When on earth they fade and perish,
Blossom in that heaven above us.'
   When he heard the owls at midnight,
Hooting, laughing in the forest,
'What is that?' he cried in terror,
'What is that?' he said, 'Nokomis?'
And the good Nokomis answered:
'That is but the owl and owlet,
Talking in their native language,
Talking, scolding at each other.'
   Then the little Hiawatha
Learned of every bird its language,
Learned their names and all their secrets,
How they built their nests in Summer,
Where they hid themselves in Winter,
Talked with them whene'er he met them,
Called them 'Hiawatha's Chickens.'
   Of all the beasts he learned the language,
Learned their names and all their secrets,
How the beavers built their lodges,
Where the squirrels hid their acorns,
How the reindeer ran so swiftly,
Why the rabbit was so timid,
Talked with them whene'er he met them,

Called them 'Hiawatha's Brothers.'
Then Iagoo, the great boaster,
He the marvellous story-teller,
He the traveller and the talker,
He the friend of old Nokomis,
Made a bow for Hiawatha;
From a branch of ash he made it,
From an oak-bough made the arrows,
Tipped with flint, and winged with feathers,
And the cord he made of deer-skin.
Then he said to Hiawatha –
'Go, my son, into the forest,
Where the red deer herd together,
Kill for us a famous roebuck,
Kill for us a deer with antlers!'
Forth into the forest straightway
All alone walked Hiawatha
Proudly, with his bow and arrows;
And the birds sang round him, o'er him,
'Do not shoot us, Hiawatha!'
Sang the robin, the Opechee,
Sang the blue-bird, the Owaissa,
'Do not shoot us, Hiawatha!'
Up the oak-tree, close beside him,
Sprang the squirrel, Adjidaumo,
In and out among the branches,
Coughed and chattered from the oak-tree,
Laughed, and said between his laughing,
'Do not shoot me, Hiawatha!'
And the rabbit from his pathway
Leaped aside, and at a distance
Sat erect upon his haunches,
Half in fear and half in frolic,
Saying to the little hunter,
'Do not shoot me, Hiawatha!'
But he heeded not, nor heard them,
For his thoughts were with the red-deer;
On their tracks his eyes were fastened,
Leading downward to the river,
To the ford across the river,
And as one in slumber walked he.
Hidden in the alder-bushes,
There he waited till the deer came,
Till he saw two antlers lifted,
Saw two eyes look from the thicket,
Saw two nostrils point to windward,
And a deer came down the pathway,
Flecked with leafy light and shadow.
And his heart within him fluttered,

Trembled like the leaves above him,
Like the birch-leaf palpitated,
As the deer came down the pathway.
Then, upon one knee uprising,
Hiawatha aimed an arrow;
Scarce a twig moved with his motion
Scarce a leaf was stirred or rustled,
But the wary roebuck started,
Stamped with all his hoofs together,
Listened with one foot uplifted,
Leaped as if to meet the arrow;
Ah! the singing, fatal arrow,
Like a wasp it buzzed and stung him.
Dead he lay there in the forest,
By the ford across the river;
Beat his timid heart no longer,
But the heart of Hiawatha
Throbbed and shouted and exulted,
As he bore the red deer homeward,
And Iagoo and Nokomis
Hailed his coming with applauses.
From the red deer's hide Nokomis
Made a cloak for Hiawatha,
From the red deer's flesh Nokomis
Made a banquet in his honour.
All the village came and feasted,
All the guests praised Hiawatha,
Called him Strong-Heart, Soan-getaha!
Called him Loon-heart, Mahn-go-tay-see!

Out of childhood into manhood
Now had grown my Hiawatha,
Skilled in all the craft of hunters,
Learned in all the lore of old men,
In all youthful sports and pastimes,
In all manly arts and labours.
Swift of foot was Hiawatha;
He could shoot an arrow from him,
And run forward with such fleetness,
That the arrow fell behind him!
Strong of arm was Hiawatha;
He could shoot ten arrows upward,
Shoot them with such strength and swiftness,
That the tenth had left the bow-string
Ere the first to earth had fallen!
He had mittens, Minjekahwun,
Magic mittens made of deer-skin;

When upon his hands he wore them,
He could smite the rocks asunder,
He could grind them into powder.
He had moccasins enchanted,
Magic moccasins of deer-skin;
When he bound them round his ankles,
When upon his feet he tied them,
At each stride a mile he measured!
  Much he questioned old Nokomis
Of his father Mudjekeewis;
Learned from her the fatal secret
Of the beauty of his mother,
Of the falsehood of his father;
And his heart was hot within him,
Like a living coal his heart was.
  Then he said to old Nokomis,
'I will go to Mudjekeewis,
See how fares it with my father,
At the doorways of the West-Wind,
At the portals of the Sunset!'
  From his lodge went Hiawatha,
Dressed for travel, armed for hunting;
Dressed in deer-skin shirt and leggings,
Richly wrought with quills and wampum;
On his head his eagle-feathers,
Round his waist his belt of wampum,
In his hand his bow of ash-wood,
Strung with sinews of the reindeer;
In his quiver oaken arrows,
Tipped with jasper, winged with feathers;
With his mittens, Minjekahwun,
With his moccasins enchanted.
  Warning, said the old Nokomis,
'Go not forth, O Hiawatha!
To the kingdom of the West-Wind,
To the realms of Mudjekeewis,
Lest he harm you with his magic,
Lest he kill you with his cunning!'
  But the fearless Hiawatha
Heeded not her woman's warning;
Forth he strode into the forest,
At each stride a mile he measured;
Lurid seemed the sky above him,
Lurid seemed the earth beneath him,
Hot and close the air around him,
Filled with smoke and fiery vapours,
As of burning woods and prairies,
For his heart was hot within him,
Like a living coal his heart was.

So he journeyed westward, westward,
Left the fleetest deer behind him,
Left the antelope and bison;
Crossed the rushing Esconaba,
Crossed the mighty Mississippi,
Passed the Mountains of the Prairie,
Passed the land of Crows and Foxes,
Passed the dwellings of the Blackfeet,
Came unto the Rocky Mountains,
To the kingdom of the West-Wind,
Where upon the gusty summits
Sat the ancient Mudjekeewis,
Ruler of the winds of heaven.
Filled with awe was Hiawatha
At the aspect of his father.
On the air about him wildly
Tossed and streamed his cloudy tresses,
Gleamed like drifting snow his tresses,
Glared the Ishkoodah, the comet,
Like the star with fiery tresses.
Filled with joy was Mudjekeewis
When he looked on Hiawatha,
Saw his youth rise up before him
In the face of Hiawatha,
Saw the beauty of Wenonah
From the grave rise up before him.
'Welcome!' said he, 'Hiawatha,
To the kingdom of the West-Wind!
Long have I been waiting for you!
Youth is lovely, age is lonely;
Youth is fiery, age is frosty;
You bring back the days departed,
You bring back my youth of passion,
And the beautiful Wenonah!'
Many days they talked together,
Questioned, listened, waited, answered;
Much the mighty Mudjekeewis
Boasted of his ancient prowess,
Of his perilous adventures,
His indomitable courage,
His invulnerable body.
Patiently sat Hiawatha,
Listening to his father's boasting;
With a smile he sat and listened,
Uttered neither threat nor menace,
Neither word nor look betrayed him,
But his heart was hot within him,
Like a living coal his heart was.
Then he said, 'O Mudjekeewis,

Is there nothing that can harm you?
Nothing that you are afraid of?'
And the mighty Mudjekeewis,
Grand and gracious in his boasting,
Answered, saying, 'There is nothing,
Nothing but the black rock yonder,
Nothing but the fatal Wawbeek!'

And he looked at Hiawatha
With a wise look and benignant,
With a countenance paternal,
Looked with pride upon the beauty
Of his tall and graceful figure,
Saying, 'O my Hiawatha!
Is there anything can harm you?
Anything you are afraid of?'

But the wary Hiawatha
Paused awhile, as if uncertain,
Held his peace, as if resolving,
And then answered, 'There is nothing,
Nothing but the bulrush yonder,
Nothing but the great Apukwa!'

And as Mudjekeewis, rising,
Stretched his hand to pluck the bulrush,
Hiawatha cried in terror,
Cried in well-dissembled terror,
'Kago! kago! do not touch it!'
'Ah, kaween,' said Mudjekeewis,
'No, indeed, I will not touch it!'

Then they talked of other matters;
First of Hiawatha's brothers,
First of Wabun, of the East-Wind,
Of the South-Wind, Shawondasee,
Of the North, Kabibonokka;
Then of Hiawatha's mother,
Of the beautiful Wenonah,
Of her birth upon the meadow,
Of her death, as old Nokomis
Had remembered and related.

And he cried, 'O Mudjekeewis,
It was you who killed Wenonah,
Took her young life and her beauty,
Broke the Lily of the Prairie,
Trampled it beneath your footsteps;
You confess it! you confess it!'
And the mighty Mudjekeewis
Tossed upon the wind his tresses,
Bowed his hoary head in anguish,
With a silent nod assented.

Then up started Hiawatha,

And with threatening look and gesture,
Laid his hand upon the black rock.
On the fatal Wawbeek laid it,
With his mittens, Minjekahwun,
Rent the jutting crag asunder,
Smote and crushed it into fragments,
Hurled them madly at his father,
The remorseful Mudjekeewis,
For his heart was hot within him,
Like a living coal his heart was.
  But the ruler of the West-Wind
Blew the fragments backward from him,
With the breathing of his nostrils,
With the tempest of his anger,
Blew them back at his assailant;
Seized the bulrush, the Apukwa,
Dragged it with its roots and fibres
From the margin of the meadow,
From its ooze, the giant bulrush;
Long and loud laughed Hiawatha!
  Then began the deadly conflict,
Hand to hand among the mountains;
From his eyrie screamed the eagle,
The Keneu, the great war-eagle;
Sat upon the crags around them,
Wheeling flapped his wings above them.
Like a tall tree in the tempest
Bent and lashed the giant bulrush;
And in masses huge and heavy
Crashing fell the fatal Wawbeek;
Till the earth shook with the tumult
And confusion of the battle,
And the air was full of shoutings,
And the thunder of the mountains,
Starting, answered, 'Baim-wawa!'
  Back retreated Mudjekeewis,
Rushing westward o'er the mountains,
Stumbling westward down the mountains,
Three whole days retreated fighting,
Still pursued by Hiawatha
To the doorways of the West-Wind,
To the portals of the Sunset,
To the earth's remotest border,
Where into the empty spaces
Sinks the sun, as a flamingo
Drops into her nest at nightfall,
In the melancholy marshes.
  'Hold!' at length cried Mudjekeewis,
'Hold, my son, my Hiawatha!

'Tis impossible to kill me,
For you cannot kill the immortal.
I have put you to this trial,
But to know and prove your courage;
Now receive the prize of valour!
'Go back to your home and people,
Live among them, toil among them,
Cleanse the earth from all that harms it,
Clear the fishing-grounds and rivers,
Slay all monsters and magicians,
All the Wendigoes, the giants,
All the serpents, the Kenabeeks,
As I slew the Mishe-Mokwa,
Slew the Great Bear of the mountains.
'And at last when Death draws near you,
When the awful eyes of Pauguk
Glare upon you in the darkness,
I will share my kingdom with you,
Ruler shall you be thenceforward
Of the Northwest-Wind, Keewaydin,
Of the home-wind, the Keewaydin.'
Thus was fought that famous battle
In the dreadful days of Shah-shah,
In the days long since departed,
In the kingdom of the West-Wind.
Still the hunter sees its traces
Scattered far o'er hill and valley;
Sees the giant bulrush growing
By the ponds and water-courses,
Sees the masses of the Wawbeek
Lying still in every valley.
Homeward now went Hiawatha;
Pleasant was the landscape round him,
Pleasant was the air above him,
For the bitterness of anger
Had departed wholly from him,
From his brain the thought of vengeance,
From his heart the burning fever.
Only once his pace he slackened,
Only once he paused or halted,
Paused to purchase heads of arrows
Of the ancient Arrow-maker,
In the land of the Dacotahs,
Where the Falls of Minnehaha
Flash and gleam among the oak-trees,
Laugh and leap into the valley.
There the ancient Arrow-maker
Made his arrow-heads of sandstone,
Arrow-heads of chalcedony,

Arrow-heads of flint and jasper,
Smoothed and sharpened at the edges,
Hard and polished, keen and costly.
  With him dwelt his dark-eyed daughter,
Wayward as the Minnehaha,
With her moods of shade and sunshine,
Eyes that smiled and frowned alternate,
Feet as rapid as the river,
Tresses flowing like the water,
And as musical a laughter;
And he named her from the river,
From the waterfall he named her,
Minnehaha, Laughing Water.
  Was it then for heads of arrows,
Arrow-heads of chalcedony,
Arrow-heads of flint and jasper,
That my Hiawatha halted,
In the land of the Dacotahs?
  Was it not to see the maiden,
See the face of Laughing Water
Peeping from behind the curtain,
Hear the rustling of her garments
From behind the waving curtain,
As one sees the Minnehaha
Gleaming, glancing through the branches,
As one hears the Laughing Water
From behind its screen of branches?
  Who shall say what thoughts and visions
Fill the fiery brains of young men?
Who shall say what dreams of beauty
Filled the heart of Hiawatha?
All he told to old Nokomis,
When he reached the lodge at sunset,
Was the meeting with his father,
Was his fight with Mudjekeewis;
Not a word he said of arrows,
Not a word of Laughing Water!

JOHN ELLERTON

The Day Thou Gavest

The day thou gavest, Lord, is ended,
  The darkness falls at thy behest;
To thee our morning hymns ascended,
  Thy praise shall sanctify our rest.

We thank thee that thy Church unsleeping,
While earth rolls onward into light,
Through all the world her watch is keeping,
And rests not now by day or night.

As o'er each continent and island
The dawn leads on another day,
The voice of prayer is never silent,
Nor dies the strain of praise away.

The sun that bids us rest is waking
Our brethren 'neath the western sky,
And hour by hour fresh lips are making
Thy wondrous doings heard on high.

So be it, Lord; thy throne shall never,
Like earth's proud empires, pass away;
Thy kingdom stands, and grows for ever,
Till all thy creatures own thy sway.

CARDINAL NEWMAN

Lead, Kindly Light

Lead, kindly Light, amid the encircling gloom,
Lead thou me on;
The night is dark, and I am far from home,
Lead thou me on.
Keep thou my feet; I do not ask to see
The distant scene; one step enough for me.

I was not ever thus, nor prayed that thou
Should'st lead me on;
I loved to choose and see my path; but now
Lead thou me on.
I loved the garish day, and, spite of fears,
Pride ruled by will: remember not past years.

So long thy power hath blest me, sure it still
Will lead me on
O'er moor and fen, o'er crag and torrent, till
The night is gone,
And with the morn those angel faces smile,
Which I have loved long since, and lost awhile.

WILLIAM WHITING

Eternal Father, Strong to Save

Eternal Father, strong to save,
Whose arm doth bind the restless wave,
Who bidd'st the mighty ocean deep
Its own appointed limits keep:
  O hear us when we cry to thee
  For those in peril on the sea.

O Saviour, whose almighty word
The winds and waves submissive heard,
Who walkedst on the foaming deep,
And calm amid its rage didst sleep:
  O hear us when we cry to thee
  For those in peril on the sea.

O sacred Spirit, who didst brood
Upon the chaos dark and rude,
Who bad'st its angry tumult cease,
And gavest light and life and peace:
  O hear us when we cry to thee
  For those in peril on the sea.

O Trinity of love and power,
Our brethren shield in danger's hour;
From rock and tempest, fire and foe,
Protect them wheresoe'er they go:
  And ever let there rise to thee
  Glad hymns of praise from land and sea.

ARTHUR HUGH CLOUGH

Duty

Duty – that's to say, complying,
  With whate'er's expected here;
On your unkown cousin's dying,
  Straight be ready with the tear;
Upon etiquette relying,
Unto usage nought denying,
Lend your waist to be embraced,
  Blush not even, never fear;
Claims of kith and kin connection,
  Claims of manners honour still,

Ready money of affection
    Pay, whoever drew the bill.
With the form conforming duly,
Senseless what it meaneth truly,
Go to church – the world require you,
    To balls – the world require you too,
And marry – papa and mamma desire you,
    And your sisters and schoolfellows do.
Duty – 'tis to take on trust.
What things are good, and right, and just;
    And whether indeed they be or be not,
    Try not, test not, feel not, see not:
    'Tis walk and dance, sit down and rise
    By leading, opening ne'er your eyes;
Stunt sturdy limbs that Nature gave,
And be drawn in a Bath chair along to the grave.
'Tis the stern and prompt suppressing,
    As an obvious deadly sin,
All the questing and the guessing
    Of the soul's own soul within:
'Tis the coward acquiescence
    In a destiny's behest,
To a shade by terror made,
Sacrificing, aye, the essence
    Of all that's truest, noblest, best:
'Tis the blind non-recognition
    Or of goodness, truth, or beauty,
Save by precept and submission;
    Moral blank, and moral void,
    Life at very birth destroyed.
Atrophy, exinanition!
Duty!
Yea, by duty's prime condition
    Pure nonentity of duty!

Say Not the Struggle Naught Availeth

Say not the struggle naught availeth,
    The labour and the wounds are vain,
The enemy faints not, nor faileth,
    And as things have been they remain.

If hopes were dupes, fears may be liars;
    It may be, in yon smoke concealed,
Your comrades chase e'en now the fliers,
    And, but for you, possess the field.

For while the tired waves, vainly breaking,
  Seem here no painful inch to gain,
Far back, through creeks and inlets making,
  Comes silent, flooding in, the main.

And not by eastern windows only,
  When daylight comes, comes in the light,
In front, the sun climbs slow, how slowly,
  But westward, look, the land is bright.

How Pleasant it is to have Money

As I sat at the café, I said to myself,
They may talk as they please about what they call pelf,
They may sneer as they like about eating and drinking,
But help it I cannot, I cannot help thinking,
  How pleasant it is to have money, heigh ho!
  How pleasant it is to have money.

I sit at my table *en grand seigneur*,
And when I have done, throw a crust to the poor;
Not only the pleasure, one's self, of good living,
But also the pleasure of now and then giving.
  So pleasant it is to have money, heigh ho!
  So pleasant it is to have money.

It was but last winter I came up to Town,
But already I'm getting a little renown;
I make new acquaintance where'er I appear;
I am not too shy, and have nothing to fear.
  So pleasant it is to have money, heigh ho!
  So pleasant it is to have money.

I drive through the streets, and I care not a damn;
The people they stare, and they ask who I am;
And if I should chance to run over a cad,
I can pay for the damage if ever so bad.
  So pleasant it is to have money, heigh ho!
  So pleasant it is to have money.

We stroll to our box and look down on the pit,
And if it weren't low should be tempted to spit;
We loll and we talk until people look up,
And when it's half over we go out and sup.
  So pleasant it is to have money, heigh ho!
  So pleasant it is to have money.

The best of the tables and best of the fare –
And as for the others, the devil may care;
It isn't our fault if they dare not afford
To sup like a prince and be drunk as a lord.
So pleasant it is to have money, heigh ho!
So pleasant it is to have money.

We sit at our tables and tipple champagne;
Ere one bottle goes, comes another again;
The waiters they skip and they scuttle about,
And the landlord attends us so civilly out.
So pleasant it is to have money, heigh ho!
So pleasant it is to have money.

It was but last winter I came up to Town,
But already I'm getting a little renown;
I get to good houses without much ado,
Am beginning to see the nobility too.
So pleasant it is to have money, heigh ho!
So pleasant it is to have money.

O dear! what a pity they ever should lose it!
For they are the gentry that know how to use it;
So grand and so graceful, such manners, such dinners,
But yet, after all, it is we are the winners.
So pleasant it is to have money, heigh ho!
So pleasant it is to have money.

Thus I sat at my table *en grand seigneur*,
And when I had done threw a crust to the poor;
Not only the pleasure, one's self, of good eating,
But also the pleasure of now and then treating.
So pleasant it is to have money, heigh ho!
So pleasant it is to have money.

They may talk as they please about what they call pelf,
And how one ought never to think of one's self,
And how pleasures of thought surpass eating and drinking –
My pleasure of thought is the pleasure of thinking
How pleasant it is to have money, heigh ho!
How pleasant it is to have money.

A gondola here, and a gondola there,
'Tis the pleasantest fashion of taking the air.
To right and to left; stop, turn, and go yonder,
And let us repeat, o'er the tide as we wander,
How pleasant it is to have money, heigh ho!
How pleasant it is to have money.

ROBERT F. MURRAY

The Wasted Day

Another day let slip! Its hours have run,
Its golden hours, with prodigal excess,
All run to waste. A day of life the less;
Of many wasted days, alas, but one!

Through my west window streams the setting sun.
I kneel within my chamber, and confess
My sin and sorrow, filled with vain distress,
In place of honest joy for work well done.

At noon I passed some labourers in a field.
The sweat ran down upon each sunburnt face,
Which shone like copper in the ardent glow.
And one looked up, with envy unconcealed,
Beholding my cool cheeks and listless pace,
Yet he was happier, though he did not know.

WATHEN MARK WILKS CALL

Summer Days

In summer, when the days were long,
We walked, two friends, in field and wood,
Our heart was light, our step was strong,
And life lay round us, fair as good,
In summer, when the days were long.

We strayed from morn till evening came,
We gathered flowers, and wove us crowns,
We walked mid poppies red as flame,
Or sat upon the yellow downs,
And always wished our life the same.

In summer, when the days were long,
We leapt the hedgerow, crossed the brook;
And still her voice flowed forth in song,
Or else she read some graceful book,
In summer, when the days were long.

And then we sat beneath the trees,
With shadows lessening in the noon;
And in the sunlight and the breeze,
We revelled, many a glorious June,
While larks were singing o'er the leas.

In summer, when the days were long,
We plucked wild strawberries, ripe and red,
Or feasted, with no grace but song,
On golden nectar, snow-white bread,
In summer, when the days were long.

We loved, and yet we knew it not,
For loving seemed like breathing then,
We found a heaven in every spot,
Saw angels, too, in all good men,
And dreamt of gods in grove and grot.

In summer, when the days are long,
Alone I wander, muse alone;
I see her not, but that old song,
Under the fragrant wind is blown,
In summer, when the days are long.

Alone I wander in the wood,
But one fair spirit hears my sighs;
And half I see the crimson hood,
The radiant hair, the calm glad eyes,
That charmed me in life's summer mood.

In summer, when the days are long,
I love her as I loved of old;
My heart is light, my step is strong,
For love brings back those hours of gold,
In summer, when the days are long.

ALFRED AUSTIN

Is Life Worth Living?

Is life worth living? Yes, so long
  As Spring revives the year,
And hails us with the cuckoo's song,
  To show that she is here;
So long as May of April takes
  In smiles and tears farewell,
And windflowers dapple all the brakes,
  And primroses the dell;
While children in the woodlands yet
  Adorn their little laps
With ladysmock and violet,
  And daisy-chain their caps;
While over orchard daffodils
  Cloud-shadows float and fleet,

And ousel pipes and laverock trills,
  And young lambs buck and bleat;
So long as that which bursts the bud
  And swells and tunes the rill
Makes springtime in the maiden's blood,
  Life is worth living still.

Life not worth living! Come with me,
  Now that, through vanishing veil,
Shimmers the dew on lawn and lea,
  And milk foams in the pail;
Now that June's sweltering sunlight bathes
  With sweat the striplings lithe,
As fall the long straight scented swathes
  Over the crescent scythe;
Now that the throstle never stops
  His self-sufficing strain,
And woodbine-trails festoon the copse,
  And eglantine the lane;
Now rustic labour seems as sweet
  As leisure, and blithe herds
Wend homeward with unweary feet,
  Carolling like the birds;
Now all, except the lover's vow,
  And nightingale, is still;
Here, in the twilight hour, allow,
  Life is worth living still.

When Summer, lingering half-forlorn,
  On Autumn loves to lean,
And fields of slowly yellowing corn
  Are girt by woods still green;
When hazel-nuts wax brown and plump,
  And apples rosy-red,
And the owlet hoots from hollow stump,
  And the dormouse makes its bed;
When crammed are all the granary floors
  And the Hunter's moon is bright,
And life again is sweet indoors,
  And logs again alight;
Ay, even when the houseless wind
  Waileth through cleft and chink,
And in the twilight maids grow kind,
  And jugs are filled and clink;
When children clasp their hands and pray
  'Be done Thy Heavenly will!'
Who doth not lift his voice, and say,
  'Life is worth living still'?

Is life worth living? Yes, so long
  As there is wrong to right,
Wail of the weak against the strong,
  Or tyranny to fight;
Long as there lingers gloom to chase,
  Or streaming tear to dry,
One kindred woe, one sorrowing face
  That smiles as we draw nigh;
Long as at tale of anguish swells
  The heart, and lids grow wet,
And at the sound of Christmas bells
  We pardon and forget;
So long as Faith with Freedom reigns,
  And loyal Hope survives,
And gracious Charity remains
  To leaven lowly lives;
While there is one untrodden tract
  For Intellect or Will,
And men are free to think and act,
  Life is worth living still.

FREDERICK LOCKER-LAMPSON

Mr Placid's Flirtation

Miss Tristram's *poulet* ended thus: 'Nota bene,
We meet for croquet in the Aldobrandini.'
Says my wife, 'Then I'll drive, and you'll ride with Selina'
(Jones's fair spouse, of the Via Sistina).

We started: I'll own that my family deem
I'm an ass, but I'm not such an ass as I seem;
As we cross'd the stones gently a nursemaid said 'La –
There goes Mrs Jones with Miss Placid's papa!'

Our friends, one or two may be mention'd anon,
Had arranged *rendezvous* at the Gate of St John:
That pass'd, off we spun over turf that's not green there,
And soon were all met at the villa. You've been there?

I'll try and describe, or I won't, if you please,
The cheer that was set for us under the trees:
You have read the *menu*, may you read it again;
Champagne, perigord, galantine, and – champagne.

Suffice is to say, I got seated between
Mrs Jones and old Brown – to the latter's chagrin.
Poor Brown, who believes in himself, and – another thing,
Whose talk is so bald, but whose cheeks are so – t'other thing.

She sang, her sweet voice fill'd the gay garden alleys;
I jested, but Brown would not smile at my sallies: –
Selina remark'd that a swell met at Rome
Is not always a swell when you meet him at home.

The luncheon despatch'd, we adjourn'd to croquet,
A dainty, but difficult sport in its way.
Thus I counsel the sage, who to play at it stoops,
Belabour thy neighbour, and spoon through thy hoops.

Then we stroll'd, and discourse found its kindest of tones:
'Oh, how charming were solitude and – Mrs Jones!'
'Indeed, Mr Placid, I dote on the sheeny
And shadowy paths of the Aldobrandini!'

A girl came with violet posies, and two
Gentle eyes, like her violets, freshen'd with dew,
And a kind of an indolent, fine-lady air, –
As if she by accident found herself there.

I bought one. Selina was pleased to accept it;
She gave me a rosebud to keep – and I've kept it
Then twilight was near, and I think, in my heart,
When she vow'd she must go, she was loth to depart.

Cattivo momento! we dare not delay:
The steeds are remounted, and wheels roll away:
The ladies *condemn* Mrs Jones, as the phrase is,
But vie with each other in chanting my praises.

'He has so much to say!' cries the fair Mrs Legge;
'How amusing he was about missing the peg!'
'What a beautiful smile!' says the plainest Miss Gunn.
All echo, 'He's charming! delightful! – What fun!'

This sounds rather *nice*, and it's perfectly clear it
Had sounded more *nice* had I happen'd to hear it;
The men were less civil, and gave me a rub,
So I happen'd to hear when I went to the Club.

Says Brown, 'I shall drop Mr Placid's society;'
(Brown is a prig of improper propriety;)
'Hang him,' said Smith (who from cant's not exempt)
'Why he'll bring immorality into contempt.'

Says I (to myself) when I found me alone,
'My dear wife has my heart, is it always her own?'
And further, says I (to myself) 'I'll be shot
If I know if Selina adores me or not.'

Says Jones, 'I've just come from the *scavi*, at Veii,
And I've bought some remarkably fine scarabæi!'

ERNEST DOWSON

'I have been faithful to thee, Cynara! in my fashion'

Last night, ah, yesternight, betwixt her lips and mine
There fell thy shadow, Cynara! thy breath was shed
Upon my soul between the kisses and the wine;
And I was desolate and sick of an old passion,
Yea, I was desolate and bowed my head:
I have been faithful to thee, Cynara! in my fashion.

All night upon mine heart I felt her warm heart beat,
Night-long within mine arms in love and sleep she lay;
Surely the kisses of her bought red mouth were sweet;
But I was desolate and sick of an old passion,
When I awoke and found the dawn was gray:
I have been faithful to thee, Cynara! in my fashion.

I have forgot much, Cynara! gone with the wind
Flung roses, roses riotously with the throng,
Dancing, to put thy pale, lost lilies out of mind;
But I was desolate and sick of an old passion,
Yea, all the time, because the dance was long:
I have been faithful to thee, Cynara! in my fashion.

I cried for madder music and for stronger wine,
But when the feast is finished and the lamps expire,
Then falls thy shadow, Cynara! the night is thine;
And I am desolate and sick of an old passion,
Yea, hungry for the lips of my desire:
I have been faithful to thee, Cynara! in my fashion.

'They are not long, the weeping and the laughter'

They are not long, the weeping and the laughter,
Love and desire and hate:
I think they have no portion in us after
We pass the gate.

They are not long, the days of wine and roses:
Out of a misty dream
Our path emerges for a while, then closes
Within a dream.

ROBERT LOUIS STEVENSON

Over the Sea to Skye

Sing me a song of a lad that is gone,
 Say, could that lad be I?
Merry of soul he sailed on a day
 Over the sea to Sky.

Mull was astern, Rum on the port,
 Eigg on the starboard bow;
Glory of youth glowed in his soul:
 Where is that glory now?

Sing me a song of a lad that is gone,
 Say, could that lad be I?
Merry of soul he sailed on a day
 Over the sea to Skye.

Give me again all that was there,
 Give me the sun that shone!
Give me the eyes, give me the soul,
 Give me the lad that's gone!

Sing me a song of a lad that is gone,
 Say, could that lad be I?
Merry of soul he sailed on a day
 Over the sea to Skye.

Billow and breeze, islands and seas,
 Mountains of rain and sun,
All that was good, all that was fair,
 All that was me is gone.

For Your Delight

I will make you brooches and toys for your delight
Of bird-song at morning and star-shine at night.
I will make a palace fit for you and me
Of green days in forests and blue days at sea.

I will make my kitchen, and you shall keep your room,
Where white flows the river and bright blows the broom,
And you shall wash your linen and keep your body white
In rainfull at morning and dewfall at night.

And this shall be for music when no one else is near,
The fine song for singing, the rare song to hear!
That only I remember, that only you admire,
Of the broad road that stretches and the roadside fire.

A. C. SWINBURNE

The Garden of Proserpine

Here, where the world is quiet;
  Here, where all trouble seems
Dead winds' and spent waves' riot
  In doubtful dreams of dreams;
I watch the green field growing
For reaping folk and sowing,
For harvest-time and mowing,
  A sleepy world of streams.

I am tired of tears and laughter,
  And men that laugh and weep;
Of what may come hereafter
  For men that sow to reap:
I am weary of days and hours,
Blown buds of barren flowers,
Desires and dreams and powers
  And everything but sleep.

Here life has death for neighbour,
  And far from eye or ear
Wan waves and wet winds labour,
  Weak ships and spirits steer;
They drive adrift, and whither
They wot not who make thither;
But no such winds blow hither,
  And no such things grow here.

No growth of moor or coppice,
  No heather-flower or vine,
But bloomless buds of poppies,
  Green grapes of Proserpine,
Pale beds of blowing rushes
Where no leaf blooms or blushes
Save this whereout she crushes
  For dead men deadly wine.

Pale, without name or number,
  In fruitless fields of corn,
They bow themselves and slumber
  All night till light is born;
And like a soul belated,
In hell and heaven unmated,
By cloud and mist abated
  Comes out of darkness morn.

Though one were strong as seven,
  He too with death shall dwell,
Nor wake with wings in heaven,
  Nor weep for pains in hell;
Though one were fair as roses,
His beauty clouds and closes;
And well though love reposes,
  In the end it is not well.

Pale, beyond porch and portal,
  Crowned with calm leaves, she stands
Who gathers all things mortal
  With cold immortal hands;
Her languid lips are sweeter
Than love's who fears to greet her
To men that mix and meet her
  From many times and lands.

She waits for each and other,
  She waits for all men born;
Forgets the earth her mother,
  The life of fruits and corn;
And spring and seed and swallow
Take wing for her and follow
Where summer song rings hollow
  And flowers are put to scorn.

There go the loves that wither,
  The old loves with wearier wings;
And all dead years draw thither,
  And all disastrous things;
Dead dreams of days forsaken,
Blind buds that snows have shaken,
Wild leaves that winds have taken,
  Red strays of ruined springs.

We are not sure of sorrow,
  And joy was never sure;
To-day will die to-morrow;
  Time stoops to no man's lure;
And love, grown faint and fretful,
With lips but half regretful
Sighs, and with eyes forgetful
  Weeps that no loves endure.

From too much love of living,
From hope and fear set free,
We thank with brief thanksgiving
Whatever gods may be
That no life lives for ever;
That dead men rise up never;
That even the weariest river
Winds somewhere safe to sea.

Then star nor sun shall waken,
Nor any change of light:
Nor sound of waters shaken,
Nor any sound or sight:
Nor wintry leaves nor vernal,
Nor days nor things diurnal;
Only the sleep eternal
In an eternal night.

WILLIAM ALLINGHAM

The Fairies

Up the airy mountain,
Down the rushy glen,
We daren't go a-hunting
For fear of little men;
Wee folk, good folk,
Trooping all together;
Green jacket, red cap,
And white owl's feather!

Down along the rocky shore
Some make their home,
They live on crispy pancakes
Of yellow tide-foam;
Some in the reeds
Of the black mountain lake,
With frogs for their watch-dogs,
All night awake.

High on the hill-top
The old King sits;
He is now so old and gray
He's nigh lost his wits.
With a bridge of white mist
Columbkill he crosses,
On his stately journeys
From Slieveleague to Rosses;

Or going up with music
  On cold starry nights,
To sup with the Queen
  Of the gay Northern Lights.

They stole little Bridget
  For seven years long;
When she came down again
  Her friends were all gone.
They took her lightly back,
  Between the night and morrow,
They thought that she was fast asleep,
  But she was dead with sorrow.
They have kept her ever since
  Deep within the lake,
On a bed of flag-leaves,
  Watching till she wake.

By the craggy hill-side,
  Through the mosses bare,
They have planted thorn-trees
  For pleasure here and there.
Is any man so daring
  As dig them up in spite,
He shall find their sharpest thorns
  In his bed at night.

Up the airy mountain,
  Down the rushy glen,
We daren't go a-hunting
  For fear of little men;
Wee folk, good folk,
  Trooping all together;
Green jacket, red cap,
  And white owl's feather!

CHRISTINA GEORGINA ROSSETTI

A Birthday

My heart is like a singing bird
  Whose nest is in a watered shoot;
My heart is like an apple-tree
  Whose boughs are bent with thickset fruit;
My heart is like a rainbow shell
  That paddles in a halcyon sea;
My heart is gladder than all these
  Because my love is come to me.

Raise me a dais of silk and down;
  Hang it with vair and purple dyes;
Carve it in doves, and pomegranates,
  And peacocks with a hundred eyes;
Work it in gold and silver grapes,
  In leaves, and silver fleurs-de-lys;
Because the birthday of my life
  Is come, my love is come to me.

Twice

I took my heart in my hand
  (O my love, O my love),
I said: Let me fall or stand,
  Let me live or die,
But this once hear me speak –
  (O my love, O my love) –
Yet a woman's words are weak;
  You should speak, not I.

You took my heart in your hand
  With a friendly smile,
With a critical eye you scanned,
  Then set it down,
And said: It is still unripe,
  Better wait awhile;
Wait while the skylarks pipe,
  Till the corn grows brown.

As you set it down it broke –
  Broke, but I did not wince;
I smiled at the speech you spoke,
  At your judgement that I heard:
But I have not often smiled
  Since then, nor questioned since,
Nor cared for corn-flowers wild,
  Nor sung with the singing bird.

I take my heart in my hand,
  O my God, O my God,
My broken heart in my hand,
  Thou has seen, judge thou.
My hope was written on sand,
  O my God, O my God:
Now let thy judgement stand –
  Yea, judge me now.

This contemned of a man,
This marred one heedless day,
This heart take thou to scan
Both within and without:
Refine with fire its gold,
Purge thou its dross away –
Yea, hold it in thy hold,
Whence none can pluck it out.

I take my heart in my hand –
I shall not die, but live –
Before thy face I stand;
I, for thou callest such:
All that I have I bring,
All that I am I give,
Smile thou and I shall sing,
But shall not question much.

Somewhere or Other

Somewhere or other there must surely be
The face not seen, the voice not heard,
The heart that not yet – never yet – ah me!
Made answer to my word.

Somewhere or other, may be near or far;
Past land and sea, clean out of sight;
Beyond the wandering moon, beyond the star
That tracks her night by night.

Somewhere or other, may be far or near;
With just a wall, a hedge, between;
With just the last leaves of the dying year
Fallen on a turf grown green.

DANTË GABRIEL ROSSETTI

Sudden Light

I have been here before,
But when or how I cannot tell:
I know the grass beyond the door,
The sweet keen smell,
The sighing sound, the lights around the shore.

You have been mine before, –
How long ago I may not know:
But just when at that swallow's soar
Your neck turned so,
Some veil did fall, – I knew it all of yore.

Has this been thus before?
And shall not thus time's eddying flight
Still with our lives our love restore
In death's despite,
And day and night yield one delight once more?

A Superscription

Look in my face; my name is Might-have-been;
I am also called No-more, Too-late, Farewell;
Unto thine ear I hold the dead-sea shell
Cast up thy Life's foam-fretted feet between;
Unto thine eyes the glass where that is seen
Which had Life's form and Love's, but by my spell
Is now a shaken shadow intolerable,
Of ultimate things unuttered the frail screen.
Mark me, how still I am! But should there dart
One moment through thy soul the soft surprise
Of that winged Peace which lulls the breath of sighs, –
Then shalt thou see me smile, and turn apart
Thy visage to mine ambush at thy heart
Sleepless with cold commemorative eyes.

MATTHEW ARNOLD

Dover Beach

The sea is calm to-night.
The tide is full, the moon lies fair
Upon the straits; – on the French coast the light
Gleams and is gone; the cliffs of England stand,
Glimmering and vast, out in the tranquil bay.
Come to the window, sweet is the night-air!
Only, from the long line of spray
Where the sea meets the moon-blanched land,
Listen! you hear the grating roar
Of pebbles which the waves draw back, and fling,
At their return, up the high strand,

Begin, and cease, then again begin,
With tremulous cadence slow, and bring
The eternal note of sadness in.

Sophocles long ago
Heard it on the Ægæn, and it brought
Into his mind the turbid ebb and flow
Of human misery; we
Find also in the sound a thought,
Hearing it by this distant northern sea.

The Sea of Faith
Was once, too, at the full, and round earth's shore
Lay like the folds of a bright girdle furled.
But now I only hear
Its melancholy, long, withdrawing roar,
Retreating, to the breath
Of the night-wind, down the vast edges drear
And naked shingles of the world.

Ah, love, let us be true
To one another! for the world, which seems
To lie before us like a land of dreams,
So various, so beautiful, so new,
Hath really neither joy, nor love, nor light,
Nor certitude, nor peace, nor help for pain;
And we are here as on a darkling plain
Swept with confused alarms of struggle and flight,
Where ignorant armies clash by night.

WILLIAM (JOHNSON) CORY

Heraclitus

They told me, Heraclitus, they told me you were dead;
They brought me bitter news to hear and bitter tears to shed.
I wept, as I remembered, how often you and I
Had tired the sun with talking and sent him down the sky.

And now that thou art lying, my dear old Carian guest,
A handful of grey ashes, long long ago at rest,
Still are thy pleasant voices, thy nightingales, awake;
For Death, he taketh all away, but them he cannot take.

SIR HENRY NEWBOLT

Vitaï Lampada

There's a breathless hush in the Close to-night –
  Ten to make and the match to win –
A bumping pitch and a blinding light,
  An hour to play and the last man in.
And it's not for the sake of a ribboned coat,
  Or the selfish hope of a season's fame,
But his Captain's hand on his shoulder smote –
  'Play up! play up! and play the game!'

The sand of the desert is sodden red, –
  Red with the wreck of a square that broke; –
The Gatling's jammed and the Colonel dead,
  And the regiment blind with dust and smoke.
The river of death has brimmed his banks,
  And England's far, and Honour a name,
But the voice of a schoolboy rallies the ranks:
  'Play up! play up! and play the game!'

This the word that year by year,
  While in her place the School is set,
Every one of her sons must hear,
  And none that hears it dare forget.
This they all with a joyful mind
  Bear through life like a torch in flame,
And falling fling to the host behind –
  'Play up! play up! and play the game!'

COVENTRY PATMORE

The Toys

My little Son, who looked from thoughtful eyes
And moved and spoke in quiet grown-up wise,
Having my law the seventh time disobeyed,
I struck him, and dismissed
With hard words and unkissed,
His Mother, who was patient, being dead.
Then, fearing lest his grief should hinder sleep,
I visited his bed,
But found him slumbering deep,
With darkened eyelids, and their lashes yet
From his late sobbing wet.

And I, with moan,
Kissing away his tears, left others of my own;

For, on a table drawn beside his head,
He had put, within his reach,
A box of counters and a red-veined stone,
A piece of glass abraded by the beach,
And six or seven shells,
A bottle with bluebells
And two French copper coins, ranged there with careful art,
To comfort his sad heart.

So when that night I prayed
To God, I wept, and said:
Ah, when at last we lie with trancèd breath,
Not vexing Thee in death,
And Thou rememberest of what toys
We made our joys,
How weakly understood,
Thy great commanded good,
Then, fatherly not less
Than I whom Thou hast moulded from the clay,
Thou'lt leave Thy wrath, and say,
'I will be sorry for their childishness.'

GERARD MANLEY HOPKINS

Patience

Patience, hard thing! the hard thing but to
But bid for, Patience is! Patience who asks
Wants war, wants wounds; weary his times, his
To do without, take tosses, and obey.

Rare patience roots in these, and, these away,
Nowhere. Natural heart's ivy, Patience masks
Our ruins of wrecked past purpose. There she basks
Purple eyes and seas of liquid leaves all day.

We hear our hearts grate on themselves: it kills
To bruise them dearer. Yet the rebellious wills
Of us we do bid God bend to him even so.

And where is he who more and more distills
Delicious kindness? – He is patient. Patience fills
His crisp combs, and that comes those ways we know.

'My own heart let me more have pity on'

My own heart let me more have pity on; let
Me live to my sad self hereafter kind,
Charitable; not live this tormented mind
With this tormented mind tormenting yet.

I cast for comfort I can no more get
By groping round my comfortless, than blind
Eyes in their dark can day or thirst can find
Thirst's all-in-all in all a world of wet.

Soul, self; come, poor Jackself, I do advise
You, jaded, let be; call off thoughts awhile
Elsewhere; leave comfort root-room; let joy size

At God knows when to God knows what; whose smile
's not wrung, see you; unforeseen times rather – as skies
Betweenpie mountains – lights a lovely mile.

God's Grandeur

The world is charged with the grandeur of God.
   It will flame out, like shining from shook foil;
   It gathers to a greatness, like the ooze of oil
Crushed. Why do men then now not reck his rod?
Generations have trod, have trod, have trod;
   And all is seared with trade; bleared, smeared with toil;
   And wears man's smudge and shares man's smell: the soil
Is bare now, nor can foot feel, being shod.

And for all this, nature is never spent;
   There lives the dearest freshness deep down things;
And though the last lights off the black West went
   Oh, morning, at the brown brink eastward, springs –
Because the Holy Ghost over the bent
   World broods with warm breast and with ah! bright wings.

The Windhover:

To Christ our Lord

I caught this morning morning's minion, king-
   dom of daylight's dauphin, dapple-dawn-drawn Falcon, in his riding
   Of the rolling level underneath him steady air, and striding
High there, how he rung upon the rein of a wimpling wing

In his ecstasy! then off, off forth on swing,
   As a skate's heel sweeps smooth on a bow-bend: the hurl and gliding
   Rebuffed the big wind. My heart in hiding
Stirred for a bird, – the achieve of, the mastery of the thing!

Brute beauty and valour and act, oh, air, pride, plume, here
   Buckle! AND the fire that breaks from thee then, a billion
Times told lovelier, more dangerous, O my chevalier!
   No wonder of it: Sheér plód makes plough down sillion
Shine, and blue-bleak embers, ah my dear,
   Fall, gall themselves, and gash gold-vermilion.

Pied Beauty

Glory be to God for dappled things –
   For skies of couple-colour as a brinded cow;
      For rose-moles all in stipple upon trout that swim;
Fresh-firecoal chestnut-falls; finches' wings;
   Landscape plotted and pieced – fold, fallow, and plough;
      And, áll trádes, their gear and tackle and trim.

All things counter, original, spare, strange;
   Whatever is fickle, freckled (who knows how?)
      With swift, slow; sweet, sour; adazzle, dim;
He fathers-forth whose beauty is past change:
                                                            Praise him.

CHARLOTTE MEW

The Quiet House

   When we were children old Nurse used to say,
   The house was like an auction or a fair
   Until the lot of us were safe in bed.
   It has been quiet as the country-side
   Since Ted and Janey and then Mother died
And Tom crossed Father and was sent away.
After the lawsuit he could not hold up his head,
   Poor Father, and he does not care
   For people here, or to go anywhere.

To get away to Aunt's for that week-end
   Was hard enough; (since then, a year ago,
   He scarcely lets me slip out of his sight –)
At first I did not like my cousin's friend,
   I did not think I should remember him:

His voice has gone, his face is growing dim
And if I like him now I do not know.
He frightened me before he smiled –
He did not ask me if he might –
He said that he would come one Sunday night,
He spoke to me as if I were a child.

No year has been like this that has just gone by;
It may be that what Father says is true,
If things are so it does not matter why:
But everything has burned, and not quite through.
The colours of the world have turned
To flame, the blue, the gold has burned
In what used to be such a leaden sky.
When you are burned quite through you die.

Red is the strangest pain to bear;
In Spring the leaves on the budding trees;
In Summer the roses are worse than these,
More terrible than they are sweet:
A rose can stab you across the street
Deeper than any knife:
And the crimson haunts you everywhere –
Thin shafts of sunlight, like ghosts of reddened swords
have struck our stair
As if, coming down, you had spilt your life.

I think that my soul is red
Like the soul of a sword or a scarlet flower:
But when these are dead
They have had their hour.

I shall have had mine, too,
For from head to feet
I am burned and stabbed half through,
And the pain is deadly sweet.

The things that kill us seem
Blind to the death they give:
It is only in our dream
The things that kill us live.

The room is shut where Mother died,
The other rooms are as they were,
The world goes on the same outside,
The sparrows fly across the Square,
The children play as we four did there,
The trees grow green and brown and bare,
The sun shines on the dead Church spire,
And nothing lives here but the fire.

While Father watches from his chair
Day follows day
The same, or now and then a different grey,
Till, like his hair,
Which Mother said was wavy once and bright,
They will all turn white.

To-night I heard a bell again –
Outside it was just the same mist of fine rain,
The lamps just lighted down the long, dim street,
No one for me –
I think it is myself I go to meet:
I do not care; some day I *shall* not think; I shall not *be*.

ROBERT BROUGH

My Lord Tomnoddy

My Lord Tomnoddy's the son of an Earl,
His hair is straight, but his whiskers curl;
His Lordship's forehead is far from wide,
But there's plenty of room for the brains inside.
He writes his name with indifferent ease,
He's rather uncertain about the 'd's', –
But what does it matter, if three or one,
To the Earl of Fitzdotterel's eldest son?

My Lord Tomnoddy to college went,
Much time he lost, much money he spent;
Rules, and windows, and heads, he broke –
Authorities winked – young men will joke!
He never peeped inside of a book –
In two years' time a degree he took;
And the newspapers vaunted the honours won
By the Earl of Fitzdotterel's eldest son.

My Lord Tomnoddy came out in the world,
Waists were tightened, and ringlets curled.
Virgins languished, and matrons smiled –
'Tis true, his Lordship is rather wild;
In very queer places he spends his life;
There's talk of some children, by nobody's wife –
But we mustn't look close into what is done
By the Earl of Fitzdotterel's eldest son.

My Lord Tomnoddy must settle down –
There's a vacant seat in the family town!
('Tis time he should sow his eccentric oats) –

He hasn't the wit to apply for votes:
He cannot e'en learn his election speech,
Three phrases he speaks – a mistake in each!
And then breaks down – but the borough is won
For the Earl of Fitzdotterel's eldest son.

My Lord Tomnoddy prefers the Guards,
(The House is a bore) so! – it's on the cards!
My Lord's a Lieutenant at twenty-three,
A Captain at twenty-six is he –
He never drew sword, except on drill;
The tricks of parade he has learnt but ill –
A full-blown Colonel at thirty-one
Is the Earl of Fitzdotterel's eldest son!

My Lord Tomnoddy is thirty-four;
The Earl can last but a few years more.
My Lord in the Peers will take his place:
Her Majesty's councils his words will grace.
Office he'll hold, and patronage sway;
Fortunes and lives he will vote away –
And what are his qualifications? – ONE!
He's the Earl of Fitzdotterel's eldest son.

JOHN DAVIDSON

Thirty Bob a Week

I couldn't touch a stop and turn a screw,
 And set the blooming world a-work for me,
Like such as cut their teeth – I hope, like you –
 On the handle of a skeleton gold key;
I cut mine on a leek, which I eat it every week:
 I'm a clerk at thirty bob as you can see.

But I don't allow it's luck and all a toss;
 There's no such thing as being starred and crossed;
It's just the power of some to be a boss,
 And the bally power of others to be bossed:
I face the music, sir; you bet I ain't a cur;
 Strike me lucky if I don't believe I'm lost!

For like a mole I journey in the dark,
 A-travelling along the underground
From my Pillar'd Halls and broad Suburbean Park,
 To come the daily dull official round;
And home again at night with my pipe all alight,
 A-scheming how to count ten bob a pound.

And it's often very cold and very wet,
  And my missis stitches towels for a hunks;
And the Pillar'd Halls is half of it to let –
  Three rooms about the size of travelling trunks.
And we cough, my wife and I, to dislocate a sigh,
  When the noisy little kids are in their bunks.

But you never hear her do a growl or whine,
  For she's made of flint and roses, very odd;
And I've got to cut my meaning rather fine,
  Or I'd blubber, for I'm made of greens and sod:
So p'r'aps we are in Hell for all that I can tell,
  And lost and damn'd and served up hot to God.

I ain't blaspheming, Mr Silver-tongue;
  I'm saying things a bit beyond your art:
Of all the rummy starts you ever sprung,
  Thirty bob a week's the rummiest start!
With your science and your books and your the'ries about spooks,
  Did you ever hear of looking in your heart?

I didn't mean your pocket, Mr, no:
  I mean that having children and a wife,
With thirty bob on which to come and go,
  Isn't dancing to the tabor and the fife:
When it doesn't make you drink, by Heaven! it makes you think,
  And notice curious items about life.

I step into my heart and there I meet
  A god-almighty devil singing small,
Who would like to shout and whistle in the street,
  And squelch the passers flat against the wall;
If the whole world was a cake he had the power to take,
  He would take it, ask for more, and eat it all.

And I meet a sort of simpleton beside,
  The kind that life is always giving beans;
With thirty bob a week to keep a bride
  He fell in love and married in his teens:
At thirty bob he stuck; but he knows it isn't luck:
  He knows the seas are deeper than tureens.

And the god-almighty devil and the fool
  That meet me in the High Street on the strike,
When I walk about my heart a-gathering wool,
  Are my good and evil angels if you like.
And both of them together in every kind of weather
  Ride me like a double-seated bike.

That's rough a bit and needs its meaning curled.
  But I have a high old hot un in my mind –

A most engrugious notion of the world,
  That leaves your lightning 'rithmetic behind:
I give it at a glance when I say 'There ain't no chance,
  Nor nothing of the lucky-lottery kind.'

And it's this way that I make it out to be:
  No fathers, mothers, countries, climates – none;
Not Adam was responsible for me,
  Nor society, nor systems, nary one:
A little sleeping seed, I woke – I did, indeed –
  A million years before the blooming sun.

I woke because I thought the time had come;
  Beyond my will there was no other cause;
And everywhere I found myself at home,
  Because I chose to be the thing I was;
And in whatever shape of mollusc or of ape
  I always went according to the laws.

I was the love that chose my mother out;
  I joined two lives and from the union burst;
My weakness and my strength without a doubt
  Are mine alone for ever from the first:
It's just the very same with a difference in the name
  As 'Thy will be done.' You say it if you durst!

They say it daily up and down the land
  As easy as you take a drink, it's true;
But the difficultest go to understand,
  And the difficultest job a man can do,
Is to come it brave and meek with thirty bob a week,
  And feel that that's the proper thing for you.

It's a naked child against a hungry wolf;
  It's playing bowls upon a splitting wreck;
It's walking on a string across a gulf
  With millstones fore-and-aft about your neck;
But the thing is daily done by many and many a one;
  And we fall, face forward, fighting, on the deck.

A Labourer's Wife

All the day I worked and played
When I was a little maid,
Soft and nimble as a mouse,
Living in my father's house.
If I lacked my liberty,
All my thoughts were free as free;

Though my hands were hacked all o'er,
Ah! my heart was never sore.

Oh! once I had my fling!
I romped at ging-go-ring;
I used to dance and sing,
And play at everything.
I never feared the light;
I shrank from no one's sight;
I saw the world was right;
I always slept at night.

What a simpleton was I
To go and marry on the sly!
Now I work and never play:
Three pale children all the day
Fight and whine; and Dick, my man,
Is drunk as often as he can.
Ah! my head and bones are sore,
And my heart is hacked all o'er.

Yet, once I had my fling;
I romped at ging-go-ring;
I used to dance and sing,
And play at everything.
Now I fear the light;
I shrink from every sight;
I see there's nothing right;
I hope to die to-night.

C. S. CALVERLEY

Peace

A Study

He stood, a worn-out City clerk –
Who'd toiled, and seen no holiday,
For forty years from dawn to dark –
  Alone beside Caermarthen Bay.

He felt the salt spray on his lips;
  Heard children's voices on the sands;
Up the sun's path he saw the ships
  Sail on and on to other lands;

And laughed aloud. Each sight and sound
  To him was joy too deep for tears;
He sat him on the beach, and bound
  A blue bandana round his ears,

And thought how, posted near his door,
  His own green door on Camden Hill,
Two bands at least, most likely more,
  Were mingling at their own sweet will

Verdi with Vance. And at the thought
  He laughed again, and softly drew
That Morning Herald that he'd bought
  Forth from his breast, and read it through.

ARTHUR SYMONS

Scènes de la Vie de Bohème

Episode of a night of May

The coloured lanterns lit the trees, the grass,
The little tables underneath the trees,
And the rays dappled like a delicate breeze
    Each wine-illumined glass.

The pink light flickered, and a shadow ran
Along the ground as couples came and went;
The waltzing fiddles sounded from the tent,
    And *Giroflée* began.

They sauntered arm in arm, these two; the smiles
Grew chilly, as the best spring evenings do.
The words were warmer, but the words came few,
    And pauses fell at whiles.

But she yawned prettily. 'Come then,' said he.
He found a chair, Veuve Clicquot, some cigars.
They emptied glasses and admired the stars,
    The lanterns, night, the sea,

Nature, the newest opera, the dog
(So clever) who could shoulder arms and dance;
He mentioned Alphonse Daudet's last romance,
    Last Sunday's river-fog,

Love, Immortality; the talk ran down
To these mere lees: they wearied each of each,
And tortured ennui into hollow speech,
        And yawned, to hide a frown.

She jarred his nerves; he bored her – and so soon.
Both were polite, and neither cared to say
The word that mars a perfect night of May.
        They watched the waning moon.

La Mélinite: Moulin-Rouge

Olivier Metra's Waltz of Roses
Sheds in rhythmic shower
The very petals of the flower;
And all is roses,
The rouge of petals in a shower.

Down the long hall the dance returning
Rounds the full circle, rounds
The perfect rose of lights and sounds,
The rose returning
Into the circle of its rounds.

Alone, apart, one dancer watches
Her mirrored, morbid grace;
Before the mirror, face to face,
Alone she watches
Her morbid, vague ambiguous grace

Before the mirror's dance of shadows
She dances in a dream,
And she and they together seem
A dance of shadows,
Alike the shadows of a dream.

The orange-rosy lamps are trembling
Between the robes that turn;
In ruddy flowers of flame that burn
The lights are trembling:
The shadows and the dancers turn

And, enigmatically smiling,
In the mysterious night,
She dances for her own delight,
A shadow smiling
Back to a shadow in the night.

OSCAR WILDE

from *The Ballad of Reading Gaol*

He did not wear his scarlet coat,
   For blood and wine are red,
And blood and wine were on his hands
   When they found him with the dead,
The poor dead woman whom he loved,
   And murdered in her bed.

He walked amongst the Trial Men
   In a suit of shabby grey;
A cricket cap was on his head,
   And his step seemed light and gay;
But I never saw a man who looked
   So wistfully at the day.

I never saw a man who looked
   With such a wistful eye
Upon that little tent of blue
   Which prisoners call the sky,
And at every drifting cloud that went
   With sails of silver by.

I walked, with other souls in pain,
   Within another ring,
And was wondering if the man had done
   A great or little thing,
When a voice behind me whispered low,
   '*That fellow's got to swing.*'

Dear Christ! the very prison walls
   Suddenly seemed to reel,
And the sky above my head became
   Like a casque of scorching steel;
And, though I was a soul in pain,
   My pain I could not feel.

I only knew what hunted thought
   Quickened his step, and why
He looked upon the garish day
   With such a wistful eye;
The man had killed the thing he loved,
   And so he had to die.

Yet each man kills the thing he loves,
   By each let this be heard,
Some do it with a bitter look,
   Some with a flattering word,

The coward does it with a kiss,
  The brave man with a sword!

Some kill their love when they are young,
  And some when they are old;
Some strangle with the hands of Lust,
  Some with the hands of Gold:
The kindest use a knife, because
  The dead so soon grow cold.

Some love too little, some too long,
  Some sell, and others buy;
Some do the deed with many tears,
  And some without a sigh:
For each man kills the thing he loves,
  Yet each man does not die.

He does not die a death of shame
  On a day of dark disgrace,
Nor have a noose about his neck,
  Nor a cloth upon his face,
Nor drop feet foremost through the floor
  Into an empty space.

Impression du Matin

The Thames nocturne of blue and gold
  Changed to a Harmony in grey:
  A barge with ochre-coloured hay
Dropped from the wharf: and chill and cold

The yellow fog came creeping down
  The bridges, till the houses' walls
  Seemed changed to shadows and St Paul's
Loomed like a bubble o'er the town.

Then suddenly arose the clang
  Of waking life; the streets were stirred
  With country waggons: and a bird
Flew to the glistening roofs and sang.

But one pale woman all alone,
  The daylight kissing her wan hair,
  Loitered beneath the gas lamps' flare,
With lips of flame and heart of stone.

FORD MADOX FORD

Sidera Cadentia

On the Death of Queen Victoria

When one of the old, little stars doth fall from its place,
    The eye,
Glimpsing aloft must sadden to see that its space
    In the sky
Is darker, lacking a spot of its ancient, shimmering grace,
And sadder, a little, for loss of the glimmer on high.

Very remote, a glitter, a mote far away, is your star,
But its glint being gone from the place where it shone
The night's somewhat grimmer and something is gone
Out of the comforting quiet of things as they are.

    A shock,
A change in the beat of the clock;
And the ultimate change that we fear feels a little less far.

THOMAS HARDY

The Darkling Thrush

I leant upon a coppice gate
  When Frost was spectre-gray,
And Winter's dregs made desolate
  The weakening eye of day.
The tangled bine-stems scored the sky
  Like strings of broken lyres,
And all mankind that haunted nigh
  Had sought their household fires.

The land's sharp features seemed to be
  The Century's corpse outleant,
His crypt the cloudy canopy,
  The wind his death-lament.
The ancient pulse of germ and birth
  Was shrunken hard and dry,
And every spirit upon earth
  Seemed fervourless as I.

At once a voice arose among
  The bleak twigs overhead
In a full-hearted evensong
  Of joy illimited;

An agèd thrush, frail, gaunt, and small,
In blast-beruffled plume,
Had chosen thus to fling his soul
Upon the growing gloom.

So little cause for carolings
Of such ecstatic sound
Was written on terrestrial things
Afar or nigh around,
That I could think there trembled through
His happy good-night air
Some blessed Hope, whereof he knew
And I was unaware.

Shut Out that Moon

Close up the casement, draw the blind,
Shut out that stealing moon,
She wears too much the guise she wore
Before our lutes were strewn
With years-deep dust, and names we read
On a white stone were hewn.

Step not forth on the dew-dashed lawn
To view the Lady's Chair,
Immense Orion's glittering form,
The Less and Greater Bear:
Stay in; to such sights we were drawn
When faded ones were fair.

Brush not the bough for midnight scents
That come forth lingeringly,
And wake the same sweet sentiments
They breathed to you and me
When living seemed a laugh, and love
All it was said to be.

Within the common lamp-lit room
Prison my eyes and thought;
Let dingy details crudely loom,
Mechanic speech be wrought:
Too fragrant was Life's early bloom,
Too tart the fruit it brought!

The Roman Road

The Roman Road runs straight and bare
As the pale parting-line in hair
Across the heath. And thoughtful men
Contrast its days of Now and Then,
And delve, and measure, and compare;

Visioning on the vacant air
Helmed legionaries, who proudly rear
The Eagle, as they pace again
The Roman Road.

But no tall brass-helmed legionnaire
Haunts it for me. Uprises there
A mother's form upon my ken,
Guiding my infant steps, as when
We walked that ancient thoroughfare,
The Roman Road.

The Oxen

Christmas Eve, and twelve of the clock.
'Now they are all on their knees,'
An elder said as we sat in a flock
By the embers in hearthside ease.

We pictured the meek mild creatures where
They dwelt in their strawy pen,
Nor did it occur to one of us there
To doubt they were kneeling then.

So fair a fancy few would weave
In these years! Yet, I feel,
If someone said on Christmas Eve,
'Come; see the oxen kneel

'In the lonely barton by yonder coomb
Our childhood used to know,'
I should go with him in the gloom,
Hoping it might be so.

The Ruined Maid

'O 'Melia, my dear, this does everything crown!
Who could have supposed I should meet you in Town?
And whence such fair garments, such prosperi-ty?' –
'O didn't you know I'd been ruined?' said she.

– 'You left us in tatters, without shoes or socks,
Tired of digging potatoes, and spudding up docks;
And now you've gay bracelets and bright feathers three!' –
'Yes: that's how we dress when we're ruined,' said she.

– 'At home in the barton you said "thee" and "thou,"
And "thik oon," and "theäs oon," and "t'other"; but now
Your talking quite fits 'ee for high compa-ny!' –
'Some polish is gained with one's ruin,' said she.

– 'Your hands were like paws then, your face blue and bleak
But now I'm bewitched by your delicate cheek,
And your little gloves fit as on any la-dy!' –
'We never do work when we're ruined,' said she.

– 'You used to call home-life a hag-ridden dream,
And you'd sigh, and you'd sock; but at present you seem
To know not of megrims or melancho-ly!' –
'True. One's pretty lively when ruined,' said she.

– 'I wish I had feathers, a fine sweeping gown,
And a delicate face, and could strut about Town!' –
'My dear – a raw country girl, such as you be,
Cannot quite expect that. You ain't ruined,' said she.

A Church Romance

(Mellstock: circa 1835)

She turned in the high pew, until her sight
Swept the west gallery, and caught its row
Of music-men with viol, book, and bow
Against the sinking sad tower-window light.

She turned again; and in her pride's despite
One strenuous viol's inspirer seemed to throw
A message from his string to her below,
Which said: 'I claim thee as my own forthright.'

Thus their hearts' bond began, in due time signed.
And long years thence, when Age had scared Romance,
At some old attitude of his or glance
That gallery-scene would break upon her mind,
With him as minstrel, ardent, young, and trim,
Bowing 'New Sabbath' or 'Mount Ephraim'.

At Castle Boterel

As I drive to the junction of lane and highway,
And the drizzle bedrenches the waggonette,
I look behind at the fading byway,
And see on its slope, now glistening wet,
Distinctly yet

Myself and a girlish form benighted
In dry March weather. We climb the road
Beside a chaise. We had just alighted
To ease the sturdy pony's load
When he sighed and slowed.

What we did as we climbed, and what we talked of
Matters not much, nor to what it led, –
Something that life will not be balked of
Without rude reason till hope is dead,
And feeling fled.

It filled but a minute. But was there ever
A time of such quality, since or before,
In that hill's story? To one mind never,
Though it has been climbed, foot-swift, foot-sore,
By thousands more.

Primaeval rocks form the road's steep border,
And much have they faced there, first and last,
Of the transitory in Earth's long order;
But what they record in colour and cast
Is – that we two passed.

And to me, though Time's unflinching rigour,
In mindless rote, has ruled from sight
The substance now, one phantom figure
Remains on the slope, as when that night
Saw us alight.

I look and see it there, shrinking, shrinking,
I look back at it amid the rain
For the very last time; for my sand is sinking,
And I shall traverse old love's domain
Never again.

On the Departure Platform

We kissed at the barrier; and passing through
She left me, and moment by moment got
Smaller and smaller, until to my view
　　She was but a spot;

A wee white spot of muslin fluff
That down the diminishing platform bore
Through hustling crowds of gentle and rough
　　To the carriage door.

Under the lamplight's fitful glowers,
Behind dark groups from far and near,
Whose interests were apart from ours,
　　She would disappear,

Then show again, till I ceased to see
That flexible form, that nebulous white;
And she who was more than my life to me
　　Had vanished quite.

We have penned new plans since that fair fond day,
And in season she will appear again –
Perhaps in the same soft white array –
　　But never as then!

– 'And why, young man, must eternally fly
A joy you'll repeat, if you love her well?'
– O friend, nought happens twice thus; why,
　　I cannot tell!

Old Furniture

I know not how it may be with others
　　Who sit amid relics of householdry
That date from the days of their mothers' mothers,
　　But well I know how it is with me
　　　　Continually.

I see the hands of the generations
　　That owned each shiny familiar thing
In play on its knobs and indentations,
　　And with its ancient fashioning
　　　　Still dallying:

Hands behind hands, growing paler and paler,
　　As in a mirror a candle-flame

Shows images of itself, each frailer
    As it recedes, though the eye may frame
        Its shape the same.

On the clock's dull dial a foggy finger,
    Moving to set the minutes right
With tentative touches that lift and linger
    In the wont of a moth on a summer night,
        Creeps to my sight.

On this old viol, too, fingers are dancing –
    As whilom – just over the strings by the nut,
The tip of a bow receding, advancing
    In airy quivers, as if it would cut
        The plaintive gut.

And I see a face by that box for tinder,
    Glowing forth in fits from the dark,
And fading again, as the linten cinder
    Kindles to red at the flinty spark,
        Or goes out stark.

Well, well. It is best to be up and doing,
    The world has no use for one to-day
Who eyes things thus – no aim pursuing!
    He should not continue in this stay,
        But sink away.

The Voice

Woman much missed, how you call to me, call to me,
Saying that now you are not as you were
When you had changed from the one who was all to me,
But as at first, when our day was fair.

Can it be you that I hear? Let me view you, then,
Standing as when I drew near to the town
Where you would wait for me: yes, as I knew you then,
Even to the original air-blue gown!

Or is it only the breeze, in its listlessness
Travelling across the wet mead to me here,
You being ever dissolved to wan wistlessness,
Heard no more again far or near?

    Thus I; faltering forward,
    Leaves around me falling,
Wind oozing thin through the thorn from norward,
    And the woman calling.

The Nettles

This, then, is the grave of my son,
Whose heart she won! And nettles grow
Upon his mound; and she lives just below.

How he upbraided me, and left,
And our lives were cleft, because I said
She was hard, unfeeling, caring but to wed.

Well, to see this sight I have fared these miles,
And her firelight smiles from her window there,
Whom he left his mother to cherish with tender care!

It is enough. I'll turn and go;
Yes, nettles grow where lone lies he,
Who spurned me for seeing what he could not see.

He Never Expected Much

A Consideration on my eighty-sixth birthday

Well, World, you have kept faith with me,
Kept faith with me;
Upon the whole you have proved to be
Much as you said you were.
Since as a child I used to lie
Upon the leaze and watch the sky,
Never, I own, expected I
That life would all be fair.

'Twas then you said, and since have said,
Times since have said,
In that mysterious voice you shed
From clouds and hills around:
'Many have loved me desperately,
Many with smooth serenity,
While some have shown contempt of me
Till they dropped underground.

'I do not promise overmuch,
Child; overmuch;
Just neutral-tinted haps and such,'
You said to minds like mine.
Wise warning for your credit's sake!
Which I for one failed not to take,
And hence could stem such strain and ache
As each year might assign.

Afterwards

When the Present has latched its postern behind my tremulous stay,
   And the May month flaps its glad green leaves like wings,
Delicate-filmed as new-spun silk, will the neighbours say,
   'He was a man who used to notice such things'?

If it be in the dusk when, like an eyelid's soundless blink,
   The dewfall-hawk comes crossing the shades to alight
Upon the wind-warped upland thorn, a gazer may think,
   'To him this must have been a familiar sight.'

If I pass during some nocturnal blackness, mothy and warm,
   When the hedgehog travels furtively over the lawn,
One may say, 'He strove that such innocent creatures should come to no
      harm,
   But he could do little for them; and now he is gone.'

If, when hearing that I have been stilled at last, they stand at the door,
   Watching the full-starred heavens that winter sees,
Will this thought rise on those who will meet my face no more,
   'He was one who had an eye for such mysteries'?

And will any say when my bell of quittance is heard in the gloom,
   And a crossing breeze cuts a pause in its outrollings,
Till they rise again, as they were a new bell's boom,
   'He hears it not now, but used to notice such things'?

WALTER DE LA MARE

Fare Well

When I lie where shades of darkness
Shall no more assail mine eyes,
Nor the rain make lamentation
      When the wind sighs;
How will fare the world whose wonder
Was the very proof of me?
Memory fades, must the remembered
      Perishing be?

Oh, when this my dust surrenders
Hand, foot, lip, to dust again,
May these loved and loving faces
      Please other men!

May the rusting harvest hedgerow
Still the Traveller's Joy entwine,
And as happy children gather
        Posies once mine.

Look thy last on all things lovely,
Every hour. Let no night
Seal thy sense in deathly slumber
        Till to delight
Thou have paid thy utmost blessing;
Since that all things thou wouldst praise
Beauty took from those who loved them
        In other days.

HILAIRE BELLOC

Henry King

Who chewed bits of String,
and was early cut off in Dreadful Agonies

The Chief Defect of Henry King
Was chewing little bits of String.
At last he swallowed some which tied
Itself in ugly Knots inside.
Physicians of the Utmost Fame
Were called at once; but when they came
They answered, as they took their Fees,
'There is no Cure for this Disease.
Henry will very soon be dead.'
His Parents stood about his Bed
Lamenting his Untimely Death,
When Henry, with his Latest Breath,
Cried – 'Oh, My Friends, be warned by me,
That Breakfast, Dinner, Lunch, and Tea
Are all the Human Frame requires . . . '
With that, the Wretched Child expires.

Lord Finchley

Lord Finchley tried to mend the Electric Light
Himself. It struck him dead: And serve him right!
It is the business of the wealthy man
To give employment to the artisan.

G. K. CHESTERTON

The Secret People

Smile at us, pay us, pass us; but do not quite forget,
For we are the people of England, that never has spoken yet.
There is many a fat farmer that drinks less cheerfully,
There is many a free French peasant who is richer and sadder than we.
There are no folk in the whole world so helpless or so wise.
There is hunger in our bellies, there is laughter in our eyes;
You laugh at us and love us, both mugs and eyes are wet:
Only you do not know us. For we have not spoken yet.

The fine French kings came over in a flutter of flags and dames.
We liked their smiles and battles, but we never could say their names.
The blood ran red to Bosworth and the high French lords went down;
There was naught but a naked people under a naked crown.
And the eyes of the King's Servants turned terribly every way,
And the gold of the King's Servants rose higher every day.
They burnt the homes of the shaven men, that had been quaint and kind,
Till there was no bed in a monk's house, nor food that man could find.
The inns of God where no man paid, that were the wall of the weak,
The King's Servants ate them all. And still we did not speak.

And the face of the King's Servants grew greater than the King:
He tricked them, and they trapped him, and stood round him in a ring.
The new grave lords closed round him, that had eaten the abbey's fruits,
And the men of the new religion, with their Bibles in their boots,
We saw their shoulders moving, to menace or discuss,
And some were pure and some were vile; but none took heed of us.
We saw the King as they killed him, and his face was proud and pale;
And a few men talked of freedom, while England talked of ale.

A war that we understood not came over the world and woke
Americans, Frenchmen, Irish; but we knew not the things they spoke.
They talked about rights and nature and peace and the people's reign:
And the squires, our masters, bade us fight; and never scorned us again.
Weak if we be for ever, could none condemn us then;
Men called us serfs and drudges; men knew that we were men.
In foam and flame at Trafalgar, on Albuera plains,
We did and died like lions, to keep ourselves in chains,
We lay in living ruins; firing and fearing not
The strange fierce face of the Frenchman who knew for what they fought,
And the man who seemed to be more than man we strained against and broke;
And we broke our own rights with him. And still we never spoke.

Our path of glory ended; we never heard guns again.
But the squire seemed struck in the saddle; he was foolish, as if in pain
He leaned on a staggering lawyer, he clutched a cringing Jew,
He was stricken; it may be, after all, he was stricken at Waterloo.

Or perhaps the shades of the shaven men, whose spoil is in his house,
Come back in shining shapes at last to spoil his last carouse:
We only know the last sad squires ride slowly towards the sea,
And a new people takes the land: and still it is not we.

They have given us into the hands of the new unhappy lords,
Lords without anger and honour, who dare not carry their swords.
They fight by shuffling papers; they have bright dead alien eyes;
They look at our labour and laughter as a tired man looks at flies.
And the load of their loveless pity is worse than the ancient wrongs,
Their doors are shut in the evening; and they know no songs.

We hear men speaking for us of new laws strong and sweet,
Yet is there no man speaketh as we speak in the street.
It may be we shall rise the last as Frenchmen rose the first,
Our wrath come after Russia's wrath and our wrath be the worst.
It may be we are meant to mark with our riot and our rest
God's scorn for all men governing. It may be beer is best.
But we are the people of England; and we have not spoken yet.
Smile at us, pay us, pass us. But do not quite forget.

A. E. HOUSMAN

On Wenlock Edge

On Wenlock Edge the wood's in trouble;
His forest fleece the Wrekin heaves;
The gale, it plies the saplings double,
And thick on Severn snow the leaves.

'Twould blow like this through holt and hanger
When Uricon the city stood:
'Tis the old wind in the old anger,
But then it threshed another wood.

Then, 'twas before my time, the Roman
At yonder heaving hill would stare:
The blood that warms an English yeoman,
The thoughts that hurt him, they were there.

There, like the wind through woods in riot,
Through him the gale of life blew high;
The tree of man was never quiet:
Then 'twas the Roman, now 'tis I.

The gale, it plies the saplings double,
It blows so hard, 'twill soon be gone:
To-day the Roman and his trouble
Are ashes under Uricon.

'Into my heart an air that kills'

Into my heart an air that kills
  From yon far country blows:
What are those blue remembered hills,
  What spires, what farms are those?

That is the land of lost content,
  I see it shining plain,
The happy highways where I went
  And cannot come again.

'Loveliest of trees, the cherry now'

Loveliest of trees, the cherry now
Is hung with bloom along the bough,
And stands about the woodland ride
Wearing white for Eastertide.

Now, of my threescore years and ten,
Twenty will not come again,
And take from seventy springs a score,
It only leaves me fifty more.

And since to look at things in bloom
Fifty springs are little room,
About the woodlands I will go
To see the cherry hung with snow.

Ludlow Fair

The lads in their hundreds to Ludlow come in for the fair,
  There's men from the barn and the forge and the mill and the fold,
The lads for the girls and the lads for the liquor are there,
  And there with the rest are the lads that will never be old.

There's chaps from the town and the field and the till and the cart,
  And many to count are the stalwart, and many the brave,
And many the handsome of face and the handsome of heart,
  And few that will carry their looks or their truth to the grave.

I wish one could know them, I wish there were tokens to tell
  The fortunate fellows that now you can never discern;
And then one could talk with them friendly and wish them farewell
  And watch them depart on the way that they will not return.

But now you may stare as you like and there's nothing to scan;
  And brushing your elbow unguessed-at and not to be told
They carry back bright to the coiner the mintage of man,
  The lads that will die in their glory and never be old.

JAMES ELROY FLECKER

The Golden Journey to Samarkand

PROLOGUE

We who with songs beguile your pilgrimage
  And swear that Beauty lives though lilies die,
We Poets of the proud old lineage
  Who sing to find your hearts, we know not why, –

What shall we tell you? Tales, marvellous tales
  Of ships and stars and isles where good men rest,
Where nevermore the rose of sunset pales,
  And winds and shadows fall toward the West:

And there the world's first huge white-bearded kings
  In dim glades sleeping, murmur in their sleep,
And closer round their breasts the ivy clings,
  Cutting its pathway slow and red and deep.

II

And how beguile you? Death has no repose
  Warmer and deeper than that Orient sand
Which hides the beauty and bright faith of those
  Who made the Golden Journey to Samarkand.

And now they wait and whiten peaceably,
  Those conquerors, those poets, those so fair:
They know time comes, not only you and I,
  But the whole world shall whiten, here or there;

When those long caravans that cross the plain
  With dauntless feet and sound of silver bells
Put forth no more for glory or for gain,
  Take no more solace from the palm-girt wells.

When the great markets by the sea shut fast
  All that calm Sunday that goes on and on:
When even lovers find their peace at last,
  And Earth is but a star, that once had shone.

ROBERT BRIDGES

Triolet

When first we met we did not guess
That Love would prove so hard a master;
Of more than common friendliness
When first we met we did not guess.
Who could foretell this sore distress,
This irretrievable disaster
When first we met? – We did not guess
That Love would prove so hard a master.

Eros

Why hast thou nothing in thy face?
Thou idol of the human race,
Thou tyrant of the human heart,
The flower of lovely youth that art;
Yea, and that standest in thy youth
An image of eternal Truth,
With thy exuberant flesh so fair,
That only Pheidias might compare,
Ere from his chaste marmoreal form
Time had decayed the colours warm;
Like to his gods in thy proud dress,
Thy starry sheen of nakedness.

Surely thy body is thy mind,
For in thy face is nought to find,
Only thy soft unchristened smile,
That shadows neither love nor guile,
But shameless will and power immense,
In secret sensuous innocence.

O king of joy, what is thy thought?
I dream thou knowest it is nought,
And wouldst in darkness come, but thou
Makest the light where'er thou go.
Ah yet no victim of thy grace,
None who e'er longed for thy embrace,
Hath cared to look upon thy face.

'My delight and thy delight'

My delight and thy delight
Walking, like two angels white,
In the gardens of the night:

My desire and thy desire
Twining to a tongue of fire,
Leaping live, and laughing higher;
Thro' the everlasting strife
In the mystery of life.

Love, from whom the world begun,
Hath the secret of the sun.

Love can tell, and love alone,
Whence the million stars were strewn,
Why each atom knows its own,
How, in spite of woe and death,
Gay is life, and sweet is breath:

This he taught us, this we knew,
Happy in his science true,
Hand in hand as we stood
Neath the shadows of the wood.
Heart to heart as we lay
In the dawning of the day.

On a Dead Child

Perfect little boy, without fault or stain on thee,
With promise of strength and manhood full and fair!
Though cold and stark and bare,
The bloom and the charm of life doth awhile remain on thee.

Thy mother's treasure wert thou; – alas! no longer
To visit her heart with wondrous joy; to be
Thy father's pride; – ah, he
Must gather his faith together, and his strength make stronger.

To me, as I move thee now in the last duty,
Dost thou with a turn or gesture anon respond;
Startling my fancy fond
With a chance attitude of the head, a freak of beauty.

Thy hand clasps, as 'twas wont, my finger, and holds it:
But the grasp is the clasp of Death, heartbreaking and stiff;
Yet feels to my hand as if
'Twas still thy will, thy pleasure and trust that enfolds it.

So I lay thee there, thy sunken eyelids closing, –
  Go lie thou there in thy coffin, thy last little bed! –
        Propping thy wise, sad head
Thy firm, pale hands across thy chest disposing.

So quiet! doth the change content thee? – Death, whither hath he taken thee?
  To a world, do I think, that rights the disaster of this?
        The vision of which I miss,
Who weep for the body, and wish but to warm thee and awaken thee?

Ah! little at best can all our hopes avail us
  To lift this sorrow, or cheer us, when in the dark,
        Unwilling, alone we embark,
And the things we have seen and have known and have heard of, fail us.

ALICE MEYNELL

Maternity

One wept whose only child was dead,
New-born, ten years ago.
'Weep not; he is in bliss,' they said.
She answered, 'Even so,

'Ten years ago was born in pain
A child, not now forlorn.
But oh, ten years ago, in vain,
A mother, a mother was born.'

E. NESBIT

The Things that Matter

Now that I've nearly done my days,
  And grown too stiff to sweep or sew,
I sit and think, till I'm amaze,
  About what lots of things I know:
Things as I've found out one by one –
  And when I'm fast down in the clay,
My knowing things and how they're done
  Will all be lost and thrown away.

There's things, I know, as won't be lost,
  Things as folks write and talk about:
The way to keep your roots from frost,
  And how to get your ink spots out.

What medicine's good for sores and sprains,
  What way to salt your butter down,
What charms will cure your different pains,
  And what will bright your faded gown.

But more important things than these,
  They can't be written in a book:
How fast to boil your greens and peas,
  And how good bacon ought to look;
The feel of real good wearing stuff,
  The kind of apple as will keep,
The look of bread that's rose enough,
  And how to get a child asleep.

Whether the jam is fit to pot,
  Whether the milk is going to turn,
Whether a hen will lay or not,
  Is things as some folks never learn.
I know the weather by the sky,
  I know what herbs grow in what lane;
And if sick men are going to die,
  Or if they'll get about again.

Young wives come in, a-smiling, grave,
  With secrets that they itch to tell:
I know what sort of times they'll have
  And if they'll have a boy or gell.
And if a lad is ill to bind,
  Or some young maid is hard to lead,
I know when you should speak 'em kind,
  And when it's scolding as they need.

I used to know where birds ud set,
  And likely spots for trout or hare,
And God may want me to forget
  The way to set a line or snare;
But not the way to truss a chick,
  To fry a fish, or baste a roast,
Nor how to tell, when folks are sick,
  What kind of herb will ease them most!

Forgetting seems such silly waste!
  I know so many little things,
And now the Angels will make haste
  To dust it all away with wings!
O God, you made me like to know,
  You kept the things straight in my head,
Please God, if you can make it so,
  Let me know *something* when I'm dead.

Song

Oh, baby, baby, baby dear,
We lie alone together here;
The snowy gown and cap and sheet
With lavender are fresh and sweet;
Through half-closed blinds the roses peer
To see and love you, baby dear.

We are so tired, we like to lie
Just doing nothing, you and I,
Within the darkened quiet room.
The sun sends dusk rays through the gloom,
Which is no gloom since you are here,
My little life, my baby dear.

Soft sleepy mouth so vaguely pressed
Against your new-made mother's breast.
Soft little hands in mine I fold,
Soft little feet I kiss and hold,
Round soft smooth head and tiny ear,
All mine, my own, my baby dear.

And he we love is far away!
But he will come some happy day,
You need but me, and I can rest
At peace with you beside me pressed.
There are no questions, longings vain,
No murmuring, nor doubt, nor pain,
Only content and we are here,
My baby dear.

RUDYARD KIPLING

Recessional

God of our fathers, known of old,
Lord of our far-flung battle-line,
Beneath whose awful Hand we hold
Dominion over palm and pine –
Lord God of Hosts, be with us yet,
Lest we forget – lest we forget!

The tumult and the shouting dies;
The Captains and the Kings depart:
Still stands Thine ancient sacrifice,
An humble and a contrite heart.

Lord God of Hosts, be with us yet,
Lest we forget – lest we forget!

Far-called, our navies melt away;
  On dune and headland sinks the fire:
Lo, all our pomp of yesterday
  Is one with Nineveh and Tyre!
Judge of the Nations, spare us yet,
Lest we forget – lest we forget!

If, drunk with sight of power, we loose
  Wild tongues that have not Thee in awe,
Such boastings as the Gentiles use,
  Or lesser breeds without the Law –
Lord God of Hosts, be with us yet,
Lest we forget – lest we forget!

For heathen heart that puts her trust
  In reeking tube and iron shard,
All valiant dust that builds on dust,
  And guarding, calls not Thee to guard,
For frantic boast and foolish word –
Thy mercy on Thy People, Lord!

Mandalay

By the old Moulmein Pagoda, lookin' lazy at the sea,
There's a Burma girl a-settin', and I know she thinks o' me;
For the wind is in the palm-trees, and the temple-bells they say:
'Come you back, you British soldier; come you back to Mandalay!'
    Come you back to Mandalay,
    Where the old Flotilla lay:
    Can't you 'ear their paddles chunkin' from Rangoon to Mandalay?
    On the road to Mandalay,
    Where the flyin'-fishes play,
    An' the dawn comes up like thunder outer China 'crost the Bay!

'Er petticoat was yaller an' 'er little cap was green,
An' 'er name was Supi-yaw-lat – jes' the same as Theebaw's Queen,
An' I seed her first a-smokin' of a whackin' white cheroot,
An' a-wastin' Christian kisses on an 'eathen idol's foot:
    Bloomin' idol made o' mud –
    Wot they called the Great Gawd Budd –
    Plucky lot she cared for idols when I kissed 'er where she stud!
    On the road to Mandalay . . .

When the mist was on the rice-fields an' the sun was droppin' slow,
She'd git 'er little banjo an' she'd sing '*Kulla-lo-lo!*'

With 'er arm upon my shoulder an' 'er cheek agin my cheek
We useter watch the steamers an' the *hathis* pilin' teak.
    Elephints a-pilin' teak
    In the sludgy, squdgy creek,
    Where the silence 'ung that 'eavy you was 'arf afraid to speak!
    On the road to Mandalay . . .

But that's all shove be'ind me – long ago an' fur away,
An' there ain't no 'buses runnin' from the Bank to Mandalay;
An' I'm learnin' 'ere in London what the ten-year soldier tells:
'If you've 'eard the East a-callin', you won't never 'eed naught else.'
    No! you won't 'eed nothin' else
    But them spicy garlic smells,
    An' the sunshine an' the palm-trees an' the tinkly temple-bells;
    On the road to Mandalay . . .

I am sick o' wastin' leather on these gritty pavin'-stones,
An' the blasted English drizzle wakes the fever in my bones;
Tho' I walks with fifty 'ousemaids outer Chelsea to the Strand,
An' they talks a lot o' lovin', but wot do they understand?
    Beefy face an' grubby 'and –
    Law! wot do they understand?
    I've a neater, sweeter maiden in a cleaner, greener land!
    On the road to Mandalay . . .

Ship me somewheres east of Suez, where the best is like the worst,
Where there aren't no Ten Commandments an' a man can raise a thirst;
For the temple-bells are callin', an' it's there that I would be –
By the old Moulmein Pagoda, looking lazy at the sea;
    On the road to Mandalay,
    Where the old Flotilla lay,
    With our sick beneath the awnings when we went to Mandalay!
    O the road to Mandalay,
    Where the flyin'-fishes play,
    An' the dawn comes up like thunder outer China 'crost the Bay!

If

If you can keep your head when all about you
    Are losing theirs and blaming it on you,
If you can trust yourself when all men doubt you,
    But make allowance for their doubting too;
If you can wait and not be tired by waiting,
    Or being lied about, don't deal in lies,
Or being hated, don't give way to hating,
    And yet don't look too good, nor talk too wise:

If you can dream – and not make dreams your master;
    If you can think – and not make thoughts your aim;

If you can meet with Triumph and Disaster
    And treat those two imposters just the same;
If you can bear to hear the truth you've spoken
    Twisted by knaves to make a trap for fools,
Or watch the things you gave your life to, broken,
    And stoop and build 'em up with worn-out tools:

If you can make one heap of all your winnings
    And risk it on one turn of pitch-and-toss,
And lose, and start again at your beginnings
    And never breathe a word about your loss;
If you can force your heart and nerve and sinew
    To serve your turn long after they are gone,
And so hold on when there is nothing in you
    Except the Will which says to them: 'Hold on!'

If you can talk with crowds and keep your virtue,
    Or walk with Kings – nor lose the common touch,
If neither foes nor loving friends can hurt you,
    If all men count with you, but none too much;
If you can fill the unforgiving minute
    With sixty seconds' worth of distance run,
Yours is the Earth and everything that's in it,
    And – which is more – you'll be a Man, my son!

Danny Deever

'What are the bugles blowin' for?' said Files-on-Parade.
'To turn you out, to turn you out,' the Colour-Sergeant said.
'What makes you look so white, so white? said Files-on-Parade.
'I'm dreadin' what I've got to watch,' the Colour-Sergeant said.
    For they're hangin' Danny Deever, you can hear the Dead March play,
    The Regiment's in 'ollow square – they're hangin' him to-day;
    They've taken of his buttons off an' cut his stripes away,
    An' they're hangin' Danny Deever in the mornin'.

'What makes the rear-rank breathe so 'ard? said Files-on-Parade.
'It's bitter cold, it's bitter cold,' the Colour-Sergeant said.
'What makes that front-rank man fall down?' said Files-on-Parade.
'A touch o' sun, a touch o' sun,' the Colour-Sergeant said.
    They are hangin' Danny Deever, they are marchin' of 'im round,
    They 'ave 'alted Danny Deever by 'is coffin on the ground;
    An' 'e'll swing in 'arf a minute for a sneakin' shootin' hound –
    O they're hangin' Danny Deever in the mornin'!

''Is cot was right-'and cot to mine,' said Files-on-Parade.
''E's sleepin' out an' far to-night,' the Colour-Sergeant said.
'I've drunk 'is beer a score o' times,' said Files-on-Parade.
''E's drinkin' bitter beer alone,' the Colour-Sergeant said.

They are hangin' Danny Deever, you must mark 'im to 'is place,
For 'e shot a comrade sleepin' – you must look 'im in the face;
Nine 'undred of 'is country an' the Regiment's disgrace,
While they're hangin' Danny Deever in the mornin'.

'What's that so black agin the sun?' said Files-on-Parade.
'It's Danny fighting' 'ard for life,' the Colour-Sergeant said.
'What's that that whimpers over'ead?' said Files-on-Parade.
'It's Danny's soul that's passin' now,' the Colour-Sergeant said.
For they're done with Danny Deever, you can 'ear the quickstep play,
The Regiment's in column, an' they're marchin' us away;
Ho! the young recruits are shakin', an' they'll want their beer to-day.
After hangin' Danny Deever in the mornin'!

Tommy

I went into a public-'ouse to get a pint o' beer,
The publican 'e up an' sez 'We serve no red-coats here.'
The girls be'ind the bar they laughed an' giggled fit to die,
I outs into the street again an' to myself sez I:
O it's Tommy this, an' Tommy that, an' 'Tommy, go away';
But it's 'Thank you, Mister Atkins,' when the band begins to play –
The band begins to play, my boys, the band begins to play,
O it's 'Thank you, Mister Atkins,' when the band begins to play.

I went into a theatre as sober as could be,
They gave a drunk civilian room but 'adn't none for me;
They sent me to the gallery or round the music-'alls,
But when it comes to fightin', Lord! they'll shove me in the stalls!
For it's Tommy this, an' Tommy that, an' 'Tommy, wait outside';
But it's 'Special train for Atkins' when the trooper's on the tide –
The troopship's on the tide, my boys, the troopship's on the tide,
O it's 'Special train for Atkins' when the trooper's on the tide.

Yes, makin' mock o' uniforms that guard you while you sleep
Is cheaper than them uniforms, an' they're starvation cheap;
An' hustlin' drunken soldiers when they're goin' large a bit
Is five times better business than paradin' in full kit.
Then it's Tommy this, an' Tommy that, an' 'Tommy, 'ow's yer soul?'
But it's 'Thin red line of 'eroes' when the drums begin to roll –
The drums begin to roll, my boys, the drums begin to roll,
O it's 'Thin red line of 'eroes' when the drums begin to roll.

We aren't no thin red 'eroes, nor we aren't no blackguards too,
But single men in barricks, most remarkable like you;
An' if sometimes our conduck isn't all your fancy paints,
Why, single men in barricks don't grow into plaster saints;

While it's Tommy this, an' Tommy that, an' 'Tommy, fall be'ind,'
But it's 'Please to walk in front, sir,' when there's trouble in the wind –
There's trouble in the wind, my boys, there's trouble in the wind,
O it's 'Please to walk in front, sir,' when there's trouble in the wind.

You talk o' better food for us, an' schools, an' fires, an' all:
We'll wait for extry rations if you treat us rational.
Don't mess about the cook-room slops, but prove it to our face
The Widow's Uniform is not the soldier-man's disgrace.
For it's Tommy this, an' Tommy that, an' 'Chuck him out, the brute!'
But it's 'Saviour of 'is country' when the guns begin to shoot;
An' it's Tommy this, an' Tommy that, an' anything you please;
An' Tommy ain't a bloomin' fool – you bet that Tommy sees!

For All We Have and Are

1914

For all we have and are,
For all our children's fate,
Stand up and take the war.
The Hun is at the gate!
Our world has passed away,
In wantonness o'erthrown.
There is nothing left to-day
But steel and fire and stone!
Though all we knew depart,
The old Commandments stand:-
'In courage keep your heart,
In strength lift up your hand.'

Once more we hear the word
That sickened earth of old:-
'No law except the Sword
Unsheathed and uncontrolled.'
Once more it knits mankind,
Once more the nations go
To meet and break and bind
A crazed and driven foe.

Comfort, content, delight,
The ages' slow-bought gain,
They shrivelled in a night.
Only ourselves remain
To face the naked days
In silent fortitude,
Through perils and dismays
Renewed and re-renewed.

Though all we made depart,
The old Commandments stand:-
'In patience keep your heart,
In strength lift up your hand.'

No easy hope or lies
Shall bring us to our goal,
But iron sacrifice
Of body, will, and soul.
There is but one task for all –
One life for each to give.
What stands if Freedom fall?
Who dies if England live?

JOHN FREEMAN

Happy is England Now

There is not anything more wonderful
Than a great people moving towards the deep
Of an unguessed and unfeared future; nor
Is aught so dear of all held dear before
As the new passion stirring in their veins
When the destroying dragon wakes from sleep.

Happy is England now, as never yet!
And though the sorrows of the slow days fret
Her faithfullest children, grief itself is proud.
Ev'n the warm beauty of this spring and summer
That turns to bitterness turns then to gladness
Since for this England the beloved ones died.

Happy is England in the brave that die
For wrongs not hers and wrongs so sternly hers;
Happy in those that give, give, and endure
The pain that never the new years may cure;
Happy in all her dark woods, green fields, towns,
Her hills and rivers and her chafing sea.

Whate'er was dear before is dearer now.
There's not a bird singing upon this bough
But sings the sweeter in our English ears:
There's not a nobleness of heart, hand, brain,
But shines the purer; happiest is England now
In those that fight, and watch with pride and tears.

E. A. MACKINTOSH

Recruiting

'Lads, you're wanted, go and help,'
On the railway carriage wall
Stuck the poster, and I thought
Of the hands that penned the call.

Fat civilians wishing they
'Could go and fight the Hun.'
Can't you see them thanking God
That they're over forty-one?

Girls with feathers, vulgar songs –
Washy verse on England's need –
God – and don't we damned well know
How the message ought to read.

'Lads, you're wanted! over there,'
Shiver in the morning dew,
More poor devils like yourselves
Waiting to be killed by you.

Go and help to swell the names
In the casualty lists.
Help to make a column's stuff
For the blasted journalists.

Help to keep them nice and safe
From the wicked German foe.
Don't let him come over here!
'Lads, you're wanted – out you go.'

There's a better word than that,
Lads, and can't you hear it come
From a million men that call
You to share their martyrdom?

Leave the harlots still to sing
Comic songs about the Hun,
Leave the fat old men to say
Now *we've* got them on the run.

Better twenty honest years
Than their dull three score and ten.
Lads, you're wanted. Come and learn
To live and die with honest men.

You shall learn what men can do
If you will but pay the price,

Learn the gaiety and strength
In the gallant sacrifice.

Take your risk of life and death
Underneath the open sky.
Live clean or go out quick –
Lads, you're wanted. Come and die.

FRANCIS LEDWIDGE

Soliloquy

When I was young I had a care
Lest I should cheat me of my share
Of that which makes it sweet to strive
For life, and dying still survive,
A name in sunshine written higher
Than lark or poet dare aspire.

But I grew weary doing well,
Besides, 'twas sweeter in that hell,
Down with the loud banditti people
Who robbed the orchards, climbed the steeple
For jackdaws' eggs and made the cock
Crow ere 'twas daylight on the clock.
I was so very bad the neighbours
Spoke of me at their daily labours.

And now I'm drinking wine in France,
The helpless child of circumstance.
Tomorrow will be loud with war,
How will I be accounted for?
It is too late now to retrieve
A fallen dream, too late to grieve
A name unmade, but not too late
To thank the gods for what is great;
A keen-edged sword, a soldier's heart,
Is greater than a poet's art.
And greater than a poet's fame
A little grave that has no name.

PATRICK SHAW-STEWART

'I saw a man this morning'

I saw a man this morning
  Who did not wish to die:
I ask, and cannot answer,
  If otherwise wish I.

Fair broke the day this morning
  Against the Dardanelles;
The breeze blew soft, the morn's cheeks
  Were cold as cold sea-shells.

But other shells are waiting
  Across the Aegean Sea,
Shrapnel and high explosive,
  Shells and hells for me.

O hell of ships and cities,
  Hell of men like me,
Fatal second Helen,
  Why must I follow thee?

Achilles came to Troyland
  And I to Chersonese:
He turned from wrath to battle,
  And I from three days' peace.

Was it so hard, Achilles,
  So very hard to die?
Thou knowest and I know not –
  So much the happier am I.

I will go back this morning
  From Imbros over the sea;
Stand in the trench, Achilles,
  Flame-capped, and shout for me.

RUPERT BROOKE

The Soldier

If I should die, think only this of me:
  That there's some corner of a foreign field
That is for ever England. There shall be
  In that rich earth a richer dust concealed;
A dust whom England bore, shaped, made aware,
  Gave, once, her flowers to love, her ways to roam,

A body of England's, breathing English air,
  Washed by the rivers, blest by suns of home.
And think, this heart, all evil shed away,
  A pulse in the eternal mind, no less
    Gives somewhere back the thoughts by England
      given;
Her sights and sounds; dreams happy as her day;
  And laughter, learnt of friends; and gentleness,
    In hearts at peace, under an English heaven.

T. M. KETTLE

To my Daughter Betty

In wiser days, my darling rosebud, blown
To beauty proud as was your Mother's prime.
In that desired, delayed, incredible time,
You'll ask why I abandoned you, my own,
And the dear heart that was your baby throne,
To dice with death. And oh! they'll give you rhyme
And reason: some will call the thing sublime,
And some decry it in a knowing tone.
So here, while the mad guns curse overhead,
And tired men sigh with mud for couch and floor,
Know that we fools, now with the foolish dead,
Died not for flag, nor King, nor Emperor,
But for a dream, born in a herdsman's shed,
And for the secret Scripture of the poor.

SIEGFRIED SASSOON

Everyone Sang

Everyone suddenly burst out singing;
And I was filled with such delight
As prisoned birds must find in freedom,
Winging wildly across the white
Orchards and dark-green fields; on – on – and
  out of sight.

Everyone's voice was suddenly lifted;
And beauty came like the setting sun:
My heart was shaken with tears; and horror
Drifted away . . . O, but Everyone
Was a bird; and the song was wordless, the singing
  will never be done.

Glory of Women

You love us when we're heroes, home on leave,
Or wounded in a mentionable place.
You worship decorations; you believe
That chivalry redeems the war's disgrace.
You make us shells. You listen with delight,
By tales of dirt and danger fondly thrilled.
You crown our distant ardours while we fight,
And mourn our laurelled memories when we're killed.
You can't believe that British troops 'retire'
When hell's last horror breaks them, and they run,
Trampling the terrible corpses – blind with blood.
    O German mother dreaming by the fire,
    While you are knitting socks to send your son
    His face is trodden deeper in the mud.

EDWARD THOMAS

'This is no case of petty right or wrong'

This is no case of petty right or wrong
That politicians or philosophers
Can judge. I hate not Germans, nor grow hot
With love of Englishmen, to please newspapers.
Beside my hate for one fat patriot
My hatred of the Kaiser is love true:-
A kind of god he is, banging a gong.
But I have not to choose between the two,
Or between justice and injustice. Dinned
With war and argument I read no more
Than in the storm smoking along the wind
Athwart the wood. Two witches' cauldrons roar.
From one the weather shall rise clear and gay;
Out of the other an England beautiful
And like her mother that died yesterday.
Little I know or care if, being dull,
I shall miss something that historians
Can rake out of the ashes when perchance
The phoenix broods serene above their ken.
But with the best and meanest Englishmen
I am one in crying, God save England, lest
We lose what never slaves and cattle blessed.
The ages made her that made us from dust:
She is all we know and live by, and we trust
She is good and must endure, loving her so:
And as we love ourselves we hate our foe.

In Memoriam (Easter, 1915)

The flowers left thick at nightfall in the wood
This Eastertide call into mind the men,
Now far from home, who, with their sweethearts, should
Have gathered them and will do never again.

ALAN SEEGER

Rendezvous

I have a rendezvous with Death
At some disputed barricade,
When Spring comes back with rustling shade
And apple-blossoms fill the air –
I have a rendezvous with Death
When Spring brings back blue days and fair.

It may be he shall take my hand
And lead me into his dark land
And close my eyes and quench my breath –
It may be I shall pass him still.
I have a rendezvous with Death
On some scarred slope of battered hill,
When Spring comes round again this year
And the first meadow-flowers appear.

God knows 'twere better to be deep
Pillowed in silk and scented down,
Where love throbs out in blissful sleep,
Pulse nigh to pulse, and breath to breath,
Where hushed awakenings are dear . . .
But I've a rendezvous with Death
At midnight in some flaming town,
When Spring trips north again this year,
And I to my pledged word am true,
I shall not fail that rendezvous.

LESLIE COULSON

From the Somme

In other days I sang of simple things,
Of summer dawn, and summer noon and night,
The dewy grass, the dew-wet fairy rings,
The lark's long golden flight.

Deep in the forest I made melody
While squirrels cracked their hazel nuts on high,
Or I would cross the wet sand to the sea
And sing to sea and sky.

When came the silvered silence of the night
I stole to casements over scented lawns,
And softly sang of love and love's delight
To mute white marble fauns.

Oft in the tavern parlour I would sing
Of morning sun upon the mountain vine,
And, calling for a chorus, sweep the string
In praise of good red wine.

I played with all the toys the gods provide,
I sang my songs and made glad holiday.
Now I have cast my broken toys aside
And flung my lute away.

A singer once, I now am fain to weep.
Within my soul I feel strange music swell,
Vast chants of tragedy too deep – too deep
For my poor lips to tell.

HAROLD MONRO

Officers' Mess

I

I search the room with all my mind,
Peering among those eyes;
For I am feverish to find
A brain with which my brain may talk,
Not that I think myself too wise,
But that I'm lonely, and I walk
Round the large place and wonder – No:
There's nobody, I fear,
Lonely as I, and here.

How they hate me. I'm a fool.
I can't play Bridge; I'm bad at Pool;
I cannot drone a comic song;
I can't talk Shop; I can't use Slang;
My jokes are bad, my stories long;
My voice will falter, break or hang,
Not blurt the sour sarcastic word,
And so my swearing sounds absurd.

II

But came the talk: I found
Three or four others for an argument.
I forced their pace. They shifted their dull ground,
And went
Sprawling about the passages of Thought.
We tugged each other's words until they tore.
They asked me my philosophy: I brought
Bits of it forth and laid them on the floor.
They laughed, and so I kicked the bits about,
Then put them in my pocket one by one,
I, sorry I had brought them out,
They, grateful for the fun.

And when these words had thus been sent
Jerking about, like beetles round a wall,
Then one by one to dismal sleep we went:
There was no happiness at all
In that short hopeless argument
Through yawns and on the way to bed
Among men waiting to be dead.

ROBERT NICHOLS

Comrades: an Episode

Before, before he was aware
The 'Verey' light had risen . . . on the air
It hung glistering . . .
And he could not stay his hand
From moving to the barbed wire's broken strand.
A rifle cracked.
He fell.
Night waned. He was alone. A heavy shell
Whispered itself passing high, high overhead.

His wound was wet to his hand: for still it bled
On to the glimmering ground.
Then with a slow, vain smile his wound he bound,

Knowing, of course, he'd not see home again –
Home whose thought he put away.
                                                    His men
Whispered: 'Where's Mister Gates?' 'Out on the wire.'
'I'll get him,' said one . . .
                                        Dawn blinked, and the fire
Of the Germans heaved up and down the line.
'Stand to!'
                    Too late! 'I'll get him.' 'O the swine!
When we might get him in yet safe and whole!'
'Corporal didn't see 'un fall out on patrol,
Or he'd 'a got 'un.' 'Sssh!'
                                        'No talking there.'
A whisper: ''A went down at the last flare.'
Meanwhile the Maxims toc-toc-tocked; their swish
Of bullets told death lurked against the wish.
No hope for him!
                                His corporal, as one shamed,
Vainly and helplessly his ill-luck blamed.

Then Gates slowly saw the morn
Break in a rosy peace through the lone thorn
By which he lay, and felt the dawn-wind pass
Whispering through the pallid, stalky grass
Of No-Man's Land . . .
                                    And the tears came
Scaldingly sweet, more lovely than a flame.
He closed his eyes: he thought of home
And grit his teeth. He knew no help could come . . .

The silent sun over the earth held sway,
Occasional rifles cracked and far away
A heedless speck, a 'plane, slide on alone,
Like a fly traversing a cliff of stone.
'I must get back,' said Gates aloud, and heaved
At his body. But it lay bereaved
Of any power. He could not wait till night . . .
And he lay still. Blood swam across his sight.
Then with a groan:
'No luck ever! Well, I must die alone.'

Occasional rifles cracked. A cloud that shone,
Gold-rimmed, blackened the sun and then was gone . . .
The sun still smiled. The grass sang in its play.
Someone whistled: 'Over the hills and far away.'
Gates watched silently the swift, swift sun
Burning his life before it was begun . . .

Suddenly he heard Corporal Timmins' voice: 'Now then,
'Urry up with that tea.'
'Hi Ginger!' 'Bill!' His men!
Timmins and Jones and Wilkinson (the 'bard'),
And Hughes and Simpson. It was hard
Not to see them: Wilkinson, stubby, grim,
With his 'No, sir,' 'Yes, sir,' and the slim
Simpson: 'Indeed, sir?' (while it seemed he winked
Because his smiling left eye always blinked)
And Corporal Timmins, straight and blond and wise,
With his quiet-scanning, level, hazel eyes;
And all the others . . . tunics that didn't fit . . .
A dozen different sorts of eyes. O it
Was hard to lie there! Yet he must. But no:
'I've got to die. I'll get to them. I'll go.'

Inch by inch he fought, breathless and mute,
Dragging his carcase like a famished brute . . .
His head was hammering, and his eyes were dim;
A bloody sweat seemed to ooze out of him
And freeze along his spine . . . Then he'd lie still
Before another effort of his will
Took him one nearer yard.
The parapet was reached.
He could not rise to it. A lookout screeched:
'Mr Gates!'
Three figures in one breath
Leaped up. Two figures fell in toppling death;
And Gates was lifted in. 'Who's hit?' said he.
'Timmins and Jones.' 'Why did they that for me? –
I'm gone already!' Gently they laid him prone
And silently watched.
He twitched. They heard him moan

'Why for me?' His eyes roamed round, and none replied.
'I see it was alone I should have died.'
They shook their heads. Then, 'Is the doctor here?'
'He's coming, sir; he's hurryin', no fear.'
'No good . . .
Lift me.' They lifted him.
He smiled and held his arms out to the dim,
And in a moment passed beyond their ken,
Hearing him whisper, 'O my men, my men!'

E. A. MACKINTOSH

In Memoriam

Private D. Sutherland killed in action in the German trench,
May 16th, 1916, and the others who died.

So you were David's father,
And he was your only son,
And the new-cut peats are rotting
And the work is left undone,
Because of an old man weeping,
Just an old man in pain,
For David, his son David,
That will not come again.

Oh, the letters he wrote you,
And I can see them still,
Not a word of the fighting
But just the sheep on the hill
And how you should get the crops in
Ere the year get stormier,
And the Bosches have got his body,
And I was his officer.

You were only David's father,
But I had fifty sons
When we went up in the evening
Under the arch of the guns,
And we came back at twilight –
O God! I heard them call
To me for help and pity
That could not help at all.

Oh, never will I forget you,
My men that trusted me,
More my sons than your fathers',
For they could only see
The little helpless babies
And the young men in their pride.
They could not see you dying,
And hold you while you died.

Happy and young and gallant,
They saw their first-born go,
But not the strong limbs broken
And the beautiful men brought low,
The piteous writhing bodies,
They screamed 'Don't leave me, sir,'
For they were only your fathers
But I was your officer.

CHARLES HAMILTON SORLEY

'When you see millions of the mouthless dead'

When you see millions of the mouthless dead
Across your dreams in pale battalions go,
Say not soft things as other men have said,
That you'll remember. For you need not so.
Give them not praise. For, deaf, how should they know
It is not curses heaped on each gashed head?
Nor tears. Their blind eyes see not your tears flow.
Nor honour. It is easy to be dead.
Say only this, 'They are dead.' Then add thereto,
'Yet many a better one has died before.'
Then, scanning all the o'ercrowded mass, should you
Perceive one face that you loved heretofore,
It is a spook. None wears the face you knew.
Great death has made all his for evermore.

ROBERT PALMER

How Long, O Lord?

How long, O Lord, how long, before the flood
Of crimson-welling carnage shall abate?
From sodden plains in West and East the blood
Of kindly men streams up in mists of hate,
Polluting Thy clean air: and nations great
In reputation of the arts that bind
The world with hopes of Heaven, sink to the state
Of brute barbarians, whose ferocious mind
Gloats o'er the bloody havoc of their kind,
Not knowing love or mercy. Lord, how long
Shall Satan in high places lead the blind
To battle for the passions of the strong?
Oh, touch Thy children's hearts, that they may know
Hate their most hateful, pride their deadliest foe.

WILFRED OWEN

Anthem for Doomed Youth

What passing bells for those who die as cattle?
Only the monstrous anger of the guns.
Only the stuttering rifles' rapid rattle
Can patter out their hasty orisons.
No mockeries for them from prayers or bells,
Nor any voice of mourning save the choirs, –
The shrill, demented choirs of wailing shells;
And bugles calling for them from sad shires.
What candles may be held to speed them all?
Not in the hands of boys, but in their eyes
Shall shine the holy glimmers of good-byes.
The pallor of girls' brows shall be their pall;
Their flowers the tenderness of patient minds,
And each slow dusk a drawing-down of blinds.

Disabled

He sat in a wheeled chair, waiting for dark,
And shivered in his ghastly suit of grey,
Legless, sewn short at elbow. Through the park
Voices of boys rang saddening like a hymn,
Voices of play and pleasure after day,
Till gathering sleep had mothered them from him.

* * *

About this time Town used to swing so gay
When glow-lamps budded in the light blue trees,
And girls glanced lovelier as the air grew dim,
– In the old times, before he threw away his knees.
Now he will never feel again how slim
Girls' waists are, or how warm their subtle hands.
All of them touch him like some queer disease.

* * *

There was an artist silly for his face,
For it was younger than his youth, last year.
Now, he is old; his back will never brace;
He's lost his colour very far from here,
Poured it down shell-holes till the veins ran dry,
And half his lifetime lapsed in the hot race
And leap of purple spurted from his thigh.
One time he liked a bloodsmear down his leg,

After the matches, carried shoulder-high.
It was after football, when he'd drunk a peg,
He thought he'd better join. – He wonders why.
Someone had said he'd look a god in kilts,
That's why; and maybe, too, to please his Meg,
Aye, that was it, to please the giddy jilts
He asked to join. He didn't have to beg;
Smiling they wrote his lie: aged nineteen years.
Germans he scarcely thought of; all their guilt
And Austria's, did not move him. And no fears
Of Fear came yet. He thought of jewelled hilts
For daggers in plaid socks; of smart salutes;
And care of arms; and leave; and pay arrears;
Esprit de corps; and hints for young recruits.
And soon, he was drafted out with drums and cheers.

* * *

Some cheered him home, but not as crowds cheer Goal.
Only a solemn man who brought him fruits
Thanked him; and then inquired about his soul.

* * *

Now, he will spend a few sick years in institutes,
And do what things the rules consider wise,
And take whatever pity they may dole.
Tonight he noticed how the women's eyes
Passed from him to the strong men that were whole.
How cold and late it is! Why don't they come
And put him into bed? Why don't they come?

FORD MADOX FORD

The Women of Flanders

This is Charing Cross;
It is midnight;
There is a great crowd
And no light.
A great crowd, all black that hardly whispers aloud.
Surely, that is a dead woman – a dead mother!
She has a dead face;
She is dressed all in black;
She wanders to the bookstall and back,
At the back of the crowd;
And back again and again back,
She sways and wanders.

This is Charing Cross;
It is one o'clock.
There is still a great cloud, and very little light;
Immense shafts of shadows over the black crowd
That hardly whispers aloud . . .
And now! . . . That is another dead mother,
And there is another and another and another . . .
And little children, all in black,
All with dead faces, waiting in all the waiting-places,
Wandering from the doors of the waiting-room
In the dim gloom.

These are the women of Flanders.
They await the lost.
They await the lost that shall never leave the dock;
They await the lost that shall never again come by the train
To the embraces of all these women with dead faces;
They await the lost who lie dead in trench and barrier and foss,
In the dark of the night.
This is Charing Cross; it is past one of the clock;
There is very little light.

There is so much pain.

JOHN MCCRAE

In Flanders Fields

In Flanders fields the poppies blow
Between the crosses, row on row
   That mark our place; and in the sky
   The larks, still bravely singing, fly
Scarce heard amid the guns below.

We are the Dead. Short days ago
We lived, felt dawn, saw sunset glow,
   Loved and were loved, and now we lie
         In Flanders fields.

Take up our quarrel with the foe:
To you from failing hands we throw
   The torch; be yours to hold it high.
   If ye break faith with us who die
We shall not sleep, though poppies grow
         In Flanders fields.

RUDYARD KIPLING

Epitaphs of the War (1914-18)

A SON

My son was killed while laughing at some jest. I would
I knew
What it was, and it might serve me in a time when jests
are few.

THE COWARD

I could not look on Death, which being known,
Men led me to him, blindfold and alone.

THE REFINED MAN

I was of delicate mind. I stepped aside for my needs,
Disdaining the common office. I was seen from afar
and killed . . .
How is this matter for mirth? Let each man be judged
by his deeds.
*I have paid my price to live with myself on the terms
that I willed.*

A SERVANT

We were together since the War began.
He was my servant – and the better man.

COMMON FORM

If any question why we died,
Tell them, because our fathers lied.

A DEAD STATESMAN

I could not dig: I dared not rob:
Therefore I lied to please the mob.
Now all my lies are proved untrue
And I must face the men I slew.
What tale shall serve me here among
Mine angry and defrauded young?

W. B. YEATS

The Wild Swans at Coole

The trees are in their autumn beauty,
The woodland paths are dry,
Under the October twilight the water
Mirrors a still sky;
Upon the brimming water among the stones
Are nine-and-fifty swans.

The nineteenth autumn has come upon me
Since I first made my count;
I saw, before I had well finished,
All suddenly mount
And scatter wheeling in great broken rings
Upon their clamorous wings.

I have looked upon those brilliant creatures,
And now my heart is sore.
All's changed since I, hearing at twilight,
The first time on this shore,
The bell-beat of their wings above my head,
Trod with a lighter tread.

Unwearied still, lover by lover,
They paddle in the cold
Companionable streams or climb the air;
Their hearts have not grown old;
Passion or conquest, wander where they will,
Attend upon them still.

But now they drift on the still water,
Mysterious, beautiful;
Among what rushes will they build,
By what lake's edge or pool
Delight men's eyes when I awake some day
To find they have flown away?

Red Hanrahan's Song About Ireland

The old brown thorn-trees break in two high over Cummen Strand,
Under a bitter black wind that blows from the left hand;
Our courage breaks like an old tree in a black wind and dies,
But we have hidden in our hearts the flame out of the eyes
Of Cathleen, the daughter of Houlihan.

The wind has bundled up the clouds high over Knocknarea,
And thrown the thunder on the stones for all that Maeve can say.
Angers that are like noisy clouds have set our hearts abeat;
But we have all bent low and low and kissed the quiet feet
Of Cathleen, the daughter of Houlihan.

The yellow pool has overflowed high up on Clooth-na-Bare,
For the wet winds are blowing out of the clinging air;
Like heavy flooded waters our bodies and our blood;
But purer than a tall candle before the Holy Rood
Is Cathleen, the daughter of Houlihan.

The Lake Isle of Innisfree

I will arise and go now, and go to Innisfree,
And a small cabin build there, of clay and wattles made:
Nine bean-rows will I have there, a hive for the honey-bee,
And live alone in the bee-loud glade.

And I shall have some peace there, for peace comes dropping slow,
Dropping from the veils of the morning to where the cricket sings;
There midnight's all a glimmer, and noon a purple glow,
And evening full of the linnet's wings.

I will arise and go now, for always night and day
I hear lake water lapping with low sounds by the shore;
While I stand on the roadway, or on the pavements grey,
I hear it in the deep heart's core.

September 1913

What need you, being come to sense,
But fumble in a greasy till
And add the halfpence to the pence
And prayer to shivering prayer, until
You have dried the marrow from the bone?
For men were born to pray and save:
Romantic Ireland's dead and gone,
It's with O'Leary in the grave.

Yet they were of a different kind,
The names that stilled your childish play,
They have gone about the world like wind,
But little time had they to pray
For whom the hangman's rope was spun,
And what, God help us, could they save?
Romantic Ireland's dead and gone,
It's with O'Leary in the grave.

Was it for this the wild geese spread
The grey wing upon every tide;
For this that all that blood was shed,
For this Edward Fitzgerald died,
And Robert Emmet and Wolfe Tone,
All that delirium of the brave?
Romantic Ireland's dead and gone,
It's with O'Leary in the grave.

Yet could we turn the years again,
And call those exiles as they were
In all their loneliness and pain,
You'd cry, 'Some woman's yellow hair
Has maddened every mother's son':
They weighed so lightly what they gave.
But let them be, they're dead and gone,
They're with O'Leary in the grave.

Easter 1916

I have met them at close of day
Coming with vivid faces
From counter or desk among grey
Eighteenth-century houses.
I have passed with a nod of the head
Or polite meaningless words,
Or have lingered awhile and said
Polite meaningless words,
And thought before I had done
Of a mocking tale or a gibe
To please a companion
Around the fire at the club,
Being certain that they and I
But lived where motley is worn:
All changed, changed utterly:
A terrible beauty is born.

That woman's days were spent
In ignorant good-will,

Her nights in argument
Until her voice grew shrill.
What voice more sweet than hers
When, young and beautiful,
She rode to harriers?
This man had kept a school
And rode our wingèd horse;
This other his helper and friend
Was coming into his force;
He might have won fame in the end,
So sensitive his nature seemed,
So daring and sweet his thought.
This other man I had dreamed
A drunken, vainglorious lout.
He had done most bitter wrong
To some who are near my heart,
Yet I number him in the song;
He, too, has resigned his part
In the casual comedy;
He, too, has been changed in his turn,
Transformed utterly:
A terrible beauty is born.

Hearts with one purpose alone
Through summer and winter seem
Enchanted to a stone
To trouble the living stream.
The horse that comes from the road,
The rider, the birds that range
From cloud to tumbling cloud,
Minute by minute they change;
A shadow of cloud on the stream
Changes minute by minute;
A horse-hoof slides on the brim,
And a horse plashes within it;
The long-legged moor-hens dive,
And hens to moor-cocks call;
Minute by minute they live:
The stone's in the midst of all.

Too long a sacrifice
Can make a stone of the heart.
O when may it suffice?
That is Heaven's part, our part
To murmur name upon name,
As a mother names her child
When sleep at last has come
On limbs that had run wild.
What is it but nightfall?

No, no, not night but death;
Was it needless death after all?
For England may keep faith
For all that is done and said.
We know their dream; enough
To know they dreamed and are dead;
And what if excess of love
Bewildered them till they died?
I write it out in a verse –
MacDonagh and MacBride
And Connolly and Pearse
Now and in time to be,
Wherever green is worn,
Are changed, changed utterly:
A terribly beauty is born.

The Great Day

Hurrah for revolution and more cannon-shot!
A beggar upon horseback lashes a beggar on foot.
Hurrah for revolution and cannon come again!
The beggars have changed places, but the lash goes on.

A Coat

I made my song a coat
Covered with embroideries
Out of old mythologies
From heel to throat;
But the fools caught it,
Wore it in the world's eyes
As though they'd wrought it.
Song, let them take it,
For there's more enterprise
In walking naked.

He Wishes for the Cloths of Heaven

Had I the heavens' embroidered cloths,
Enwrought with golden and silver light,
The blue and the dim and the dark cloths
Of night and light and the half-light,
I would spread the cloths under your feet:
But I, being poor, have only my dreams;
I have spread my dreams under your feet;
Tread softly because you tread on my dreams.

The Second Coming

Turning and turning in the widening gyre
The falcon cannot hear the falconer;
Things fall apart; the centre cannot hold;
Mere anarchy is loosed upon the world,
The blood-dimmed tide is loosed, and everywhere
The ceremony of innocence is drowned;
The best lack all conviction, while the worst
Are full of passionate intensity.

Surely some revelation is at hand;
Surely the Second Coming is at hand.
The Second Coming! Hardly are those words out
When a vast image out of *Spiritus Mundi*
Troubles my sight: somewhere in sands of the desert
A shape with lion body and the head of a man,
A gaze blank and pitiless as the sun,
Is moving its slow thighs, while all about it
Reel shadows of the indignant desert birds.
The darkness drops again; but now I know
That twenty centuries of stony sleep
Were vexed to nightmare by a rocking cradle,
And what rough beast, its hour come round at last,
Slouches towards Bethlehem to be born?

No Second Troy

Why should I blame her that she filled my days
With misery, or that she would of late
Have taught to ignorant men most violent ways,
Or hurled the little streets upon the great,
Had they but courage equal to desire?
What could have made her peaceful with a mind
That nobleness made simple as a fire,
With beauty like a tightened bow, a kind
That is not natural in an age like this,
Being high and solitary and most stern?
Why, what could she have done, being what she is?
Was there another Troy for her to burn?

Sailing to Byzantium

That is no country for old men. The young
In one another's arms, birds in the trees
– Those dying generations – at their song,
The salmon-falls, the mackerel-crowded seas,
Fish, flesh, or fowl, commend all summer long
Whatever is begotten, born, and dies.
Caught in that sensual music all neglect
Monuments of unageing intellect.

An aged man is but a paltry thing,
A tattered coat upon a stick, unless
Soul clap its hands and sing, and louder sing
For every tatter in its mortal dress,
Nor is there singing school but studying
Monuments of its own magnificence;
And therefore I have sailed the seas and come
To the holy city of Byzantium.

O sages standing in God's holy fire
As in the gold mosaic of a wall,
Come from the holy fire, perne in a gyre,
And be the singing-masters of my soul.
Consume my heart away; sick with desire
And fastened to a dying animal
It knows not what it is; and gather me
Into the artifice of eternity.

Once out of nature I shall never take
My bodily form from any natural thing,
But such a form as Grecian goldsmiths make
Of hammered gold and gold enamelling
To keep a drowsy Emperor awake;
Or set upon a golden bough to sing
To lords and ladies of Byzantium
Of what is past, or passing, or to come.

The Choice

The intellect of man is forced to choose
Perfection of the life, or of the work,
And if it take the second must refuse
A heavenly mansion, raging in the dark.

When all that story's finished, what's the news?
In luck or out the toil has left its mark:
That old perplexity an empty purse,
Or the day's vanity, the night's remorse.

The Fascination of What's Difficult

The fascination of what's difficult
Has dried the sap out of my veins, and rent
Spontaneous joy and natural content
Out of my heart. There's something ails our colt
That must, as if it had not holy blood
Nor on Olympus leaped from cloud to cloud,
Shiver under the lash, strain, sweat and jolt
As though it dragged road metal. My curse on plays
That have to be set up in fifty ways,
On the day's war with every knave and dolt,
Theatre business, management of men.
I swear before the dawn comes round again
I'll find the stable and pull out the bolt.

A Prayer for My Daughter

Once more the storm is howling, and half hid
Under this cradle-hood and coverlid
My child sleeps on. There is no obstacle
But Gregory's wood and one bare hill
Whereby the haystack- and roof-levelling wind,
Bred on the Atlantic, can be stayed;
And for an hour I have walked and prayed
Because of the great gloom that is in my mind.

I have walked and prayed for this young child an hour
And hear the sea-wind scream upon the tower,
And under the arches of the bridge, and scream
In the elms above the flooded stream;
Imagining in excited reverie
That the future years had come,
Dancing to a frenzied drum,
Out of the murderous innocence of the sea.

May she be granted beauty and yet not
Beauty to make a stranger's eye distraught,
Or hers before a looking-glass, for such,
Being made beautiful overmuch,
Consider beauty a sufficient end,
Lose natural kindness and maybe
The heart-revealing intimacy
That chooses right, and never find a friend.

Helen being chosen found life flat and dull
And later had much trouble from a fool,

While that great Queen, that rose out of the spray,
Being fatherless could have her way
Yet chose a bandy-leggèd smith for man.
It's certain that fine women eat
A crazy salad with their meat
Whereby the Horn of Plenty is undone.

In courtesy I'd have her chiefly learned;
Hearts are not had as a gift but hearts are earned
By those that are not entirely beautiful;
Yet many, that have played the fool
For beauty's very self, has charm made wise,
And many a poor man that has roved,
Loved and thought himself beloved,
From a glad kindness cannot take his eyes.

May she become a flourishing hidden tree
That all her thoughts may like the linnet be,
And have no business but dispensing round
Their magnanimities of sound,
Nor but in merriment begin a chase,
Nor but in merriment a quarrel.
O may she live like some green laurel
Rooted in one dear perpetual place.

My mind, because the minds that I have loved,
The sort of beauty that I have approved,
Prosper but little, has dried up of late,
Yet knows that to be choked with hate
May well be of all evil chances chief.
If there's no hatred in a mind
Assault and battery of the wind
Can never tear the linnet from the leaf.

An intellectual hatred is the worst,
So let her think opinions are accursed.
Have I not seen the loveliest woman born
Out of the mouth of Plenty's horn,
Because of her opinionated mind
Barter that horn and every good
By quiet natures understood
For an old bellows full of angry wind?

Considering that, all hatred driven hence,
The soul recovers radical innocence
And learns at last that it is self-delighting,
Self-appeasing, self-affrighting,
And that its own sweet will is Heaven's will;
She can, though every face should scowl

And every windy quarter howl
Or every bellows burst, be happy still.

And may her bridegroom bring her to a house
Where all's accustomed, ceremonious;
For arrogance and hatred are the wares
Peddled in the thoroughfares.
How but in custom and in ceremony
Are innocence and beauty born?
Ceremony's a name for the rich horn,
And custom for the spreading laurel tree.

JAMES JOYCE

'I hear an army charging upon the land'

I hear an army charging upon the land
   And the thunder of horses plunging, foam about their knees.
Arrogant, in black armour, behind them stand,
   Disdaining the reins, with fluttering whips, the charioteers.

They cry unto the night their battlename:
   I moan in sleep when I hear afar their whirling laughter.
They cleave the gloom of dreams, a blinding flame,
   Clanging, clanging upon the heart as upon an anvil.

They come shaking in triumph their long green hair;
   They come out of the sea and run shouting by the shore.
My heart, have you no wisdom thus to despair?
   My love, my love, my love, why have you left me alone?

Watching the Needleboats at San Sabba

I heard their young hearts crying
Loveward above the glancing oar
And heard the prairie grasses sighing:
No more, return no more!

O hearts, O sighing grasses,
Vainly your loveblown bannerets mourn!
No more will the wild wind that passes
Return, no more return.

She Weeps Over Rahoon

Rain on Rahoon falls softly, softly falling,
Where my dark lover lies,
Sad is his voice that calls me, sadly calling,
At grey moonrise.

Love, hear thou
How soft, how sad his voice is ever calling,
Ever unanswered, and the dark rain falling,
Then as now.

Dark too our hearts, O love, shall lie and cold
As his sad heart has lain
Under the moongrey nettles, the black mould
And muttering rain.

Gas from a Burner

Ladies and gents, you are here assembled
To hear why earth and heaven trembled
Because of the black and sinister arts
Of an Irish writer in foreign parts.
He sent me a book ten years ago:
I read it a hundred times or so,
Backwards and forwards, down and up,
Through both the ends of a telescope.
I printed it all to the very last word
But by the mercy of the Lord
The darkness of my mind was rent
And I saw the writer's foul intent.
But I owe a duty to Ireland:
I hold her honour in my hand,
This lovely land that always sent
Her writers and artists to banishment
And in a spirit of Irish fun
Betrayed her own leaders, one by one.
'Twas Irish humour, wet and dry,
Flung quicklime into Parnell's eye;
'Tis Irish brains that save from doom
The leaky barge of the Bishop of Rome
For everyone knows the Pope can't belch
Without the consent of Billy Walsh.
O Ireland my first and only love
Where Christ and Caesar are hand and glove!
O lovely land where the shamrock grows!
(Allow me, ladies, to blow my nose)
To show you for strictures I don't care a button

I printed the poems of Mountainy Mutton
And a play he wrote (you've read it, I'm sure)
Where they talk of '*bastard*', '*bugger*' and '*whore*',
And a play on the Word and Holy Paul
And some woman's legs that I can't recall,
Written by Moore, a genuine gent
That lives on his property's ten per cent:
I printed mystical books in dozens:
I printed the table-book of Cousins
Though (asking your pardon) as for the verse
'Twould give you a heartburn on your arse:
I printed folklore from North and South
By Gregory of the Golden Mouth:
I printed poets, sad, silly and solemn:
I printed Patrick What-do-you-Colm:
I printed the great John Milicent Synge
Who soars above on an angel's wing
In the playboy shift that he pinched as swag
From Maunsel's manager's travelling-bag.
But I draw the line at that bloody fellow
That was over here dressed in Austrian yellow,
Spouting Italian by the hour
To O'Leary Curtis and John Wyse Power
And writing of Dublin, dirty and dear,
In a manner no blackamoor printer could bear.
Shite and onions! Do you think I'll print
The name of the Wellington Monument,
Sydney Parade and Sandymount tram,
Downes's cakeshop and Williams's jam?
I'm damned if I do – I'm damned to blazes!
Talk about *Irish Names of Places*!
It's a wonder to me, upon my soul,
He forgot to mention Curly's Hole.
No, ladies, my press shall have no share in
So gross a libel on Stepmother Erin.
I pity the poor – that's why I took
A red-headed Scotchman to keep my book.
Poor sister Scotland! Her doom is fell;
She cannot find any more Stuarts to sell.
My conscience is fine as Chinese silk:
My heart is as soft as buttermilk.
Colm can tell you I made a rebate
Of one hundred pounds on the estimate
I gave him for his *Irish Review*.
I love my country – by herrings I do!
I wish you could see what tears I weep
When I think of the emigrant train and ship.
That's why I publish far and wide
My quite illegible railway guide,

In the porch of my printing institute
The poor and deserving prostitute
Plays every night at catch-as-catch can
With her tight-breeched British artilleryman
And the foreigner learns the gift of the gab
From the drunken draggletail Dublin drab.
Who was it said: Resist not evil?
I'll burn that book, so help me devil.
I'll sing a psalm as I watch it burn
And the ashes I'll keep in a one-handled urn.
I'll penance do with farts and groans
Kneeling upon my marrowbones.
This very next lent I will unbare
My penitent buttocks to the air
And sobbing beside my printing press
My awful sin I will confess.
My Irish foreman from Bannockburn
Shall dip his right hand in the urn
And sign crisscross with reverent thumb
Memento homo upon my bum.

Ecce Puer

Of the dark past
A child is born;
With joy and grief
My heart is torn.

Calm in his cradle
The living lies.
May love and mercy
Unclose his eyes!

Young life is breathed
On the glass;
The world that was not
Come to pass.

A child is sleeping:
An old man gone.
O, father forsaken,
Forgive your son!

'Strings in the earth and air'

Strings in the earth and air
  Make music sweet;
Strings by the river where
  The willows meet.

There's music along the river,
  For Love wanders there,
Pale flowers on his mantle,
  Dark leaves on his hair.

All softly playing,
  With head to the music bent,
And fingers straying
  Upon an instrument.

D. H. LAWRENCE

Piano

Softly, in the dusk, a woman is singing to me;
Taking me back down the vista of years, till I see
A child sitting under the piano, in the boom of the tingling strings
And pressing the small, poised feet of a mother who smiles as she sings.

In spite of myself, the insidious mastery of song
Betrays me back, till the heart of me weeps to belong
To the old Sunday evenings at home, with winter outside
And hymns in the cosy parlour, the tinkling piano our guide.

So now it is vain for the singer to burst into clamour
With the great black piano appassionato. The glamour
Of childish days is upon me, my manhood is cast
Down in the flood of remembrance, I weep like a child for the past.

The Collier's Wife

Somebody's knocking' at th' door
  Mother, come down an' see!
– I's think it's nobbut a beggar;
  Say I'm busy.

It's not a beggar, mother; hark
  How 'ard 'e knocks!
– Eh, tha'rt a mard-arsed kid,
  'E'll gie thee socks!

Shout an' ax what 'e wants,
    I canna come down.
– 'E says, is it Arthur Holliday's?
    – Say Yes, tha clown.

'E says: Tell your mother as 'er mester's
    Got hurt i' th' pit –
What? Oh my Sirs, 'e never says that.
    That's not it!

Come out o' th' way an' let me see!
    Eh, there's no peace!
An' stop thy scraightin', childt,
    Do shut thy face!

'Your mester's 'ad a accident
    An' they ta'ein' 'im i' th' ambulance
Ter Nottingham.' – Eh dear o' me,
    If 'e's not a man for mischance!

Wheer's 'e hurt this time, lad?
    – I dunna know,
They on'y towd me it wor bad –
    It would be so!

Out o' my way, childt! dear o' me, wheer
    'Ave I put 'is clean stockin's an' shirt?
Goodness knows if they'll be able
    To take off 'is pit-dirt!

An' what a moan 'e'll make! there niver
    Was such a man for fuss
If anything ailed 'im; at any rate
    I shan't 'ave 'im to nuss.

I do 'ope as it's not very bad!
    Eh, what a shame it seems
As some should ha'e hardly a smite o' trouble
    An' others 'as reams!

It's a shame as 'e should be knocked about
    Like this, I'm sure it is!
'E's 'ad twenty accidents, if 'e's 'ad one;
    Owt bad, an' it's his!

There's one thing, we s'll 'ave a peaceful 'ouse f'r a bit,
    Thank heaven for a peaceful house!
An' there's compensation, sin' it's accident,
    An' club-money – I won't growse.

An' a fork an' a spoon 'e'll want – an' what else?
I s'll never catch that train!
What a traipse it is, if a man gets hurt!
I sh'd think 'e'll get right again.

A Young Wife

The pain of loving you
Is almost more than I can bear.

I walk in fear of you.
The darkness starts up where
You stand, and the night comes through
Your eyes when you look at me.

Ah never before did I see
The shadows that live in the sun!

Now every tall glad tree
Turns round its back to the sun
And looks down on the ground, to see
The shadow it used to shun.

At the foot of each glowing thing
A night lies looking up.

Oh, and I want to sing
And dance, but I can't lift up
My eyes from the shadows: dark
They lie spilt round the cup.

What is it? – Hark
The faint fine seethe in the air!

Like the seething sound in a shell!
It is death still seething where
The wild-flower shakes its bell
And the skylark twinkles blue –

The pain of loving you
Is almost more than I can bear.

What Would You Fight For?

I am not sure I would always fight for my life.
Life might not be worth fighting for.

I am not sure I would always fight for my wife.
A wife isn't always worth fighting for.

Nor my children, nor my country, nor my fellow-men.
It all depends whether I found them worth fighting for.

The only thing men invariably fight for
is their money. But I doubt if I'd fight for mine, anyhow
not to shed a lot of blood over it.

Yet one thing I do fight for, tooth and nail, all the time.
And that is my bit of inward peace, where I am at one
with myself.

And I must say, I am often worsted.

To Women, As Far As I'm Concerned

The feelings I don't have I don't have.
The feelings I don't have, I won't say I have.
The feelings you say you have, you don't have.
The feelings you would like us both to have, we
neither of us have.
The feelings people ought to have, they never have.
If people say they've got feelings, you may be pretty
sure they haven't got them.
So if you want either of us to feel anything at all
you'd better abandon all idea of feelings altogether.

Intimates

Don't you care for my love? she said bitterly.

I handed her the mirror, and said:
Please address these questions to the proper person!
Please make all requests to head-quarters!
In all matters of emotional importance
please approach the supreme authority direct! –
So I handed her the mirror.

And she would have broken it over my head,
but she caught sight of her own reflection
and that held her spellbound for two seconds
while I fled.

Bavarian Gentians

Not every man has gentians in his house
in soft September, at slow, sad Michaelmas.

Bavarian gentians, big and dark, only dark
darkening the day-time torch-like with the smoking blueness of Pluto's gloom,
ribbed and torch-like, with their blaze of darkness spread blue
down flattening into points, flattened under the sweep of white day
torch-flower of the blue-smoking darkness, Pluto's dark-blue daze,
black lamps from the halls of Dis, burning dark blue,
giving off darkness, blue darkness, as Demeter's pale lamps give off light,
lead me then, lead me the way.

Reach me a gentian, give me a torch
let me guide myself with the blue, forked torch of this flower
down the darker and darker stairs, where blue is darkened on blueness,
even where Persephone goes, just now, from the frosted September
to the sightless realm where darkness is awake upon the dark
and Persephone herself is but a voice
or a darkness invisible enfolded in the deeper dark
of the arms Plutonic, and pierced with the passion of dense gloom,
among the splendour of torches of darkness, shedding darkness on the lost bride and
her groom.

Sicilian Cyclamens

When he pushed his bush of black hair off his brow:
When she lifted her mop from her eyes, and screwed it in a knob behind
– O act of fearful temerity!
When they felt their foreheads bare, naked to heaven, their eyes revealed:
When they felt the light of heaven brandished like a knife at their defenceless eyes,
And the sea like a blade at their face,
Mediterranean savages:
When they came out, face-revealed, under heaven, from the shaggy undergrowth of
their own hair
For the first time,
They saw the tiny rose cyclamens between their toes, growing
Where the slow toads sat brooding on the past.

Slow toads, and cyclamen leaves
Stickily glistening with eternal shadow
Keeping to earth.
Cyclamen leaves
Toad-filmy, earth-iridescent
Beautiful
Frost-filigreed
Spumed with mud

Snail-nacreous
Low down.

The shaking aspect of the sea
And man's defenceless bare face
And cyclamens putting their ears back.

Long, pensive, slim-muzzled greyhound buds
Dreamy, not yet present,
Drawn out of earth
At his toes.

Dawn-rose
Sub-delighted, stone-engendered
Cyclamens, young cyclamens
Arching
Waking, pricking their ears
Like delicate very-young greyhound bitches
Half-yawning at the open, inexperienced
Vista of day,
Folding back their soundless petalled ears.

Greyhound bitches
Bending their rosy muzzles pensive down,
And breathing soft, unwilling to wake to the new day
Yet sub-delighted.
Ah Mediterranean morning, when our world began!
Far-off Mediterranean mornings,
Pelasgic faces uncovered,
And unbudding cyclamens.

The hare suddenly goes uphill
Laying back her long ears with unwinking bliss.

And up the pallid, sea-blanched Mediterranean stone-slopes
Rose cyclamen, ecstatic fore-runner!
Cyclamens, ruddy-muzzled cyclamens
In little bunches like bunches of wild hares
Muzzles together, ears-aprick,
Whispering witchcraft
Like women at a well, the dawn-fountain.

Greece, and the world's morning
Where all the Parthenon marbles still fostered the roots of the cyclamen.
Violets
Pagan, rosy-muzzled violets
Autumnal
Dawn-pink,
Dawn-pale
Among squat toad-leaves sprinkling the unborn
Erechtheion marbles.

Self-Pity

I never saw a wild thing
sorry for itself.
A small bird will drop frozen dead from a bough
without ever having felt sorry for itself.

The Gazelle Calf

The gazelle calf, O my children,
goes behind its mother across the desert,
goes behind its mother on blithe bare foot
requiring no shoes, O my children!

Little Fish

The tiny fish enjoy themselves
in the sea.
Quick little splinters of life,
their little lives are fun to them
in the sea.

The Mosquito Knows

The mosquito knows full well, small as he is
he's a beast of prey.
But after all
he only takes his bellyful,
he doesn't put my blood in the bank.

E. E. CUMMINGS

'16 heures'

16 heures
l'Etoile

the communists have fine Eyes

some are young some old none
look alike the flics rush

batter the crowd sprawls collapses
singing knocked down trampled the kicked by
flics rush(the

Flics,tidiyum,are
very tidiyum reassuringly similar,
they all have very tidiyum
mustaches,and very
tidiyum chins,and just above
their very tidiyum ears their
very tidiyum necks begin)
let us add

that there are 50(fifty)flics for every
one(1)communist and
all the flics are very organically
arranged
and their nucleus(composed
of captains in freshly-creased
-uniforms with only-just-
shined buttons
tidiyum
before and behind)has a nucleolus:

the Prefect of Police

(a dapper derbied
creature,swaggers daintily
twiddling
his tiny cane
and,mazurkas about tweak-
ing his wing collar pecking at his im
-peccable cravat directing being
shooting his cuffs
saluted everywhere saluting
reviewing processions of minions
tappingpeopleontheback

"allezcirculez")

–my he's brave. . .
the
communists pick
up themselves friends
& their hats legs &

arms brush dirt coats
smile looking hands
spit blood teeth

the Communists have(very)fine eyes
(which stroll hither and thither through the
evening in bruised narrow questioning faces)

ROBERT GRAVES

To Whom Else?

To whom else other than,
To whom else not of man
Yet in human state,
Standing neither in stead
Of self nor idle godhead,
Should I, man in man bounded,
Myself dedicate?

To whom else momently,
To whom else endlessly,
But to you, I?
To you who only,
To you who mercilessly,
To you who lovingly,
Plucked out the lie?

To whom else less acquaint,
To whom else without taint
Of death, death-true?
With great astonishment
Thankfully I consent
To my estrangement
From me in you.

LANGSTON HUGHES

Dream Variation

To fling my arms wide
In some place of the sun,
To whirl and to dance
Till the white day is done.
Then rest at cool evening
Beneath a tall tree
While night comes on gently,
  Dark like me –
That is my dream!

To fling my arms wide
In the face of the sun,
Dance! Whirl! Whirl!

Till the quick day is done.
Rest at pale evening . . .
A tall, slim tree . . .
Night coming tenderly
   Black like me.

ROBERT FROST

The Road Not Taken

Two roads diverged in a yellow wood,
And sorry I could not travel both
And be one traveler, long I stood
And looked down one as far as I could
To where it bent in the undergrowth;

Then took the other, as just as fair,
And having perhaps the better claim,
Because it was grassy and wanted wear;
Though as for that the passing there
Had worn them really about the same,

And both that morning equally lay
In leaves no step had trodden black.
Oh, I kept the first for another day!
Yet knowing how way leads on to way,
I doubted if I should ever come back.

I shall be telling this with a sigh
Somewhere ages and ages hence:
Two roads diverged in a wood, and I –
I took the one less traveled by,
And that has made all the difference.

EZRA POUND

That Lake Isle

O God, O Venus, O Mercury, patron of thieves,
Give me in due time, I beseech you, a little tobacco-shop,
With the little bright boxes
      piled up neatly upon the shelves
And the loose fragrant cavendish
      and the shag,
And the bright Virginia
      loose under the bright glass cases,

And a pair of scales not too greasy,
And the whores dropping in for a word or two in passing,
For a flip word, and to tidy their hair a bit.
O God, O Venus, O Mercury, patron of thieves,
Lend me a little tobacco-shop,
        or install me in any profession
Save this damn'd profession of writing,
        where one needs one's brains all the time.

In a Station of the Metro

The apparition of these faces in the crowd;
Petals on a wet, black bough.

Plunge

I would bathe myself in strangeness:
These comforts heaped upon me, smother me!
I burn, I scald so for the new,
New friends, new faces,
Places!
Oh to be out of this,
This that is all I wanted
        – save the new.

And you,
Love, you the much, the more desired!
Do I not loathe all walls, streets, stones,
All mire, mist, all fog,
All ways of traffic?
You, I would have flow over me like water,
Oh, but far out of this!
Grass, and low fields, and hills,
And sun,
Oh, sun enough!
Out, and alone, among some
Alien people!

T. S. ELIOT

Prelude

The winter evening settles down
With smells of steaks in passageways.
Six o'clock.
The burnt-out ends of smoky days.
And now a gusty shower wraps
The grimy scraps
Of withered leaves about his feet
And newspapers from vacant lots;
The showers beat
On broken blinds and chimney pots,
And at the corner of the street
A lonely cab-horse steams and stamps.
And then the lighting of the lamps.

Journey of the Magi

'A cold coming we had of it,
Just the worst time of the year
For a journey, and such a long journey:
The ways deep and the weather sharp,
The very dead of winter.'
And the camels galled, sore-footed, refractory,
Lying down in the melting snow.
There were times we regretted
The summer palaces on slopes, the terraces,
And the silken girls bringing sherbet.
Then the camel men cursing and grumbling
And running away, and wanting their liquor and women,
And the night-fires going out, and the lack of shelters,
And the cities hostile and the towns unfriendly
And the villages dirty and charging high prices:
A hard time we had of it.
At the end we preferred to travel all night,
Sleeping in snatches,
With the voices singing in our ears, saying
That this was all folly.

Then at dawn we came down to a temperate valley,
Wet, below the snow line, smelling of vegetation;
With a running stream and a water-mill beating the darkness,
And three trees on the low sky,
And an old white horse galloped away in the meadow.
Then we came to a tavern with vine-leaves over the lintel,

Six hands at an open door dicing for pieces of silver,
And feet kicking the empty wine-skins.
But there was no information, and so we continued
And arrived at evening, not a moment too soon
Finding the place; it was (you may say) satisfactory.

All this was a long time ago, I remember,
And I would do it again, but set down
This set down
This: were we led all that way for
Birth or Death? There was a Birth, certainly,
We had evidence and no doubt. I had seen birth and death,
But had thought they were different; this Birth was
Hard and bitter agony for us, like Death, our death.
We returned to our places, these Kingdoms,
But no longer at ease here, in the old dispensation,
With an alien people clutching their gods.
I should be glad of another death.

LOUIS MACNEICE

Snow

The room was suddenly rich and the great bay-window was
Spawning snow and pink roses against it
Soundlessly collateral and incompatible:
World is suddener than we fancy it.

World is crazier and more of it than we think,
Incorrigibly plural. I peel and portion
A tangerine and spit the pips and feel
The drunkenness of things being various.

And the fire flames with a bubbling sound for world
Is more spiteful and gay than one supposes –
On the tongue on the eyes on the ears in the palms of one's hands –
There is more than glass between the snow and the huge roses.

LAURIE LEE

Home from Abroad

Far-fetched with tales of other worlds and ways,
My skin well-oiled with wines of the Levant,
I set my face into a filial smile
To greet the pale, domestic kiss of Kent.

But shall I never learn? That gawky girl,
Recalled so primly in my foreign thoughts,
Becomes again the green-haired queen of love
Whose wanton form dilates as it delights.

Her rolling tidal landscape floods the eye
And drowns Chianti in a dusky stream;
The flower-flecked grasses swim with simple horses,
The hedges choke with roses fat as cream.

So do I breathe the hayblown airs of home,
And watch the sea-green elms drip birds and shadows,
And as the twilight nets the plunging sun
My heart's keel slides to rest among the meadows.

JOHN MASEFIELD

Cargoes

Quinquireme of Nineveh from distant Ophir
Rowing home to haven in sunny Palestine,
With a cargo of ivory,
And apes and peacocks,
Sandalwood, cedarwood, and sweet white wine.

Stately Spanish galleon coming from the Isthmus,
Dipping through the Tropics by the palm-green shores,
With a cargo of diamonds,
Emeralds, amethysts,
Topazes, and cinnamon, and gold moidores.

Dirty British coaster with a salt-caked smoke stack
Butting through the Channel in the mad March days,
With a cargo of Tyne coal,
Road-rail, pig-lead,
Firewood, iron-ware, and cheap tin trays.

JOHN BETJEMAN

The Metropolitan Railway

Baker Street Station Buffet

Early Electric! With what radiant hope
  Men formed this many-branched electrolier,
Twisted the flex around the iron rope
  And let the dazzling vacuum globes hang clear,
And then with hearts the rich contrivance fill'd
Of copper, beaten by the Bromsgrove Guild.

Early Electric! Sit you down and see,
  'Mid this fine woodwork and a smell of dinner,
A stained-glass windmill and a pot of tea,
  And sepia views of leafy lanes in PINNER, –
Then visualize, far down the shining lines,
Your parents' homestead set in murmuring pines.

Smoothly from HARROW, passing PRESTON ROAD,
  They saw the last green fields and misty sky,
At NEASDEN watched a workmen's train unload,
  And, with the morning villas sliding by,
They felt so sure on their electric trip
That Youth and Progress were in partnership.

And all that day in murky London Wall
  The thought of RUISLIP kept him warm inside;
At FARRINGDON that lunch hour at a stall
  He bought a dozen plants of London Pride;
While, she, in arc-lit Oxford Street adrift,
Soared through the sales by safe hydraulic lift.

Early Electric! Maybe even here
  They met that evening at six-fifteen
Beneath the hearts of this electrolier
  and caught the first non-stop to WILLESDEN GREEN,
Then out and on, through rural RAYNER'S LANE
To autumn-scented Middlesex again.

Cancer has killed him. Heart is killing her.
  The trees are down. An Odeon flashes fire
Where stood their villa by the murmuring fir
  When 'they would for their children's good conspire'.
Of all their loves and hopes on hurrying feet
Thou art the worn memorial, Baker Street.

In a Bath Teashop

'Let us not speak, for the love we bear one another –
    Let us hold hands and look.'
She, such a very ordinary little woman;
    He, such a thumping crook;
But both, for a moment, little lower than the angels
    In the teashop's ingle-nook.

CHRISTOPHER ISHERWOOD

On His Queerness

When I was young and wanted to see the sights,
They told me: 'Cast an eye over the Roman Camp
If you care to,
But plan to spend most of your day at the Aquarium –
Because, after all, the Aquarium –
Well, I mean to say, the Aquarium –
Till you've seen the Aquarium you ain't seen nothing.'

So I cast an eye over
The Roman Camp –
And that old Roman Camp,
That old, old Roman Camp
Got me
Interested.

So that now, near closing-time,
I find that I still know nothing –
And am not even sorry that I know nothing –
About fish.

W. H. AUDEN

Night Mail

Commentary for a G.P.O. Film)

I

This is the Night Mail crossing the Border,
Bringing the cheque and the postal order,

Letters for the rich, letters for the poor,
The shop at the corner, the girl next door.

Pulling up Beattock, a steady climb:
The gradient's against her, but she's on time.

Past cotton-grass and moorland boulder,
Shovelling white steam over her shoulder,

Snorting noisily, she passes
Silent miles of wind-bent grasses.

Birds turn their heads as she approaches,
Stare from bushes at her blank-faced coaches.

Sheep-dogs cannot turn her course;
They slumber on with paws across.

In the farm she passes no one wakes,
But a jug in a bedroom gently shakes.

II

Dawn freshens. Her climb is done.
Down towards Glasgow she descends,
Towards the steam tugs yelping down a glade of cranes,
Towards the fields of apparatus, the furnaces
Set on the dark plain like gigantic chessmen.
All Scotland waits for her:
In dark glens, beside pale-green lochs,
Men long for news.

III

Letters of thanks, letters from banks,
Letters of joy from girl and boy,
Receipted bills and invitations
To inspect new stock or to visit relations,
And applications for situations,
And timid lovers' declarations,
And gossip, gossip from all the nations,
News circumstantial, news financial,
Letters with holiday snaps to enlarge in,
Letters with faces scrawled on the margin,
Letters from uncles, cousins and aunts,
Letters to Scotland from the South of France,
Letters of condolence to Highlands and Lowlands,
Written on paper of every hue,
The pink, the violet, the white and the blue,
The chatty, the catty, the boring, the adoring,
The cold and official and the heart's outpouring,
Clever, stupid, short and long,
The typed and the printed and the spelt all wrong.

IV

Thousands are still asleep,
Dreaming of terrifying monsters
Or a friendly tea beside the band in Cranston's or Crawford's:
Asleep in working Glasgow, asleep in well-set Edinburgh,
Asleep in granite Aberdeen,
They continue their dreams,
But shall wake soon and hope for letters,
And none will hear the postman's knock
Without a quickening of the heart.
For who can bear to feel himself forgotten?

'Yes, we are going to suffer, now'

Yes, we are going to suffer, now; the sky
Throbs like a feverish forehead; pain is real;
The groping searchlights suddenly reveal
The little natures that will make us cry,

Who never quite believed they could exist,
Not where we were. They take us by surprise
Like ugly long-forgotten memories,
And like a conscience all the guns resist.

Behind each sociable home-loving eye
The private massacres are taking place;
All women, Jews, the Rich, the Human Race.

The mountains cannot judge us when we lie:
We dwell upon the earth; the earth obeys
The intelligent and evil till they die.

NOËL COWARD

'Lie in the dark and listen'

Lie in the dark and listen,
It's clear tonight so they're flying high
Hundreds of them, thousands perhaps,
Riding the icy, moonlight sky.
Men, material, bombs and maps
Altimeters and guns and charts
Coffee, sandwiches, fleece-lined boots
Bones and muscles and minds and hearts
English saplings with English roots
Deep in the earth they've left below

Lie in the dark and let them go
Lie in the dark and listen.

Lie in the dark and listen
They're going over in waves and waves
High above villages, hills and streams
Country churches and little graves
And little citizens' worried dreams.
Very soon they'll have reached the sea
And far below them will lie the bays
And coves and sands where they used to be
Taken for summer holidays.
Lie in the dark and let them go
Lie in the dark and listen.

Lie in the dark and listen
City magnates and steel contractors,
Factory workers and politicians
Soft, hysterical little actors
Ballet dancers, 'Reserved' musicians,
Safe in your warm, civilian beds.
Count your profits and count your sheep
Life is flying above your heads
Just turn over and try to sleep.
Lie in the dark and let them go
Theirs is a world you'll never know
Lie in the dark and listen.

JOHN GILLESPIE MAGEE

High Flight (An Airman's Ecstasy)

Oh, I have slipped the surly bonds of earth
And danced the skies on laughter-silvered wings;
Sunward I've climbed and joined the tumbling mirth
Of sun-split clouds – and done a hundred things
You have not dreamed of; wheeled and soared and swung
High in the sun-lit silence. Hovering there
I've chased the shouting wind along, and flung
My eager craft through footless halls of air;
Up, up the long, delirious, burning blue
I've topped the wind-swept heights with easy grace,
Where never lark nor even eagle flew;
And while, with silent lifting mind I've trod
The high untrespassed sanctity of space,
Put out my hand, and touched the face of God.

RUTHVEN TODD

These Are Facts

These are facts, observe them how you will:
Forget for a moment the medals and the glory,
The clean shape of the bomb, designed to kill,
And the proud headlines of the papers' story.

Remember the walls of brick that forty years
Had nursed to make a neat though shabby home;
The impertinence of death, ignoring tears,
That smashed the house and left untouched the Dome.

Bodies in death are not magnificent or stately,
Bones are not elegant that blast has shattered;
This sorry, stained and crumpled rag was lately
A man whose life was made of little things that mattered;

Now he is just a nuisance, liable to stink,
A breeding-ground for flies, a test-tube for disease:
Bury him quickly and never pause to think,
What is the future worth to men like these?

People are more than places, more than pride;
A million photographs record the works of Wren;
A city remains a city on credit from the tide
That flows among its rocks, a sea of men.

JOHN JARMAIN

El Alamein

There are flowers now, they say, at Alamein;
Yes, flowers in the minefields now.
So those that come to view that vacant scene
Where death remains and agony has been
Will find the lilies grow –
Flowers, and nothing that we know.

So they rang the bells for us and Alamein,
Bells which we could not hear:
And to those who heard the bells what could it mean,
That name of loss and pride, El Alamein?
– Not the murk and harm of war,
But their hope, their own warm prayer.

It will become a staid historic name,
That crazy sea of sand!
Like Troy or Agincourt its single fame
Will be the garland for our brow, our claim,
On us a fleck of glory to the end:
And there our dead will keep their holy ground.

But this is not the place that we recall,
The crowded desert crossed with foaming tracks,
The one blotched building, lacking half a wall,
The grey-faced men, sand powdered over all;
The tanks, the guns, the trucks,
The black, dark-smoking wrecks.

So be it: none but us has known that land:
El Alamein will still be only ours
And those ten days of chaos in the sand.
Others will come who cannot understand,
Will halt beside the rusty minefield wires
And find there – flowers.

DENYS L. JONES

Cain in the Jungle

I have killed my brother in the jungle;
Under the green liana's clammy tangle
I hid, and pressed my trigger, and he died.

Smooth as the spotted panther crept my brother,
Never a creak of his equipment's leather,
Never a leaf dislodged nor bird offended.

With his palaeozoic prototype
My mother shared her own ungainly shape
In caverns on some slow Silurian stream;

And with the cublings played my father's sons,
Shoulder to shoulder chipped their flints and bones
Or scraped a greasy ichthyosaurus hide.

And, when the floods of purple slime receded
My brother's hutments by the apes were raided,
I lay beneath my brother's legs and cried.

Yet I have fought my brother for the planets;
I have never stopped to hear the linnets,
Or watch the cocos grow against the moon.

I have only slain him in the shadows,
I have made his slant-eyed women widows
And inherited his empty meadows.

GORDON SYMES

Song

Sailor, harrowing the seas,
Your eyebrows caked with salt
No harbour siren's kiss
Shall ever melt.

Soldier, snatching the bitter
Open-mouthed sleep,
For you the cosy taproom
No refreshment keeps.

Airman, down to earth,
Painting the town red,
Swingbands merely enlarge the hollow
Singing in your head.

And your hearths shall be baffled, wherever
You settle, north or south,
By that airy keening, stiff alien
Salt, and the gall in your mouth.

DYLAN THOMAS

'Do not go gentle into that good night'

Do not go gentle into that good night,
Old age should burn and rave at close of day;
Rage, rage against the dying of the light.

Though wise men at their end know dark is right,
Because their words have forked no lightning they
Do not go gentle into that good night.

Good men, the last wave by, crying how bright
Their frail deeds might have danced in a green bay,
Rage, rage against the dying of the light.

Wild men who caught and sang the sun in flight,
And learn, too late, they grieved it on its way,
Do not go gentle into that good night.

Grave men, near death, who see with blinding sight
Blind eyes could blaze like meteors and be gay,
Rage, rage against the dying of the light.

And you, my father, there on the sad height,
Curse, bless, me now with your fierce tears, I pray.
Do not go gentle into that good night.
Rage, rage against the dying of the light.

PHILIP LARKIN

Days

What are days for?
Days are where we live.
They come, they wake us
Time and time over.
They are to be happy in:
Where can we live but days?

Ah, solving that question
Brings the priest and the doctor
In their long coats
Running over the fields.

ALLEN GINSBERG

In Back of the Real

railroad yard in San José
        I wandered desolate
in front of a tank factory
        and sat on a bench
near the switchman's shack.

A flower lay on the hay on
        the asphalt highway
– the dread hay flower
        I thought – It had a
brittle black stem and
        corolla of yellowish dirty
spikes like Jesus' inchlong
        crown, and a soiled
dry center cotton tuft
        like a used shaving brush

that's been lying under
    the garage for a year.

Yellow, yellow flower, and
    flower of industry,
tough spiky ugly flower,
    flower nonetheless,
with the form of the great yellow
    Rose in your brain!
This is the flower of the World.

DEREK WALCOTT

Dark August

So much rain, so much life like the swollen sky
of this black August. My sister, the sun,
broods in her yellow room and won't come out.

Everything goes to hell; the mountains fume
like a kettle, rivers over-run, still,
she will not rise and turn off the rain.

She's in her room, fondling old things,
my poems, turning her album. Even if thunder falls
like a crash of plates from the sky,

she does not come out.
Don't you know I love you but am hopeless
at fixing the rain? But I am learning slowly

to love the dark days, the steaming hills,
the air with gossiping mosquitoes,
and to sip the medicine of bitterness,

so that when you emerge, my sister,
parting the beads of the rain,
with your forehead of flowers and eyes of forgiveness,

all will not be as it was, but it will be true,
(you see they will not let me love
as I want), because my sister, then

I would have learnt to love black days like bright ones,
the black rain, the white hills, when once
I loved only my happiness and you.

SYLVIA PLATH

Mirror

I am silver and exact. I have no preconceptions.
Whatever I see I swallow immediately
Just as it is, unmisted by love or dislike.
I am not cruel, only truthful –
The eye of a little god, four-cornered.
Most of the time I meditate on the opposite wall.
It is pink, with speckles. I have looked at it so long
I think it is a part of my heart. But it flickers.
Faces and darkness separate us over and over.

Now I am a lake. A woman bends over me,
Searching my reaches for what she really is.
Then she turns to those liars, the candles or the moon.
I see her back, and reflect it faithfully.
She rewards me with tears and an agitation of hands.
I am important to her. She comes and goes.
Each morning it is her face that replaces the darkness.
In me she has drowned a young girl, and in me an old woman
Rises toward her day after day, like a terrible fish.

STEVIE SMITH

Not Waving but Drowning

Nobody heard him, the dead man,
But still he lay moaning:
I was much further out than you thought
And not waving but drowning.

Poor chap, he always loved larking
And now he's dead
It must have been too cold for him his heart gave way,
They said.

Oh, no no no, it was too cold always
(Still the dead one lay moaning)
I was much too far out all my life
And not waving but drowning.

OGDEN NASH

To My Valentine

More than a catbird hates a cat,
Or a criminal hates a clue,
Or the Axis hates the United States,
That's how much I love you.

I love you more than a duck can swim,
And more than a grapefruit squirts,
I love you more than gin rummy is a bore,
And more than a toothache hurts.

As a shipwrecked sailor hates the sea,
Or a juggler hates a shove,
As a hostess detests unexpected guests,
That's how much you I love.

I love you more than a wasp can sting,
And more than the subway jerks,
I love you as much as a beggar needs a crutch,
And more than a hangnail irks.

I swear to you by the stars above,
And below, if such there be,
As the High Court loathes perjurious oaths,
That's how you're loved by me.

The Cobra

This creature fills its mouth with venum
And walks upon its duodenum.
He who attempts to tease the cobra
Is soon a sadder he, and sobra.

The Pig

The pig, if I am not mistaken,
Supplies us sausage, ham, and bacon.
Let others say his heart is big –
I call it stupid of the pig.

CHARLES CAUSLEY

I Saw a Jolly Hunter

I saw a jolly hunter
With a jolly gun
Walking in the country
In the jolly sun.

In the jolly meadow
Sat a jolly hare.
Saw the jolly hunter.
Took jolly care.

Hunter jolly eager –
Sight of jolly prey.
Forgot gun pointing
Wrong jolly way.

Jolly hunter jolly head
Over heels gone.
Jolly old safety-catch
Not jolly on.

Bang went the jolly gun.
Hunter jolly dead.
Jolly hare got clean away.
Jolly good, I said.

GEORGE MACBETH

The Miner's Helmet

My father wore it working coal at Shotts
When I was one. My mother stirred his broth
And rocked my cradle with her shivering hands
While this black helmet's long-lost miner's-lamp
Showed him the road home. Through miles of coal
His fragile skull, filled even then with pit-props,
Lay in a shell, the brain's blue-printed future
Warm in its womb. From sheaves of saved brown paper,
Baring an oval into weeks of dust,
I pull it down: its laced straps move to admit
My larger brows; like an abdicated king's
Gold crown of thirty years ago, I touch it
With royal fingers, feel its image firm –
Hands grown to kings' hands calloused on the pick,
Feet slow like kings' feet on the throneward gradient

Up to the coal-face – but the image blurs
Before it settles: there were no crusades.
My father died a draughtsman, drawing plans
In an airy well-lit office above the ground
Beneath which his usurpers, other kings,
Reigned by the fallen helmet he resigned
Which I inherit as a concrete husk.
I hand it back to gather dust on the shelf.

ROGER MCGOUGH

'Let me die a youngman's death'

Let me die a youngman's death
not a clean and inbetween
the sheets holywater death
not a famous-last-words
peaceful out of breath death

When I'm 73
and in constant good tumour
may I be mown down at dawn
by a bright red sports car
on my way home
from an allnight party

Or when I'm 91
with silver hair
and sitting in a barber's chair
may rival gangsters
with hamfisted tommyguns burst in
and give me a short back and insides

Or when I'm 104
and banned from the Cavern
may my mistress
catching me in bed with her daughter
and fearing for her son
cut me up into little pieces
and throw away every piece but one

Let me die a youngman's death
not a free from sin tiptoe in
candle wax and waning death
not a curtains drawn by angels borne
'what a nice way to go' death

Comeclose and Sleepnow

it is afterwards
and you talk on tiptoe
happy to be part
of the darkness
lips becoming limp
a prelude to tiredness.
Comeclose and Sleepnow
for in the morning
when a policeman
disguised as the sun
creeps into the room
and your mother
disguised as birds
calls from the trees
you will put on a dress of guilt
and shoes with broken high ideals
and refusing coffee
run
alltheway
home.

ADRIAN MITCHELL

Fifteen Million Plastic Bags

I was walking in a government warehouse
Where the daylight never goes.
I saw fifteen million plastic bags
Hanging in a thousand rows.

Five million bags were six feet long
Five million were five foot five
Five million were stamped with Mickey Mouse
And they came in a smaller size.

Were they for guns or uniforms
Or a dirty kind of party game?
Then I saw each bag had a number
And every bag bore a name.

And five million bags were six feet long
Five million were five foot five
Five million were stamped with Mickey Mouse
And they came in a smaller size

So I've taken my bag from the hanger
And I've pulled it over my head
And I'll wait for the priest to zip it
So the radiation won't spread

Now five million bags are six feet long
Five million are five foot five
Five million are stamped with Mickey Mouse
And they come in a smaller size.

MARGARET ATWOOD

A Holiday

My child in the smoke of the fire
playing at barbarism,
the burst meat dripping down her
chin, soot smearing
her cheek and her hair infested with twigs,
under a huge midsummer-leafed tree
in the rain, the shelter
of poles and canvas down
the road if needed:

This could be where we
end up, learning the minimal
with maybe no tree, no rain,
no shelter, no roast carcasses
of animals to renew us

at a time when language
will shrink to the word *hunger*
and the word *none.*

Mist lifts from the warm lake
hit by the cold drizzle:
too much dust in the stratosphere
this year, they say. Unseasonal.

GILLIAN CLARKE

The Hare

(for Frances Horovitz)

That March night I remember how we heard
a baby crying in a neighbouring room
but found him sleeping quietly in his cot.

The others went to bed and we sat late
talking of children and the men we loved.
You thought you'd like another child. 'Too late'

you said. And we fell silent, thought a while
of yours with his copper hair and mine,
a grown daughter and sons.

Then, that joke we shared, our phases of the moon.
'Sisterly lunacy' I said. You liked
the phrase. It became ours. Different

as earth and air, yet in one trace that week
we towed the calends like boats reining
the oceans of the world at the full moon.

Suddenly from the fields we heard again
a baby cry, and standing at the door
listened for minutes, ears and eyes soon used

to the night. It was cold. In the east
the river made a breath of shining sound.
The cattle in the field were shadow black.

A cow coughed. Some slept and some pulled grass.
I could smell blossom from the blackthorn
and see their thorny crowns against the sky.

And then again, a sharp cry from the hill.
'A hare', we said together, not speaking
of fox or trap that held it in a lock

of terrible darkness. Both admitted,
next day, to lying guilty hours awake
at the crying of the hare. You told me

of sleeping at last in the jaws of a bad dream.
'I saw all the suffering of the world
in a single moment. Then I heard

a voice say "But this is nothing, nothing
to the mental pain".' I couldn't speak of it.
I thought about your dream when you lay ill.

In the last heavy nights before full moon,
when its face seems sorrowful and broken,
I look through binoculars. Its seas flower

like clouds over water, it wears its craters
like silver rings. Even in dying you
menstruated as a woman in health

considering to have a child or no.
When they hand me insults or little hurts
and I'm on fire with my arguments

at your great distance you can calm me still.
Your dream, my sleeplessness, the cattle
asleep under a full moon,

and out there
the dumb and stiffening body of the hare.

PAUL DURCAN

Hymn to a Broken Marriage

Dear Nessa – Now that our marriage is over
I would like you to know that, if I could put back the clock
Fifteen years to the cold March day of our wedding,
I would wed you again and, if that marriage also broke,
I would wed you yet again and, if it a third time broke,
Wed you again, and again, and again, and again, and again:
If you would have me which, of course, you would not.
For, even you – in spite of your patience and your innocence
(Strange characteristics in an age such as our own) –
Even you require to shake off the addiction of romantic love
And seek, instead, the herbal remedy of a sane affection
In which are mixed in profuse and fair proportion
Loverliness, brotherliness, fatherliness:
A sane man could not espouse a more intimate friend than you.

CRAIG RAINE

A Martian Sends a Postcard Home

Caxtons are mechanical birds with many wings
and some are treasured for their markings –

they cause the eyes to melt
or the body to shriek without pain.

I have never seen one fly, but
sometimes they perch on the hand.

Mist is when the sky is tired of flight
and rests its soft machine on ground:

then the world is dim and bookish
like engravings under tissue paper.

Rain is when the earth is television.
It has the property of making colours darker.

Model T is a room with the lock inside –
a key is turned to free the world

for movement, so quick there is a film
to watch for anything missed.

But time is tied to the wrist
or kept in a box, ticking with impatience.

In homes, a haunted apparatus sleeps,
that snores when you pick it up.

If the ghost cries, they carry it
to their lips and soothe it to sleep

with sounds. And yet, they wake it up
deliberately, by tickling with a finger.

Only the young are allowed to suffer
openly. Adults go to a punishment room

with water but nothing to eat.
They lock the door and suffer the noises

alone. No one is exempt
and everyone's pain has a different smell.

At night, when all the colours die,
they hide in pairs

and read about themselves –
in colour, with their eyelids shut.

BENJAMIN ZEPHANIAH

As a African

As a African I danced to riddims wild in Nicaragua
I overstood dem well.
As a African I did not celebrate 200 years of Australia,
I overstand its history is black.
As a African I went to find Palestine,
I got confused on de West Bank,
An as a African Palestine is important.

As a African I grew old,
I went an sat down wid an reasoned wid Mr Ayatollah.
Mr Ayatollah told me fe mind me own business,
An so did Mr President USA.
Mrs Thatcher didn't even talk to me.

As a African a plastic bullet hit me in Northern Ireland,
But me children overstood an dey grew strong,
As a African I was a woman in a man's world,
A man in a computer world,
A fly on de wall of China,
A Rastafarian diplomat,
An a miner in Wales.
I was a red hot Eskimo,
A peace luvin hippie,
A honest newcaster,
A city dwelling peasant,
I was a Arawak,
A unwanted baby,
A circumcised lady,
I was all a dis
An still a African.

LINTON KWESI JOHNSON

Wat about di Workin Claas?

fram Inglan to Poelan
evry step acraas di oweshan
di rulin claases dem is in a mess – o yes
di capitalis system a regress
But di Soviet system naw progress
soh which wan a dem yu tink is bes
wen a di two a dem di workahs a cantess

wen crisis is di aadah af di day
wen soh much people crying out fi change nowaday?

soh wat about di workin claas
comred chairman
wat about di workin claas?
dey pay di caas
dey carry di craas
an dem naw goh figet
dem tanks in Gdansk
dem naw goh figet dem tanks

fram di east to di wes
to di lan I love di bes
di rulin claases dem is in a mess – o yes
crisis is di aadah af di day
di workahs dem demandin more pay evryday
di pezants want a lat more say nowaday
di yout dem rebelin evrywhey
evrywhey insohrecksahn is di aadah af di day
is a lat a people cryin out fi change nowaday

noh baddah blame it pan di black workin claas
mistah racist
blame it pan di rulin claas
blame it pan yu capitalis baas
wi pay di caas
wi suffah di laas
an wi naw goh figet New Craas
nat a raas
wi naw goh figet new craas

FIONA PITT-KETHLEY

Sky Ray Lolly

A toddler on a day out in Herne Bay,
on seeing an ancient, civil-servant-type,
I held my Sky Ray lolly – red, yellow
and green striped, pointed, dripping down between
my legs and walked bandy. My Ma and Pa,
(old-fashioned innocents like Rupert Bear's),
just didn't notice this and ambled on,
that is, until they saw the old man's face,
jaw dislocated in surprise. They grabbed
that Martian's willy from my little hand.

The world still sees me as a nasty kid
usurping maleness. A foul brat to be
smacked down by figures of authority.
All things most natural in men, in me
are vice – having no urge to cook or clean,
lacking maternal instincts.

And they would take my pride, my rocket
of ambition, amputate my fun and geld
my laughter, depriving me of colour.
And smirk to see my little lolly melt,
me left with a stick.

JOHN HEGLEY

Popping Out for a Paper

I won't be going in my car
because it isn't very far
and because I haven't got a car
I'm not stopping out,
I'm just popping out
for a paper,
shopping for a reality shaper.

Glasses Good, Contact Lenses Bad

In the embrace of my glasses
I openly accept my vulnerability
and affirm my acceptance of outside help.
As well as providing open acknowledgment
of the imperfection in my eyesight
my glasses are a symbolic celebration
of the wider imperfection that is the human condition.
In contrast contact lenses are a hiding of the fault
they pretend the self-sufficiency of the individual
and minister unto the cult of stultifying normality,
they are that which should be cast out of your vision:
they are a denial of the self,
they are a denial of the other,
they are a betrayal of humanity.

WENDY COPE

A Policeman's Lot

The progress of any writer is marked by those moments
when he manages to outwit his own inner police system.
Ted Hughes

Oh, once I was a policeman young and merry (young and merry),
Controlling crowds and fighting petty crime (petty crime),
But now I work on matters literary (litererry)
And I am growing old before my time ('fore my time).
No, the imagination of a writer (of a writer)
Is not the sort of beat a chap would choose (chap would choose)
And they've assigned me a prolific blighter ('lific blighter) –
I'm patrolling the unconscious of Ted Hughes.

It's not the sort of beat a chap would choose (chap would choose) –
Patrolling the unconscious of Ted Hughes.

All our leave was cancelled in the lambing season (lambing season),
When bitter winter froze the drinking trough (drinking trough),
For our commander stated, with good reason (with good reason),
That that's the kind of thing that starts him off (starts him off).
But anything with four legs causes trouble (causes trouble) –
It's worse than organizing several zoos (several zoos),
Not to mention mythic creatures in the rubble (in the rubble),
Patrolling the unconscious of Ted Hughes.

It's worse than organizing several zoos (several zoos),
Patrolling the unconscious of Ted Hughes.

Although it's disagreeable and stressful (bull and stressful)
Attempting to avert poetic thought ('etic thought),
I could boast of times when I have been successful (been successful)
And conspiring compound epithets were caught ('thets were caught).
But the poetry statistics in this sector (in this sector)
Are enough to make a copper turn to booze (turn to booze)
And I do not think I'll make it to inspector (to inspector)
Patrolling the unconscious of Ted Hughes.

It's enough to make a copper turn to booze (turn to booze) –
Patrolling the unconscious of Ted Hughes.

after W. S. Gilbert

Acknowledgements

The publishers wish to thank the following for their permission to reproduce poems in this volume: the Literary Trustees of Walter de la Mare and the Society of Authors as their representatives for 'Farewell' by Walter de la Mare; Peters Fraser and Dunlop Group Ltd for 'Henry King' and 'Lord Finchley' by Hilaire Belloc (*Complete Verse*, Pimlico); George Sassoon for 'Everyone Sang' and 'Glory of Women' by Siegfried Sassoon; W.W. Norton and Co. Ltd and Liveright Publishing Corporation for '16 heures' by e.e. cummings (*Complete Poems, 1904–1962*); A.P. Watt Ltd on behalf of the Robert Graves Copyright Trust for 'To Whom Else' by Robert Graves; David Higham Associates and Random House Inc. Alfred A. Knopf Inc. for 'Dream Variation' by Langston Hughes (*Selected Poems*, Vintage Books); Random House UK Ltd and Henry Holt and Co. Inc. for 'The Road Not Taken' by Robert Frost (*The Poetry of Robert Frost*, ed. Edward Connery Lathem, Jonathan Cape); Faber and Faber Ltd for 'The Lake Isle', 'In a Station of the Metro' and 'The Plunge' by Ezra Pound (*Collected Shorter Poems*), and for 'Prelude' and 'Journey of the Magi' by T.S. Eliot (*Collected Poems, 1909–1962*), and for 'Snow' by Louis MacNeice (*Collected Poems*, ed. E.R. Dobbs); Penguin Books Ltd for 'Home from Abroad' by Laurie Lee (André Deutsch, copyright © 1983 Laurie Lee); the Society of Authors as the literary representative of the Estate of John Masefield for 'Cargoes' by John Masefield; John Murray for 'The Metropolitan Railway' and 'In a Bath Teashop' by John Betjeman; Reed Consumer Books and Curtis Brown Group Ltd on behalf of the Estate of Christopher Isherwood for 'On his Queerness' by Christopher Isherwood (*Exhumations*, Methuen London); Faber and Faber Ltd for 'Night Mail' and 'In Time of War XIV' (first line 'Yes, we are going to suffer, now') by W.H. Auden (*The English Auden*); Michael Imison Playwrights Ltd for 'Lie in the dark and listen' by Noël Coward (copyright © 1984 the Estate of the late Noël Coward); David Higham Associates for 'These are Facts' by Ruthven Todd (J.M. Dent and Sons), and for 'Do not go gentle into that good night' by Dylan Thomas (*The Poems*, J.M. Dent and Sons); Faber and Faber Ltd for 'Days' by Philip Larkin

(*The Whitsun Weddings*); Penguin Books Ltd for 'In Back of the Real' by Allen Ginsberg (*Collected Poems, 1947–1980*, Viking); Random House UK Ltd for 'Dark August' by Derek Walcott (*Sea Grapes*, Jonathan Cape); Faber and Faber Ltd for 'Mirror' by Sylvia Plath (*Collected Poems*); New Directions Publishing Corporation for 'Not Waving but Drowning' by Stevie Smith (*Collected Poems*, copyright © 1972 Stevie Smith); André Deutsch Ltd for 'To My Valentine', 'The Pig' and 'The Cobra' by Ogden Nash (*I Wouldn't Have Missed It – Selected Poems*, André Deutsch Ltd, 1983); David Higham Associates for 'I Saw a Jolly Hunter' by Charles Causley (*Figgie Hobbin*, Macmillan); Sheil Land Associates for 'The Miner's Helmet' by George MacBeth (*Collected Poems, 1958–1982*, Hutchinson, copyright © 1989 George MacBeth); Peters Fraser and Dunlop Group Ltd for 'Let me die a youngman's death' and 'Comeclose and Sleepnow' by Roger McGough (*Blazing Fruit*, Penguin), and for 'Fifteen Million Plastic Bags' by Adrian Mitchell (none of Adrian Mitchell's poems are to be used in connection with any examination whatsoever); Curtis Brown Group Ltd and Oxford University Press Canada for 'A Holiday' by Margaret Atwood (*Interlunar*, copyright © 1984 Margaret Atwood); Carcanet Press Ltd for 'The Hare' by Gillian Clarke (*Selected Poems*); The Blackstaff Press for 'Hymn to a Broken Marriage' by Paul Durcan (*The Berlin Wall Café*, 1985); Oxford University Press for 'A Martian Sends a Postcard Home' by Craig Raine (*A Martian Sends a Postcard*, copyright © 1979, Craig Raine); Bloodaxe Books for 'Wat About di Workin Claas' by Linton Kwesi Johnson (*Tings and Times*, 1991), and for 'As a African' by Benjamin Zephaniah (*City Psalms*, 1992); Sheil Land Associates for 'Sky Ray Lolly' by Fiona Pitt-Kethley (*Sky Ray Lolly*, Abacus); Reed Consumer Books for 'Popping out for a Paper' and 'Glasses Good, Contact Lenses Bad' by John Hegley (*Five Sugars Please*, Methuen London); Faber and Faber Ltd for 'A Policeman's Lot' by Wendy Cope (*Making Cocoa for Kingsley Amis*). The publishers have made every effort to trace copyright-holders, and trust that their apologies will be accepted for any errors or omissions.

Index of Authors